ESCAPE THE GAY
STRAITJACKET

It is strongly recommended that this book

is read in sequence from the beginning.

Neither the publisher nor the author

can be responsible for any ill effects

caused by dipping in to the book

or browsing through it.

Publication of the name of any person

or organisation or of a photograph of

any person in this book should not

be construed as an indication of the

religious, political or sexual orientation

of that person or organisation unless

it is specifically stated as such.

ESCAPE THE GAY STRAITJACKET

DONALD BLACK

POWER BOOKS
LONDON

First published in Great Britain by Power Books in 2002

© 2002 by Donald Black

All rights reserved.

No part of this publication may be reproduced, stored in a retrieval system or transmitted, in any form or by any means without the prior permission in writing of the publisher, nor be otherwise circulated in any form of binding or cover other than that in which it is published and without a similar condition including this condition being imposed on the subsequent purchaser.

A CIP catalogue record for this book
is available from the British Library.

ISBN 0 9506782 2 8

Printed and bound in Finland by
W S Bookwell

POWER BOOKS

54 Balham Park Road, London SW12 8DU

CONTENTS

Front cover and chapter heading photographs by Jay Eff

    Models: Danni, Kevin, Steve

Text photographs by André Napier

    Models: Kevin, Leon

    Sports facilities courtesy of Balham Leisure Centre

CONTENTS

Preface	xi
1. The Gay Straitjacket	1
2. The Nature of Homosexuality and Bisexuality	43
3. Digging Deeper	87
4. Escaping the Gay Straitjacket	119
5. Spreading Your Wings and Flexing Your Muscles	159
Glossary	211
Appendix A: Mouth-to-Mouth Resuscitation	225
Appendix B: Body Opponent Bag (BOB) addresses	229
Bibliography	233
Index	247

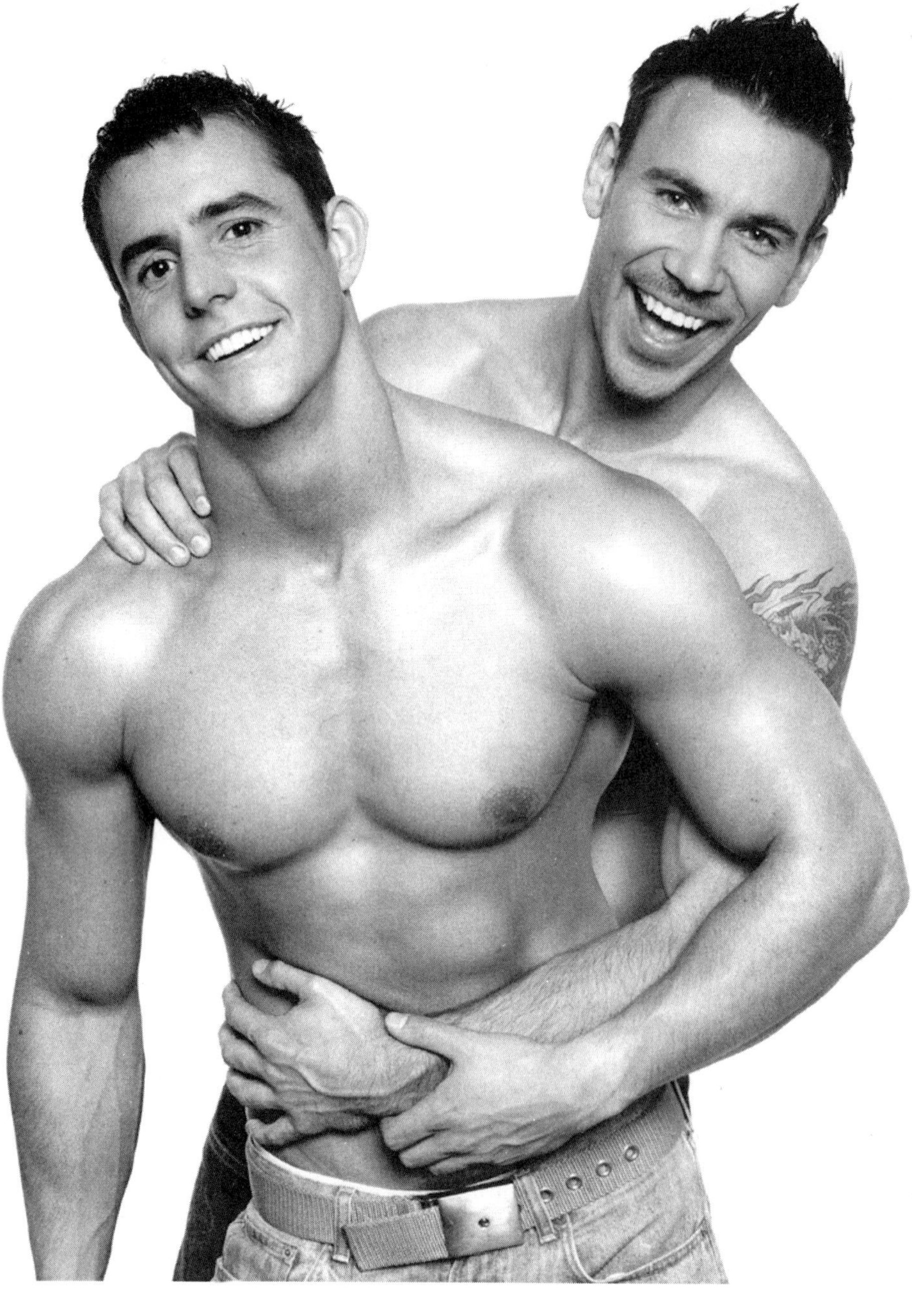

Preface

MANY people, including heterosexuals, suffer from neuroses that may prevent them from doing things but do not consider themselves to be "sick". Many may not even be at all aware that they suffer from a neurosis. Certainly, militant homosexuals have shown that they are not prepared to be described as "sick", and many heterosexuals like to think of themselves as only in a state of good health.

Most gay men have a fear of violence and have difficulty in expressing anger. The former manifests itself as a fear of other men and the latter results in a long list of horrendous and pervasive problems that we will need to look at. This results in a helplessness that is like a straitjacket that prevents gay men from doing things that other (straight) men can do, and from enjoying life the way others can.

I am not a psychiatrist or psychologist in an ivory tower being critical of gay life and passing judgment on you from on high. I am an ordinary gay man who has experienced this all myself. I am not trying to point a finger at other gay men saying, "I am well and you are sick!" Like most gay men I too suffered from this fear of violence and difficulty with expressing my anger up until 1970 when I was in psychotherapy at the Tavistock Clinic in London and these two problems were cured for me, proving that they are merely neuroses.

Knowing the psychological pain and anguish that I have endured earlier in my life because of these two neuroses, I cannot bear to think that other gay men may be enduring the same. I do not want to label anyone as "sick". What I want is for you to be *free* – free of the gay straitjacket and the resulting helplessness and fear of other men that it brings, so that you can enjoy life to the full.

Beware of those gay militants who want to damn this book because (they will say) it implies you are sick. They are part of the gay straitjacket. They would prefer you to endure the horrors of the gay straitjacket rather than admit that you have problems, and have them cured. They want you to believe that you are "normal". Normal people *have* problems. It would be a strange person indeed who has no problems. Maybe God gives us problems so that we will turn to Him for help. I cannot pretend that I managed to cure my neuroses without using the power of prayer. Do not worry, this is not a religious book. I just have to acknowledge credit where credit is due.

There will be references to my own life throughout this book. Not all of what I experienced may apply to you but I hope it will provide you with a springboard to help you realise what kinds of problems you may be facing, besides helping you to understand why other people may behave in an extraordinary way. I am writing about my own experiences as a gay man and am describing the way it is, or was, for me.

And how it is, still, for most gay men.

Or is it? Times have changed, haven't they? Can what happened to me thirty years ago still be relevant today?

The French have a saying "The more things change, the more they stay the same". Actually it was Alphonse Karr (1808–1890) who said it.

Since Stonewall in the US and the change in the law in Britain making homosexual acts between two consenting men permissible in private there has been the Gay Liberation movement. Homosexuals have become more visible and accepted by the general public.

Polls taken annually among the US general population (the General Social Survey) between 1972 and 1991 show that on average 73% of the population think that homosexuality is wrong. At the same time, sometimes a minority, sometimes a majority have opposed discrimination against homosexuals (Laumann *et al.* 1994). In Britain the British Social Attitudes survey shows that the number of people who saw homosexuality as "not wrong" were just under 20% in 1990 and grew to just over 30% in 1998 (Stonewall 2001), presumably leaving nearly 70% who think it is wrong.

Young gay men who have never experienced the gay repression that existed before Stonewall in the US and before the 1967 change in the law in Britain now feel free to "come out" while they are still at school but are then taken aback by the reaction of their straight schoolmates and the bullying they are made to suffer as a result of their sexual orientation.

Can the changes that happened to me in 1970 still be relevant to young gay men today?

To answer that question let us describe a gay theorem.

Most gay men do not play body-contact sports.

The reason these gay men are unable to participate in body-contact sports is because they are unable to be aggressive.

Aggression is an offshoot of anger.

If these gay men can not express aggression it must be because they cannot express their anger.

If they cannot express their anger it must be that they have repressed their anger.

Q.E.D. (*Quod erat demonstrandum* or Which was to be shown.)

This book will tell you how to unrepress your anger safely.

If it appears that nowadays more gay men are visiting gyms to build up their muscles and more gay men are playing sports, one only has to look at a Gay Pride procession (or the ensuing fête) to see that those showing evidence of weight-training are very few indeed and that those who are unable to be aggressive because they have repressed their anger are still the great majority.

The first chapter of this book, therefore, looks at the various problems that beset gay men which are all caused by their repressing their anger.

Chapter 2 describes the nature of homosexuality and bisexuality to explain how it is that these two neuroses (repression of anger and fear of "violence") develop in such a large sector of gay men.

Chapter 3 looks at further ramifications of these two neuroses and how their consequences affect the lives of gay men.

In Chapter 4 we come to the psychotherapy that cured these neuroses for me and will, I hope, do the same for you.

We next learn how to express anger safely and, as a result, how to become more self-assertive.

Chapter 5 explores some of the things that will become possible for you to do that will further improve your life and your enjoyment once you have cured these two neuroses.

Chapters 4 and 5 are subdivided into stages that do not coincide with the chapters. As one cannot achieve psychological insight or acquire physical skills overnight, the growth that you may be about to undertake may take you as long as five years, though I have compressed it all into one book. When you reach the end of one stage (I will tell you when you have reached the end of a stage) you may need to put down the book for as long as six months or a year until you feel comfortable with the changes you have made and are ready to explore and benefit from the next stage.

Unfortunately, since psychotherapy is more of an art than a science, and some people need to maintain the *status quo* whatever the cost, and since some people fear change because of the price that it might incur, neither the author nor the publisher can *guarantee* any result for you, but that does not mean there may be no benefit from your reading this book. Timing is often crucial, so do not despair if you need to wait before the timing is right for you so that you can profit from the revelations. In the meantime you can benefit from learning about the path that is there for you and where it may lead when you are ready to take it.

As the mind often takes time to accept new ideas or different perspectives of the same thing and to adjust to them; and as this book is in effect a course in psychotherapy which would, in real time, take perhaps four or five years to accomplish (as it did for me), it is in your own interest that you should read it in sequence from the beginning and not browse through it or delve into the end to see how it works out.

The ground needs to be prepared, ploughed and loosened, then have fertiliser and humus added and mixed together before one can plant seedlings and hope for them to grow. If you plant seedlings on hard soil that has not been ploughed you cannot expect them to take root or grow.

In psychological terms we are talking about denial. Some ideas may be too painful to accept when you are first confronted with them so it is necessary to prepare people to lessen the shock so that they are able to cope with a revelation more easily when they encounter it. Otherwise they simply deny that a fact is so, no matter how true it is. If you do this, you will have wasted your money and your time . . . and perhaps your future happiness, too.

I attended the Tavistock Clinic in group psychotherapy for almost five years. I am telling you this because I fully expect you, when you read what I have to say about these two neuroses, to throw up your hands in horror and exclaim, "What absolute nonsense! What rubbish! I wasted my money buying this book!" I expect that because, whenever the psychiatrist who led our group made an interpretation to explain why we were behaving in a particular (irrational) way, each person would retort, "That is just utter nonsense!" or words to that effect.

However, a week later, after we had had time to think about it we were ready to admit that what the psychiatrist had said might apply to other members of the group but definitely not to us individually! Another week later we were prepared to admit that it might actually also apply to us . . . but only occasionally. And after a further week's cogitation and adaptation we would finally admit that he had been perfectly correct in what he had said originally and, of course, it did apply to all of us all the time.

With that experience behind me I fully expect you to behave in the same way and dispute everything in this book, only to find that, a year later you have come around to agreeing with everything I say. Well, with *almost* everything I say.

The mind is in balance. It creates its own balance according to life's circumstances, our own experiences and the conclusions we come to as a result. Therefore it resists any change which may upset the balance, but it may then well accept the change after it has had time to adjust in preparation for accommodating the new concept.

If you feel upset by what I have to say, do not throw the book away or burn it, because you may well want to pick it up again after a period of time to read the next section once you feel you have come to understand and even agree with what I said. When this happens you may even want to re-read the previous section. You may then feel it is important for you to understand everything I said so that you can extract the most from the book.

Where words in British usage may not be readily understood by American readers I have provided what I hope is the US equivalent after an oblique/slash (thus).

I am indebted to Cathy Birch, Butterworth-Heinemann and Century Incorporated for permission they have granted to use copyright material in this book.

For most of the psychological interpretations quoted in this book I am indebted to Dr David Malan, late Chief Medical Officer at the Tavistock Clinic, since retired and author of *Individual Psychotherapy and the Science of Psychodynamics*. On recently discussing with him my text of the principal interpretation, he said that the time of development at which such feelings arise in the baby is a matter of controversy and that there are some people who think that such feelings do not arise while you still call the child a baby. Since what I remember him as saying (thirty-three years ago) is what cured me, I do not think my readers need worry about this. I am also indebted to Professor Richard Green, author of the book *The "Sissy Boy Syndrome" and the Development of Homosexuality*, to the late Dr Eric Berne, founder of Transactional Analysis and author of *Games People Play* and to other psychiatrists too numerous to mention.

Where I use a person's first name only, it is an alias to avoid family embarrassment.

I am grateful to Hank Trout who has allowed me to quote him, and to the many anonymous friends who feature as examples in the narrative.

I am indebted to Juris Lavrikovs of Stonewall Lobby Group, London, to Hennie Brandhorst of Homodok-LAA, Amsterdam, and to Alex Beyer for providing information that I required, and I would like to thank Tony

Jenkins and John Stevenson for reading the draft and making many helpful suggestions, and John Banks for also making valuable suggestions and putting the final gloss on the text.

THE GAY

STRAITJACKET

WHEN I was in my teens I was walking outside the shops in our village one day and passed a woman who was pushing a pram with a baby in it. The baby had long, pretty, blonde ringlets reminiscent of Shirley Temple, the child film-star of the 1930s, and I could not help remarking to her "What a pretty girl you have!"

Much to my surprise she retorted, "It's a boy!"

"Oh, I'm sorry", I stammered, backtracking quickly.

I was quite surprised and at the same time really alarmed because I could imagine what would happen if he turned up on his first day at school with long ringlets like that, and what the other boys would do.

"Won't it affect him having ringlets like that?" I asked her.

"I don't care if it does!" was her reply.

That a mother could be so selfish and insensitive, not to say twisted, was quite a shock to me. I had not yet learned how manipulative mothers could be.

I had also not yet learned about the deep psychological problems this mother was making for her son. I will explain what they are further on – in fact it will take two-thirds of the book to do so. I had realised by that time that I was gay and I suppose something told me that this baby in the pram would grow up to be gay too.

This true story illustrates very vividly what this whole book is about. It was the beginning of a chain of events that has brought me to writing this book some fifty years later.

I was eleven years old when I discovered I was gay and it happened in a rather curious way.

I was at boarding school at the time and on Saturday afternoons the boarders went as a group to watch rugby during the winter months and to the beach to swim during the summer months.

On our first weekend back after the Christmas holidays we went to the beach (this was in the southern hemisphere where the seasons are reversed)

The Gay Straitjacket 1

and during the afternoon I came across two older schoolmates wrestling on the sand. This was no playful romp. The two boys hated each other and their feelings had been escalating at school until it was bound to explode in a fight. I did not see the start of the fight so I do not know what sparked it off but, as it was a grudge fight to settle a score, a small crowd had gathered eagerly around to cheer them on and to see one of them get what was coming to him.

I eagerly joined the crowd to see what they were watching.

One of the fighters had the other in a body scissors with his opponent between his thighs and his legs locked together at the ankles. He was squeezing his victim's body as tightly as he could to squeeze the breath out of him. He did not have the advantage for long, however. Each of them was giving vent to his anger, even rage, spurred on by the crowd, and straining every muscle in the desperate struggle to get the better of his enemy. Each was striving to punish the other, to pay him back and to obtain satisfaction.

What I saw aroused me sexually, and this was the first time in my life that I can remember having an erection. Although I was wearing only my swimming trunks at the time, I did not feel embarrassed as I realised the eyes of the crowd were all on the two figures wrestling on the sand and no one was likely to notice the swelling in my swimming trunks. Though I did not understand what was happening, I knew that their fight gave me a wonderful feeling of excitement and pleasure.

In squalid cafés where I went to buy a Coca-Cola or an ice-cream cone near the local train station I found *The Ring* magazine and *Your Physique* magazine hanging up overhead tantalisingly out of reach. I spent my meagre pocket money to get my hands on them and then, in secret moments, pored over the pictures of men with bulging muscles, photos of lean bodies in satin shorts rippling with muscles tensed in contorting the opponent's face. A shiny, pumped-up boxing glove smashed into the distorted face of another aggressive-looking boxer sent shivers of excitement and ecstasy down my spine to stimulate a response in my groin.

As I could not look at all the best pictures in the magazines at the same time I soon started cutting out what I wanted and throwing the rest away. I rubbed my erect penis against my stomach or between my thighs. Women simply did not come into what I was experiencing. Especially if they were encouraging me to be a nice, polite, well-behaved, little boy.

Why was I aroused by muscular bodies wrestling and men boxing? It will all become clear later when I explain the relevance it has for you with regard to the gay straitjacket.

Escape the Gay Straitjacket

It was the very conflict between this attraction for and desire to become a masculine, testosterone-sweating superman and the shy, timid, polite, inhibited man that I actually was that, over the years, drove me to discover what the difference between straight men and gay men actually was. Before I could learn the difference, I needed to discover what the nature of being homosexual was so that I could compare it with male heterosexuality and discover in what way gay men were different.

For me wrestling was synonymous with sex. I wanted to wrestle! I went through a desperate struggle trying to break out of the unaggressive boy that I was (and that most gay men are) and it was through my need to become, instead, one of the most aggressive of sportsmen – a wrestler! – that I discovered the straitjacket that most gay men are locked inside. Indeed, I also tried to become a boxer (an even *more* aggressive breed) but, owing to being short-sighted from about ten years of age my chances of success in that sport made it a non-starter. I could not box in spectacles and, without them, I could not see what my opponent was doing so as to know when to dodge his punches. When I was thirty-two I acquired contact lenses and thought that at last I would be able to box, but a boxing doctor told me I would not get a licence to box as they had already had cases of contact lenses breaking during contests in the ring.

If I had not been into wrestling I would never have made the discoveries which have enabled me to write this book, and I think it is important to explain to you how this knowledge developed and how the realisation eventually came about.

When I came across those schoolmates wrestling in the sand I had already had two previous wrestling experiences in which I had not come off very well and which had perhaps fired my desire to come off better in future.

I had an uncle who wrestled until he was prevented from participating in the sport by a heart attack. I never saw him wrestle as they lived three hundred miles away from our family in South Africa and, by the time I was trying to take up the sport, he had already had to stop wrestling.

When I was three or four I was sitting on a rug in their backyard with my aunt and another boy of my own age when my aunt suggested we wrestle. I had never heard the word before, had never seen wrestling and did not know what I was supposed to do. The other boy was therefore able to push me over and press my shoulders down to the ground in a pinfall when I suddenly realised what it was all about, but by then I had been declared the loser and it was all over.

When I was six our family, except for my mother, was picnicking one day on the beach. My father, who was gay (but that is another story), had a boyfriend along, and I was peeved that they had not kept their promise to take me further down the beach to show me a cave that was there, as I had never seen one before.

My dad's mate was sitting on a rock and caught me between his legs. I was furious and struggled for all my worth to get free but to no avail. Every time I was on the point of escaping he trapped me again in another way.

This was an extremely traumatic experience for me and was retold many times in my later life to different psychiatrists until I had realised all the significance of the event and how it had affected me . . . and my life even in later years.

Back at home, aged six, I asked the boy next door to wrestle with me but he refused as he said I would only cry. I promised I wouldn't. So, in a gap in the hedge between our houses, we closed with one another and, as we fell over and he landed on top of me, I began to cry and that was the end of that.

WHAT IS A GAY STRAITJACKET?

In the meantime I can feel your impatience growing as I seem to be avoiding the theme of this book. "What is a gay straitjacket?" is the first question I can hear you ask.

This is the helplessness that 90% of gay men suffer from, caused by their not being able to express their anger and resulting in all kinds of problems for them.

Expressing anger? What anger? I never had a problem with expressing anger, I mistakenly believed when I was in my twenties. On the rare occasions that I did go off pop at someone, I felt butterflies in my stomach and felt ill and exhausted for the rest of the day or even for the rest of the week. Perhaps *you* feel that all this does not apply to you either because you do not have any anger.

It must be impossible to go through life without people making you angry. They push you around, they (try to) manipulate you, they exploit you, they are rude to you, they oppress you. According to research (Averill 1983), most people experience mild to moderate anger quite frequently: from three times a week to as much as three times a day. In fact, Averill surveyed research into anger done over the last 75 years by Anastasi *et al.* (1948), Averill (1979, 1982), Gates (1926), Meltzer (1933), and Richardson (1918) and it appears to have remained constant over a long period.

If you never feel angry it can mean only one thing. You are pushing your anger out of your mind or, in psychological terms, you are repressing your anger. In this case what you must have been doing all your life is avoiding situations, as far as you can, where people make you angry; if they do, you simply avoid facing the anger and push it straight out of your mind.

"So what's wrong with repressing anger? Who wants to get involved in anger?" I hear you say. "Anger is a very destructive emotion. Even dangerous. And how do you know it is 90% of gay men who have a problem with expressing their anger? *I* don't have a problem with anger. I'm just never angry. And what about the other 10%?"

Let me take your questions one at a time.

I am sure you would accept that most gay men avoid sports, especially body-contact sports. Yes, I know there are a few gay footballers and boxers, but they are a *few* and fall into the ten per cent of gay men who have no problems with sports, as will be explained in Chapter 2. Perhaps you would acknowledge that the main reason that most gay men avoid body-contact sports is that these gay men are not aggressive, they feel they do not want to be aggressive, and so avoid competing with other (usually straight) men who, on the whole, have no problems with being aggressive and so enjoy playing competitive sports.

Who wants to be aggressive?

On my first day at primary/junior school I was amazed at the number of my peers who were running about kicking a football. How did they know what to do? Who had told them how to play the game? When I was ten years old the sports-master at the country school I was at in Kuils River just outside Cape Town asked me if I could fill in for one of the boys on the rugby team who was away. My best friend encouraged me to have a go. They knew I had never played before and explained what I needed to do. I agreed.

Playing rugby in a country school in South Africa meant running barefoot around a field that was covered in two kinds of thorns. One was the size of a pea and was covered all over in hooks to attach itself to you, but the other, called *duiweltjies* (little devils), had three or four thorns like rose thorns that would impale the sole of your foot and cause you to stop running while you extracted it.

They put me in wing position, which meant that I was often the last person to get my hands on the ball. I had to tackle my opposing number in the other team and got kicked in the chest for my trouble. I did not think I had played very well. Afterwards they said they were pleased with the way I had played and told me the next game would be in a week's time.

That evening at home I announced to my family over the dinner table the news that I had played my first game of rugby. My tale was met with complete silence from the other members of the family. No one made any comment at all about it. I was terribly hurt.

The next week when I was due to play in the next game the sports-master told me that the boy I had replaced was back so I would not be needed.

It was only when I was fifty years old that I fathomed out why everybody behaved as they did. In case you have not already guessed I will explain later.

When I was thirty-two years old my life seemed to be in a complete mess and one of my problems then was that, although I had been interested in wrestling from an early age, I had difficulty in learning the sport. I was not so much interested as turned on by wrestling, especially professional wrestling. Although I had trained in the professional style for a couple of years I did not seem to be making a success of it. In fact, some of the guys I was training with complained that I was "holding back" when I wrestled with them.

There was a man at work who was winding me up, sending me up to be more precise, in front of other workmates. He was asking for it, but he did it only because he knew he would get away with it as I would not be able to do anything to retaliate and, of course, he was right . . . I couldn't.

I thought he would stop teasing me if I punched him on the jaw (I had done some boxing with friends) but I was frightened I might break his jaw (an acquaintance had told me it had happened to him at work) and that there would be a court case, the police would probably come to work to interview us and I might get the sack.

Or worse, with my knowledge of wrestling, if I tried a wrestling takedown on him so that I could put a submission hold on him to force him to apologise, he might fall badly, breaking a leg or banging his head against the wall and have to go to hospital with a fractured skull, and the ambulance would have to come to take him away, there would be a court case and I would get the sack, and so on . . . all the thoughts of what might happen just left me powerless to do anything.

And I was being subjected to this teasing simply because my tormentor knew that I would not be able to do anything about it and that he would therefore get away with it. This event was crucial in having my fear of violence cured, so we will meet it again later in Chapter 4.

It is this type of helplessness that I later realised is like a straitjacket that prevents many gay men from taking the right kind of action to be successful in their lives. Instead, they allow themselves to be put upon by other people, or society, because their "straitjacket" prevents them from doing what other (straight) men would quite naturally get on and do without thinking twice about it.

This fear that I experienced in standing up for myself is what most gay men also experience but would call "a fear of violence" when referring to themselves. It seems to be at the base of the gay man's withdrawal from competing with other men not only, but especially, in sports. But we need to look at this a little more closely as there is a chain reaction taking place which goes on to create the fully-blown gay straitjacket.

BEING BULLIED

It will come as no surprise if I tell you then that I was bullied at school. A lot of young gay men are.

I was sent to boarding school when I was eleven years old and two lads who were also boarders began tormenting me. It was not simply my previous wrestling experiences, having ended always in humiliation for me, that left me feeling that I *ought* to be bullied. I did not match up to my peers who were all playing football/soccer or rugby. I was not able to interact with them. What was going on around me was all going on over my head. Without being able to put it into words I felt as though I was watching it from the gutter and I was on a level with vermin. The only time people turned their attention to me was to stamp on me. I felt I deserved to be punished. I deserved to be bullied, and I simply did not know what to do about it.

My mother was a Christian Scientist and suggested that if I ignored them and left them alone they would go away. Mary Baker Eddy, who founded Christian Science, maintained that "God is Love" and that anything that was not Love was Error (of thinking).

My mother's friends would take delight in describing how their sons were able to stand up for themselves. I detested this as, without saying anything, they were implying by default that I was useless in standing up for myself and this must have reinforced my low self-esteem. I hated myself so much I felt as though I *ought* to be punished, which was what being bullied amounted to.

Miraculously, one day, one of the older boarders, who was not much taller than me but was one of the most muscular and good-looking whom I had admired from a distance, put a pair of boxing gloves on me in the locker room and donned a pair himself and with the best intentions in the world tried to get me to box and "stand up for myself".

I did not want to hit him. He was like a demi-god on a pedestal that I should worship genuflecting or be allowed only to touch or caress. I tried to punch him but my punches were falling short.

"You're not punching far enough", he admonished me, "Punch right *through* me!" I could not tell him that I did not want to punch him. I just wanted him to be my friend. Then one of his punches landed on my nose. Blood streamed out and ran down my mouth. Terrified of staining the brand-new gloves that he had borrowed without permission from someone else, he whipped them off me. And it all ended as suddenly and unexpectedly as it had begun.

It is some comfort to me that later in life during my time as a weight-training instructor some of my young pupils who had reputations for being violent trouble-makers in their class at school have looked at me and talked to me with the awe that I must have displayed towards the boy who tried to teach me to box. One of them who did not know my name called me "Muscles". But that was much much later.

Why was I so helpless? The boys who bullied me did not pick on anyone else. Clearly my schoolmates knew something about how to rid themselves of attempted bullying that I did not know and my bullies also knew that. Somehow I think I wanted to be punished. That feeling became very strong later in life and I realised I was masochistic. But why?

I need to stress here that while a withdrawal from competitive sports is *one* element of the gay straitjacket it is by no means the *only* element – the effects of the gay straitjacket are far-reaching in the lives of gay men, as we shall see.

Gay men withdraw from sports because they are unable to be aggressive which is needed to compete against other men. Aggression is actually a physical expression of anger and gay men cannot be aggressive because they cannot express their anger in the first place.

I looked at anger earlier and suggested that, as it is so destructive, we are probably better off by not being angry. As most gay men are frightened of the aggression or confrontation that their anger might lead them into, they probably feel it is safer not to be angry. But *is* it safer?

THE VALUE OF ANGER

Anger is actually a good emotion. It is nature's way of preventing us from being pushed around, being put upon, being manipulated or being exploited. If you are unable to express your anger the result is that you will have to endure all these things: being put upon, being exploited, being manipulated and being pushed around without being able to do anything about it or to prevent it happening.

That is a terrible position to be in, and does not result only in being pushed around, being exploited, being put upon and being manipulated. It also results in a drop in your self-esteem, especially when you see others standing up for themselves all around you and dealing with problems that you are completely unable to deal with yourself. Instead of the problems bouncing off you the way they do with other (straight) men, they seem to come down on top of you and crush you completely. The consequence of this for you is a feeling of inferiority because you seem to be so helpless compared to most other men. This is like having a straitjacket wrapped around us making us helpless.

Winifred Rushforth in her book *Something is Happening* likens burying anger in the subconscious (see Glossary page 221) to sending troublesome children down into the cellar and locking them in. At last everything is quiet and peaceful in the house, you think, until the children find the mains switches for the electric power and heating and the mains valves for the water, and turn everything off, causing you far worse suffering. This is another way of describing the gay straitjacket.

LEVELS OF ANGER

The word "anger" may make you think of people losing their temper, shouting and screaming and behaving violently, even smashing things but this is only one level of anger. This is when people *lose control* of their anger and is an extreme state where they often are not even aware of what they are doing perhaps to try to escape the situation. All the anger that they have not expressed for years suddenly comes out at the same time.

Going down the scale one step, people shout at other people because they are angry and throw plates or other objects. They feel the need to do something to express their anger but they are well aware of what they are doing. They are expressing their anger in a seemingly-violent, but controlled, way. They are using their anger for effect or to achieve something. At this level you find sportsmen who are using their anger against the opponent also in a controlled way to run faster, jump higher or push harder in order to prevent being beaten.

Then one step down the scale, people shout to express their anger but do not actually *do* anything.

Going another step down the scale, people *do* something because they do not want to shout – for instance, slamming the phone down or slamming the door behind them.

Another step down the scale, people use their anger to say firmly but politely, "I'm afraid you can't push into the queue/line – we've been waiting here for an hour and a half" to prevent themselves from being put upon.

Another step down the scale, people can be perfectly polite when they express their anger without animosity, saying for instance, "I'd love to help you but I am afraid I can't" and thus prevent themselves from being manipulated. Or they may say, "Yes, I can see you are enjoying yourselves but you will have to find somewhere else to play football as you are kicking sand into our food and picnic things."

Below that is a step where people are well aware of their anger but have made a conscious decision that, on this occasion, no useful purpose would be served if they said, or did, anything. They are aware of their anger but feel quite happy in not expressing it.

One step below that we begin getting into trouble again with people who are aware of their anger but do not express it. Instead, they sulk. They think that "I shouldn't have to tell them why I am angry – they should *know*." What they are trying to do is to punish the perpetrator but, as we shall see, for relationships to survive there needs to be communication between the parties. This tactic indicates a severe breakdown in communications, and can end in the relationship self-destructing.

Another step down we find people saying, "I'm not angry at all" but then behaving in some odious way in revenge or to get their own back, such as what is called passive-aggressive behaviour or acting out. I will describe this when we look at these behaviours more closely.

Below that level of anger, of course, are the people who are unable to say or do any of these things and, instead, *repress* their anger with all the consequences that Rushforth describes. They think that they can get rid of their anger simply by "putting it out of their mind". Instead the anger mounts up inside them in their subconscious minds until something small upsets them and we find that the scale we have been descending one step at a time is actually a circular scale. What happens is that they explode uncontrollably and we find they are now at the first step at the top of the scale, having come full circle.

Ninety per cent of gay men are in the position of not being able to express their anger. Why this is so and why 10% of gay men are not afflicted is what this book is all about, and these two points will be explained in due course. How this inability to express anger can be cured will be examined in Chapter 4.

GETTING RID OF ANGER

You do not want to be aggressive, because this may bring you into conflict with other men, so you become frightened of feeling angry as this may put you on the slippery slope that will bring you into conflict and violence.

As you have been doing this since you were a baby you will not probably even be aware when you are angry as you are so skilled in pushing it down into your subconscious mind or pushing it out of your mind and dealing with the situation in another way (probably by walking away from it or avoiding situations where you may become angry) and hoping that, if you forget your anger, it will go away.

Unfortunately, there is only *one way* to get rid of anger, and these methods are not it. The only way one can really get anger to go away is to *express* it. It is so important for you to realise this that I am going to say it again. The only way one can *really* get anger to go away is to *express* it.

All that these other methods achieve is repression of one's anger. That is, bottling it up in one's subconscious mind where it mounts up over time, festers and spoils the quality of our lives. You may not be aware of all the anger inside you because it is in your subconscious mind and the job of the subconscious mind is to keep from us emotions that are too painful for us to live with.

What you end up with is a life, as Rushforth suggests, that is like having the electricity, the heating and the water all turned off. Or like being in a straitjacket. What can you do about that? Read on and you will eventually get to the solution.

Most (straight) men have no trouble in expressing their anger at any of the points of the scale I have described above. If there is some excess anger

The Gay Straitjacket

they have not been able to express, they will be able to channel it into sports and then expressing it (usually safely) by playing football, rugby, judo, boxing or wrestling, etc. Indeed, some of them will admit they could not keep sane if they did not have a safety valve where they can let their anger out. Hence the motto: A healthy mind in a healthy body.

I should perhaps explain why it is that rugby or football matches sometimes erupt into fisticuffs on the field. What level of anger is that? Is that supposed to be expressing anger safely? Or in a controlled way?

These games are supposed to be played by the rules, but some sportsmen (perhaps if they are frightened of being beaten, I don't know) realise that if they stamp on the foot of the fastest man in the opposing team when they think the referee cannot see, he will not be able to run so fast for the rest of the game and will become easier to beat. I am told that all kinds of felonies are committed in a rugby scrum when the referee cannot see them.

And, of course, one of the delights of getting punched by someone is that his action gives you the right to hit him back; this is an enjoyable prospect if you are able to hit him back much harder than he hit you in the first place. On the other hand, if you are trapped in a straitjacket it will not be much fun as you will have to endure it without being able to do anything at all.

It is this undercurrent of fouling that occurs throughout some matches that sometimes erupts into an open fight when one of the players can take no more or simply feels an opposing player has gone too far and is asking for it.

Gay men, helpless in their straitjacket do not feel they can hit back so they never get the chance to retaliate that straight men get. There are indeed a few gay men who *are* able to express their anger through playing sports and who will not understand why this book has been written. We will discuss later the difference between those gay men who *can* express anger and most gay men who *cannot* when we will also learn why it is that most gay men become trapped in this straitjacket in the first place.

As we have seen, this way of expressing anger is not open to most gay men who, instead, have to live with their anger building up inside themselves, poisoning their lives. Although repressing anger is only one thing, the *effects* of repressing one's anger, as Rushforth says, are many and far-reaching.

In her book *Managing Anger*, Rebecca Luhn says that anger brings on tension which develops into headaches and tension in the upper body, limiting your breathing and causing back pain. The amount of glucose in your blood rises, as does your pulse rate and blood pressure. You sweat more. The effect on your mind is to prevent concentration and cause sleeplessness, making you depressed, tired and irritable, nervous, worried and strained. You lose focus. The effect on your behaviour is that you turn to drugs, eat too much, drink and smoke. You become restless, impulsive and compulsive. You end up withdrawn and isolated. Luhn says that the overall effect of chronic anger makes you unable to work, continually dissatisfied, prone to accidents, prone to bad relationships, eager to settle your problems in court and prone to changing your job.

In their book *A Straight Talk About Anger* Christine Dentemaro and Rachel Krantz repeat many of the above effects but add some more: repressed anger causes people to be constantly late for appointments, to cause or frequently have accidents, to forget appointments (which may be a way of acting out one's anger), to have migraines, stomach aches, ulcers, colitis or heart disease. It also causes one to make silly mistakes, have misunderstandings, bad feelings between friends, anxiety, feelings of hopelessness, depression and guilt. It causes one to get angry at nothing or to become angry with people who have not deserved it. They say people can end up hurting themselves physically and emotionally.

Nobody is saying that if you repress your anger you will suffer from *all* these bad effects. That would be more than anyone could bear. Different people react to stress in different ways, so different people might end up with different effects from repressing their anger: these are the sort of effects Rushforth was referring to (page 9) when she likened repressing anger to sending troublesome children down into the cellar, locking them in, and ending up with the electricity, heating and water all turned off. Suffering from any two from these long lists of symptoms could make your life a misery . . . and probably has!

If you are repressing your anger you will not feel angry. If you suffer from any of these symptoms you will not realise that they are being caused by all the (repressed) anger inside you. What then will you blame the symptoms on? You may feel that it is Peter and Paul who are being so difficult that they are causing you all these problems. You may feel it is society that is oppressing you. You simply will not realise the real cause of the symptoms . . . because you do not *feel* angry!

Of course, I may hear you say these symptoms do not apply to or affect many gay men. Most people would consider the use of poppers, to take the first effect on your behaviour as an example, to be drug abuse. Straight men often take up fashions in clothes, music or jewellery started by gay men. They have not found it necessary to take to using poppers as far as

I know. If you cannot guess the reason for that I will spell it out for you later. It is true that a few straight men experiment with poppers in discos that have a mixed clientele of gays and straights, but whether they use them as a sex aid is doubtful.

By repressing your anger you may think you have got rid of it because it is no longer in your (conscious) mind, but you have not got rid of it. Remember, the only way to get rid of anger is to *express* it.

What repressing your anger does is to lumber you with something you are not aware of. That makes it a thousand times more difficult to deal with. I am not angry, you say. And for the sick man who believes he is well there is no cure.

These labels that Luhn, for instance, uses may be meaningless and impenetrable for most people, so let us look at them in more familiar terms. Let us look at them as they occur on the gay scene.

Repressing anger causes bitchiness (resulting in bad relationships), a feeling of helplessness and frustration when other people around one can express their anger (especially if it is directed at yourself); resulting in a feeling of low self-esteem. Repressing anger causes a bondage fetish and, as we have already seen, causes us to take a long time, or have problems with, reaching a sexual climax (impotence) and the need to use poppers (drug abuse) to overcome it.

Surprising it may seem. I will explain everything. Just read on.

ALL OR NOTHING

The problem with repressing one's anger is that for many people it is not possible to be selective with your emotions. If you repress one emotion you can end up repressing more than you intended to.

Repressing one's anger (and other emotions) results in personalities that are cold, stiff, silent and lacking in spontaneity. The "gay" façade that we all know so well may be just that. A façade.

The person is so careful to hold in his anger, and it is usually anger that people want to repress, that they end up holding back a lot more. They are frightened that, if they let any emotion out, their anger might escape and come out too. This is not a conscious decision they make, you understand, this is going on in their minds at a subconscious level.

This is particularly troublesome for a large proportion of gay men and we will need to look at how this works and how it affects them.

IMPOTENCE AND DRUG ABUSE

As I have already explained, repressing anger can cause sexual impotence and drug abuse.

Surprised? Incredulous? How many gay men do you know who use poppers because it helps them to reach a sexual climax?

William Skinner and Melanie Otis conducted research in two southern-state cities of the US which they compared to the (US) National Household Survey on Drug Abuse (NHSDA) as a control. They found that overall, 29.8% of the gay men in their study used poppers (amyl nitrite or butyl nitrite) compared to 1.9% of the NHSDA respondents. This, despite the fact that amyl nitrite is known to suppress the immune system. When you look only at the gay men in the study aged 18–25 the figure rises to an alarming 36.6%

For many people, particularly on the gay scene, their sexuality has become entwined with their anger. This means that by repressing their anger they are automatically repressing their sexual feelings at the same time. This is why many gay men need to use poppers to try to get in touch with their repressed sexual feelings when they want to.

Bahr and Weeks (1989) report that there are some gay men who are *not* in therapy who have a sexual dysfunction but do not mention this as a problem. Dr Andrew Behrendt and Professor Kenneth George (1995) say that gay men rarely complain about inhibited sexual desire in themselves, and that it is more common for a partner to identify the problem. Simon Rosser (1994) conducted a study of two hundred men who were at a sexual education class and found that 97.5% reported a sexual dysfunction at some time during their lives while 52.3% reported worries about current sexual dysfunction. Clearly this is a taboo in the gay world. Perhaps militant gays have persuaded gay men for so long that they are normal, that many have come to believe that having difficulty in reaching an orgasm is normal. Drs Eli Coleman and B.R. Simon Rosser (1996) feel that gay men may be prevented from getting the high-quality medical assessment, care and treatment that they need as a result of homophobic attitudes amongst physicians (Dardick and Grady 1980; Pauly and Goldstein 1970). While attitudes may have changed, homophobia does not die so easily.

A number of guys that I have had sex with had tremendous difficulty in reaching an orgasm even with the use of poppers. My impression is that without the poppers they would have been impotent, but they insisted that the poppers were only an aid, not an enabler.

How many straight men do you know who use poppers? Straight men do not use poppers because generally they have no problem with reaching a sexual climax. They can express their anger. This means they are also free to express their sexual feelings unless perhaps they have drunk too much or have other emotional problems.

Instead of being very sensitive and easily aroused sexually when they want to be, for many gay men who have repressed their anger, reaching a sexual climax becomes difficult and, for some, even impossible. This occurs, as I know from my own experience, only when one is with a sexual partner, not when one masturbates on one's own. In the latter case one is able to fantasise releasing one's anger (or to look at pictures that portray this: e.g. boxing, fighting or wrestling) in a way that is not possible with another guy who might become terrified if you did release your anger in front of him, never mind *at* him.

When I was in my twenties and thirties I found gay men that I would have liked to have a relationship with. Unfortunately, when we got into bed together I could have an erection but never an orgasm. I just somehow could not get my mind into gear to get there. This was rather strange because when I found a guy who would wrestle with me first, usually a renter/hustler, I had very little problem in reaching an orgasm. I could never understand why it did not work for me as easily with my gay friends.

In Britain we have a National Health Service of which the object is to give everyone free medical attention. One cannot help wondering where the National Health Service has been with so many gay men having difficulty reaching an orgasm. Straight men who have such problems have been given Viagra, but what have these gay men been given?

Looking at the use of other drugs by gay men in Skinner and Otis's study we find that overall marijuana was used by 36.5%, alcohol by 89.2% and cocaine by 9.7%. When we look at the 18–25 age group of gay men there is a higher use: marijuana by 53.8%, poppers by 36.6%, cocaine by 15.2% and alcohol by 96.8%!

Luis Palacios, a psychotherapist and drug-treatment specialist in New York City, is reported in an article by G. DeSlefano in *The Advocate* in 1986 as describing the different uses for which different drugs are used. He says people use narcotics (heroin and other opiates) or hypnotics (Valium and Quaaludes) against feelings of shame, rage, jealousy and overwhelming

Escape the Gay Straitjacket

anxiety. Stimulants (such as cocaine and amphetamines) are used to alleviate depression, feelings of helplessness and a sense of inner emptiness. Psychedelics (such as LSD and mescaline, and disco drugs such as MDA and Ecstasy) are used to relieve boredom, apathy, and feelings of detachment and isolation. Alcohol is often taken to allay guilt, self-punishment, loneliness and longing. The problem is, as he says, that "many people use different drugs simultaneously, or at different times in their lives to address different feelings".

What this tells us is that so many gay men are taking drugs because they are feeling shame, rage, jealousy, overwhelming anxiety, depression, helplessness, inner emptiness, boredom, apathy, detachment, isolation, guilt, longing, loneliness and a need for punishment. The inability to express anger has suddenly exploded into a constellation of problems! Clearly Luhn, Dentemaro and Krantz (pages 12–13) were not so wrong after all.

Not only is psychiatry in its infancy but there are nowhere near enough psychiatrists or psychotherapists to go around. I was recently given a textbook on psychology. I looked in vain in the index for repressed anger. Not even anger was listed in the index! This is such an important topic for so many people. It should not be neglected any longer.

Men who are functioning normally and are content with themselves do not want to take drugs as the drugs will only spoil their enjoyment by making them feel woozy or dizzy. The fact that people need to take drugs to enjoy themselves is a clear indication that those people have psychological problems that prevent them enjoying themselves without the aid of drugs. Much of this, I believe, can be traced back to having its roots in the gay straitjacket.

Besides poppers many gay men need other ways of reaching an orgasm which we will come to examining later, such as bondage, mummification, sadism, masochism, flagellation, humiliation and so on.

You should not think that I am going to try to persuade you to give up these means of reaching an orgasm "for your own good" or anything like that. To suggest that would be utterly stupid and completely futile. I needed to wrestle to be able to reach an orgasm and I fully realise that, without such aids, you may find it just as impossible as *I* did to reach an orgasm.

Up to now you have not understood *why* you need to use such aids or why you have difficulty in reaching an orgasm, but once you understand all the reasons you will be in a position to undo the mechanism if you want to, so that you will be able to reach sexual satisfaction as most people do without needing bizarre means as an essential crutch.

Once you reach that stage you will find you will be able to reach sexual satisfaction without your usual aids but not because I *tell* you that that is what you should do. Your poppers, restraints, handcuffs, burning candles and other drugs will just lie in the drawer where you keep them because there will be no reason for you to get them out especially when you will be able to reach more exciting multiple orgasms without them.

For some people their feelings are so bottled up that it is not being able to reach an orgasm that is a problem but not being able to feel any tender feelings of love for anyone else. People are different, and repressing one's anger can affect different people in different ways.

ANDY

How subtle the effect of this repression of one's anger can be is demonstrated very clearly in what happened between me and Andy, whom I have been friends with for over thirty years.

I met Andy in a pub/bar frequented by gays in London's West End when he was eighteen and I was thirty-six. I was attracted to him because he was a young and handsome Scotsman with that lean hungry look and plenty of tattoos.

He had "LOVE" tattooed on the fingers of one hand and "HATE" on the fingers of the other hand. These alone would have been evidence of his anger which, as much as he tried to repress it, was coming out of his ears. So angry was he that every other word he uses is "f-----g".

Andy was in one way very similar to me (repressed anger combined with repressed sexual feelings and therefore itching for a fight) so I understood him very well. In another way he was the exact opposite of me: thin and handsome, tough (he never shows *any* signs of pain), violent, unemployable and living with his girlfriend; whereas I was very polite, had a good job, my own pad, a muscular body (from weight-training), a motor-bike and no live-in lover.

Opposites attract and Andy had all the things I longed to have. I suspect I have all the things he longs to have though he has never admitted it. (He has certainly never denied it.)

The attraction of opposites is an excellent biological mechanism because in heterosexual couples it brings together a wider range of attributes for the offspring of the couple than if like was only attracted to like. I was attracted to Andy but I was also terribly jealous of the qualities that he had that I wished I had. If I could not have the qualities he had, I certainly wanted to punish him for the advantage he had over me.

The first time Andy came back with me we wrestled and I trapped him in what is called an Indian Deathlock. It is certainly not at all as dangerous as the name suggests. (You need to remember that professional wrestling is all histrionics.) You wrap your opponent's legs into a cross-legged sitting position (which is not a difficult position to sit in) with one of your own legs through the middle to prevent him *un*crossing his legs. If he sits up you can knee him in the stomach and if he lies back to avoid being kneed in the stomach it puts extra strain on his legs as the muscles get squeezed between the bones of *your* leg and *his* legs.

Andy thought I was going to break his leg and pleaded cramp so I released him. For years he longed to pay me back though he never admitted it. I slowly began to suspect it.

Soon after I met Andy he was imprisoned for two-and-a-half years because he had been in a fight and, when the other guy had defended himself with a wooden pole, Andy had hit him with an iron bar. His real parents had allowed him to be adopted and he may have been hoping when he came back with me on that first occasion that I would be the loving father figure that he lacked, only to be bitterly disappointed when he became frightened I was trying to break his leg.

He was also terrified that if he became involved in another fight he would end up in prison again, so it was years before he could trust me enough to engage in some body-punching and then it was in a very controlled manner in the "you punch me twice and then I'll punch you twice" fashion. He did not want to wrestle with me again presumably because he was still frightened I might break his leg.

I told Andy he could punch me (to the body not to the face) whenever he liked except, of course, at times when it was inappropriate. For example, when we were riding my motorbike it could result in an accident, when I was holding a cup of tea it could result in a spillage and broken crockery and so on. It took me a long time to realise why it was that I enjoyed being punched and I shall explain the reason for that in due course if you have not already twigged it.

If he had tried to repress his anger before going to prison, after being released he was even more frightened of becoming involved in a fight as he did not relish having to go back to prison again. Repressing his anger meant that he showed very little sexual activity with me (or, I imagine, with anyone else).

I kept wondering if he was really only heterosexual and not bisexual (he always had a girlfriend he was living with) but then his adoptive parents were homophobic. My phone would often ring after eleven o'clock at night (when the pubs/bars in Britain were required by law to close) and it would be Andy slightly or very much inebriated. It seemed to me it must be flattering that when he was drunk, *in vino veritas*, he was thinking of me. Over the twenty-nine years girlfriends came and went but our friendship has endured.

After twenty years he admitted that he had not had cramp when we wrestled at our first meeting but that he was afraid I was going to break his leg. Instead of wrestling we took to punching each other as this brought my anger to the surface more quickly and, with it, my sexual feelings so that I could reach an orgasm. This had a miraculous effect on Andy.

Psychiatrists know when they have mentioned something that a patient has repressed in his/her subconscious because laughter is the reflex that occurs when someone unexpectedly hears something that they have repressed in their subconscious. (Freud has explained that this is the basis of humour.) The patient just cannot help laughing even though it may be a soft laugh.

On the occasion that Andy and I first had a competition of punching each other on the upper arm he ended up laughing and laughing so hysterically that, for a time, I became quite worried that the balance of his mind had been disturbed. I also realised that the need to pay me back, which he had just done, was something that he must have been repressing for a long time.

The result of punching me was that he unexpectedly had a hard-on (for the first time with me) and was able to reach an orgasm with ease. Clearly, I had been right in that he had been repressing his anger with me. By punching me, he was expressing his anger and this allowed his sexual feelings to come to the surface too.

In this he was very much like I was. I needed someone to make me angry so that I would release my anger in a fight: my sexual feelings would come to the surface at the same time and enable me to perform sexually. This was why I enjoyed being punched at any time. Though not in the face, you understand. For years I did not realise that it was helping to bring my repressed sexual feelings to the surface and that that was why I enjoyed it so much. For me it was a preparation for sex. An aphrodisiac.

MAKING ANGER EVAPORATE

After a friendship that has lasted for over thirty years I came to wonder why it was that I still wanted to punish him and, apparently, he still wanted to punish me. Then, as Andy got older, he developed arthritis in his hands which made punching painful. Without the punching it was impossible for me to reach an orgasm with him. Or he with me.

I began again to ask myself why we needed to punch each other as a prelude to sex. I decided it was (as I have said above) that I was angry with him for two reasons: because he had qualities that I was envious of, that I felt I lacked, and secondly, because he did not show that he loved me.

Remember I said that Andy never shows pain no matter how much he is hurt? Well, by repressing his pain he was also repressing his other emotions. Remember the "all or nothing" law? This was a terrible price he was paying for repressing his pain.

About a year ago he left his latest girlfriend and got his own pad, so I made the trip from London to Hove on the south coast to visit him but found myself amongst a group of his friends who were high on cider. He told them that he and I were going to Rio for a holiday. When he asked me to confirm it I denied that we were going. I had never lied to Andy and I did not see why I should lie to his friends.

He must have been furious at me for showing him up in front of his friends because he did not speak to me for the next hour and a half by which time I was so bored with the alcoholic drivel and incensed with the frustration of getting nowhere after all that time that I just left and went back home to London although he ran after me to try to stop me leaving.

When I sat down and considered calmly what had happened, I realised I had made him angry by showing him up in front of his friends. The next time we spoke on the phone I told him that I knew he was angry with me. He denied it. He said he could not remember having told his friends that we were going to Rio on holiday or my having denied it. I remembered that for years he had claimed it was cramp that he had when I put him in an Indian Deathlock, so I was not taken in by his current loss of memory.

Apart from wanting to punish him because he does not love me I feel threatened by the qualities he has that I lack. That is why I was still angry with him. I decided to tell him why I was angry with him. Once I had told him my anger evaporated, and therefore my need to punish him evaporated too and I feel more tender towards him. That this should happen is not surprising as it is what psychotherapy is all about.

Unfortunately, Andy does not like people delving into his psyche (probably because he feels frightened that they will find out what he is *really* like and will then want to abandon him as his biological parents did) so it is impossible to persuade him to explain or talk about how he really feels. However, shortly after I admitted to him that I was jealous of him and angry that he did not love me we had a brief but momentous conversation on the telephone.

I said to him, "I told you that I was angry with you."

"Yes."

"Are *you* angry with *me*?"

"No, not at all."

"I think you *are* angry with me", referring to showing him up in front of his friends with regard to the supposed Rio holiday.

"Okay. I am angry with you."

"I thought you were."

It did not seem like much at the time, but, after over thirty years, for the first time he expressed his anger in a very simple phrase: "I am angry with you" spoken more resignedly than angrily.

This is a superb lesson in how anger can be expressed calmly and safely.

At our next meeting Andy was very easily aroused sexually and reached a climax without any delay or hesitation. As he had expressed his anger with me, he had no difficulty in expressing his sexual feelings as well though for the previous thirty years this had been a problem for him most of the time, as it had been with me.

As I say, a large proportion of gay men suffer from some form of impotency or lack of tender feelings for another person as a result of repressing their anger. This one can deduce from the large quantities of amyl nitrite that are sold even if one had not seen the statistics quoted above.

There are many other gay men who have no problems when it comes to reaching a sexual climax. This is due to their sexual feelings not being intertwined with their anger and, consequently, not being repressed when they repress their anger.

BONDAGE FETISH

One way of being able to reach a sexual climax, for some people who have stifled their sexual feelings together with their anger, is to allow themselves to be tied up or restrained.

In that situation they need not be frightened of doing anything violent or destructive, should their anger come out at the same time as their tender sexual feelings are expressed. Being tied up prevents that happening and so reassures them that it is safe to let their tender sexual feelings out together with their anger.

The greater their repressed anger the greater the amount of restraint they need before they feel safe enough to let out their sexual feelings – witness those gay men who have to be practically mummified in polycarbonate vinyl. It is only in that situation that they feel safe to let go of their emotions sufficiently to be able to reach a sexual climax.

Of course, some gay men need to be tied up and then use poppers as well, in order to reach a sexual climax, so repressed are their anger and sexual feelings.

GAY ADOLESCENCE

Adolescence is a difficult phase for all children to navigate through but especially difficult for young gay men and lesbians. By puberty most gay men realise that they are different, but everybody *else* in the world – their parents, their teachers, their peers – is expecting them to be heterosexual and grooming them for this role. Probably all of us start off by dating girls to please everyone else but soon most of us realise that there is not going to be any future in that. But what to do?

One may have been called a "sissy" as a child, perhaps at school, but by puberty most gay men are becoming aware of the continuing antipathy of many straight people to the homosexual way of life. In spite of feeling that homosexuals should have equal rights and be treated in the same way as heterosexuals, many straight people feel the idea of homosexuality abhorrent. Some do not hesitate to engage in name-calling using words such as "fag", "poofter", "pansy" and so on. There are those who engage in queer-bashing. The gay man, trapped in a straitjacket and unable to use his anger to protect himself, can only run away and hide or be beaten up. Often he realises it is wiser to pretend to be heterosexual or at least not admit to being homosexual in front of his parents, his workmates, and many friends and acquaintances, and say nothing when they denigrate gays.

During childhood there is a strong need to be accepted by one's parents. During adolescence there is a strong need to belong – to be accepted by one's peer group.

Dr Richard Friedman, a psychiatrist, in research he did (1988) with "masculine, psychologically well-adjusted lifelong homosexuals" who were not patients found that 12 of the 13 subjects had the lowest possible peer status during juvenile and early adolescent years and were alternately ostracised and scapegoated, and exposed to continual humiliation. This may strike a chord in readers who passed through adolescence before 1990 but be less familiar to younger readers owing to the changes in society that have taken place.

As nearly 30% of people now believe homosexuality is acceptable (page 24) many young men now find it very easy to "come out" especially after they have left school, but, remember, 70% of the population in Britain (and the percentage is probably similar in the US) still regard homosexuality as wrong and even abhorrent, so how easy do gay men in *those* families find it to "come out"? In extreme cases they find it impossible. Those young men who find it easy to come out will feel at home on the gay scene and be very visible, whereas those who find it impossible to "come out" will never even get on the scene.

Almost every issue of Gay Times in Britain carries reports of gay-bashing in some part of the country. An extreme case of homophobia was the bombing of a gay pub/bar in Soho in London's West End, the *Admiral Duncan*, by David Copeland on 30 April 1999 when 3 people were killed and more than 80 injured.

In the face of all this homophobia which he can do nothing about, it is very difficult for some of this homophobia not to rub off on the gay man, leaving him with self-hatred (called negative homophobia) making him feel that he *is* as bad as people think and, considering how he has to hide his true self most of the time, he must be. This self-hatred stems not simply from being what others despise but also from not matching up to one's peers, from not being able to interact with (most of) one's peers (top of this page), from being so helpless – and from feeling inadequate because of this. And I have not even got to religion yet.

These sentiments are so strong in most people because the Christian religion has been preaching for nearly two thousand years, and Judaism for a lot longer, that homosexuality and sodomy are sins. These precepts have stuck in our society even though church-going has diminished since the Second World War.

For gay men who are religious or are being raised in religious families the pressures are even greater. They often have to choose between heterosexuality and being damned to Hell for eternity.

Helen McDonald and Audrey Steinhorn, counsellors, narrate the sad story of Bobbie Griffith in their book *Understanding Homosexuality*. He was the third child in a Christian Fundamentalist family. His family pressured him to pray every day not to be homosexual and he recorded his torments in his diary up until the time he committed suicide at the age of 20 on 27 August, 1983 (*San Francisco Examiner*, 18 June, 1989 page A-12). His mother, Mary Griffith, later wrote, "I firmly believe – though I did not back then – that my son Bobby's suicide is the end result of homophobia and ignorance within most Protestant and Catholic churches, and consequently within society, our public schools, our own family."

Gay or bi youths may feel the need to come out to someone they are attracted to. In some cases their feelings are reciprocated and so all goes well but, often, they are rebuffed and this is followed by rejection, public humiliation, and being ostracised at a time when they need to feel accepted by their peers. They may well eventually be accepted by their gay peers but one should not lose sight of the fact that, even so, they are still being rejected by probably the majority (90%–98%) of their peers who are straight.

They cannot but help feeling inferior as this majority who reject them are able to do so much that gay men, trapped in their straitjackets, are unable to do: they can stand up for themselves against other men and against their own families, they can make babies, they can play body-contact sports. How can the gay man, faced with his inability to do these things, not feel inferior? Of course, he does not go about his life saying to himself, "I feel inferior" but the realisation is pushed out of his mind and buried in his subconscious mind together with his repressed anger where it will poison his life.

A study made as long ago as 1972 into gay male youths aged 16–22 by T. Roesler and R. Deisher found that 31% had made a suicide attempt. Alfred Kinsey *et al.* in their report on the sex life of the American male (Bell & Weinberg 1978) found that 20% of the gay men studied reported a suicide attempt. In 1988 A.D. Martin and E.S. Hetrick reported that 21% of their clients at a social services agency for troubled youth had made a suicide attempt; and in 1993 Gilbert Herdt and Andrew Boxer reported in their book *Children of Horizons* that "about a third" of the gay youth who attended the Horizons' Social Services agency in Chicago to help them to come out, had made a suicide attempt in the past.

In 1989 P. Gibson examined earlier studies and reports from community agencies in the US and speculated that gay and bisexual youth are two to three times more likely to commit suicide than their straight peers; that gay and bisexual men may comprise up to 30% of all completed youth suicides; and that 20%–35% of gay and bisexual youth have made suicide attempts. G. Remafedi (1987a, 1987b) found that 34% of his adolescent gay male subjects had attempted suicide. In 1991 he undertook a larger study and found that 30% of his subjects had attempted suicide.

In 1989 Schneider *et al.* made a study of gay youth in which 23% had made a suicide attempt at least once, while 59% showed they had thought about it seriously. In 1993 A.R. D'Augelli and S.L. Herschberger studied gay youth in fourteen metropolitan areas and discovered that 42% had made a suicide attempt.

Most children who have problems of this magnitude can turn to their parents for support, reassurance and group identification. For gay young people this is not possible.

Where parents voice their hopes for their son of going to university/college, meeting "a nice girl", marrying her and providing grandchildren, or where parents declare their abhorrence of "queers" it only increases the burden on the young gay man. Many children do commit suicide during adolescence but it is not known how many of these might have been caused by problems with their sexual orientation. The books of authors such as Friedman, and McDonald and Steinhorn bear witness to the suffering and anguish, the torment and suicidal thoughts that many young gay men experience that one never hears about on the gay scene.

ALCOHOL ABUSE

On the one hand, gay men lack access to a wide selection of ways of socialising, many of which do not include alcohol, that heterosexuals enjoy. On the other hand, for historical reasons, the pub/bar was always the place where homosexuals could meet as long as a century ago, when homosexuality was "the love that dare not speak its name", to be amongst like-minded people and to be themselves and not have to pretend to be something that they were not. The pub/bar, therefore, became the hub of the gay scene, and still is. It is the place where one can meet new people, rendezvous with old friends, exchange gossip and news, and where no one will mind what you say or how you behave.

Since Stonewall in the US and the change in the law in Britain in 1967 there has been a proliferation of other venues and special-interest clubs where gay men can socialise without a need to consume alcohol, but the gay pub/bar retains its pull as a place to meet (or find) sexual partners and to visit before or after the other venue.

I have already mentioned the horrendous problem that some gay men find themselves in of a family that is so homophobic that the gay son cannot even come out. They are so "close" or "protective" of him that he cannot go to gay bars or buy gay literature or have gay friends for fear that they will find out about his sexuality. He is, in fact, unable to escape an ever-present homophobic family. The gay son therefore simply has to pretend to be straight. Knowing that he is something that the family despises aggravates the self-loathing and increases the need to escape into alcohol or drugs as he cannot escape from the family any other way. These are problems we will look at more closely later.

It is therefore not surprising that many gay men drown their problems in drink. Early research by Fifield (1975), who interviewed bartenders and their customers in Los Angeles, not surprisingly, came up with alarming figures. He concluded that 10% were in the "crisis stage" of alcoholism and 21% in a "high risk" category. Lohrenz studied gay men in the American midwest in 1978 and came up with similar figures, classifying 29% as alcoholics. Weinberg and Williams studied approximately 2500 gay men in the United States, the Netherlands and Denmark in 1975. They reported that 29% drank more than they should, and 31% of these said they did it "pretty often".

Given all the homophobia and negative homophobia that gay men can experience plunging them into low self-esteem and self-loathing right from puberty, given their victimisation and rejection, and their proximity in a gay bar to alcohol, it is not surprising that the Pride Institute of Minneapolis (the first drug rehabilitation centre in the US to be dedicated exclusively to gay men and lesbians) give the statistics in their publication *Our Voice* (1989) of 33% of the gay and lesbian population being "chemically dependent", compared to 10% to 12% of the population at large.

M.T. Saghir *et al.* (1970) and C.W. Lewis *et al.* (1982) compared a sample of gay men and lesbians from a homophile organisation with a control group of people living in an apartment complex and found that only 19% of the gay men were heavy drinkers compared to 11% of the straight control group.

The Skinner and Otis research (page 15) done in 1996 in two southern-state metropolitan areas of the US found that 18.3% of the gay men had consumed 5 or more alcoholic drinks on between 1 and 4 days of the past month and 11.4% had consumed 5 or more drinks on between 5 and 19 days of the past month; whereas for the NHSDA figures for the population at large the figures for men were 13.6% and 9.4% respectively.

Other more recent studies have shown that while an only slightly larger percentage of gay men drink alcohol than straight men, there are a great many more moderate and heavy drinkers amongst the gay men.

In *Textbook of Homosexuality and Mental Health* Robert Cabaj reports an estimated 28%–35% of gay men abusing drugs of all types. He arrives at these figures from a concensus of studies (Beatty 1983; Diamond and Wilsnack 1978, Lewis *et al*. 1982; Lohrenz *et al*. 1978; McKirman and Peterson 1989; Mosbacher 1988; Pillard 1988; Saghir and Robins 1973), reports (L. Fifield *et al*. unpublished observations 1975; Lesbian and Gay Substance Abuse Planning Group, unpublished observations, August 1991) reviews of literature (E.S. Morales *et al*. unpublished observations 1983; Weinberg and Williams 1974) and the experiences of most clinicians with gay male patients (Cabaj 1992; Finnegan and McNally 1987). This incidence compares with 10%–12% in the US general public. McDonald and Steinhorn agree that use of drugs is three times greater with gay men than with straight men. They go on to say that, because of the dangers of HIV infection, many gay men now try to avoid alcohol and drugs because they realise that these will lower their inhibitions and make them more likely to indulge in unsafe, unprotected sex. However, that was ten years ago and the present younger generation will not remember the huge television campaign that was mounted about AIDS in the 1980s and may feel that, as long as they have sex only with young men, they will not become infected with HIV and therefore do not need to practise safe sex. They have perhaps not realised that there are still syphilis and gonorrhoea that they need to protect themselves against

The problem with interviewing bartenders and their customers in gay bars in a large city is that only a proportion of the gay population is visible in the gay community. There is a hidden population of gay men of who-knows-what proportion that never frequents gay pubs/bars or shops for two reasons: either they abhor other gay men because they cannot bear the repressed anger that leaks out of their ears and other symptoms of their straitjacket, or their parents do not permit them to come out.

BITCHING

If you cannot express your anger and aggression to compete openly with other men and become better than someone else, then another way you can end up being in a superior position is by pulling the other person down.

This is done by making derogatory remarks – commonly known as "bitching". Unfortunately, while it may cause a great deal of laughter, people who are bitchy tend to alienate the very people they would like to make into friends. The "gay" façade is just a façade.

Channelling one's anger in this way can make you the star of the party but once the party is over it is usually not much of a success. You end up being the loser.

VEILED COMPETITIVENESS

While some may quite openly make derogatory remarks other people who are frightened of appearing in such a bad light or competing openly, resort to competing with others in a veiled way. Everything they do is better, everything they own is better, and their friends are more famous, more important or cleverer.

They put down everything you have, the friends you know, or the holidays or trips you take. If you are, for instance, planning a trip to Barcelona the response you get will be: "Oh, I'm tired of Barcelona. We just found it so dull last year. We went to Mykonos this year. It's full of rich/ beautiful people." ". . .Like us" or ". . . who instantly became our friends" is, of course, implied.

This kind of veiled competitiveness is equally unattractive. The people who engage in it end up by alienating those whom they are trying to impress. There are some gay men who loathe the gay scene and never appear on it. I think it is this kind of thing that they cannot tolerate.

FEELING OPPRESSED

Back in 1967 homosexuality had become legal in England and Wales for consenting men over the age of twenty-one though only in private, and the gay movement was well under way by 1976. There were a Gay Walkers' Group, a Gay Nudist Group, a Gay Swimmers' Group, and I thought: Why shouldn't there be a wrestling group? All we needed was a venue. I went to investigate the South London Gay Community Centre.

This was a shop in Railton Road, Brixton, a run-down suburb of London, that had been squatted (possession taken illegally of vacant premises). An unbelievably amazing array of characters, some quite bizarre, many unemployed, frequented it. There was, for instance, a young man with long ginger hair down to his shoulders who wore a white Roman toga and who many people thought resembled Christ. There was a young man who always wore face make-up that was somewhere between women's make-up and a clown's make-up, incorporating, as it did, sequins and glitter. There was one young man who always wore a lounge suit "to keep up appearances" while in the streets outside down-and-outs and drunks roamed about. In later years the district was the scene of violent race riots.

The Centre was run by a committee that consisted of literally anyone who happened to be there at the time. There was a tiny basement where discos were held on Saturday nights and I applied to use the basement for a gay wrestling group on Sunday nights.

There was a great scream of protest from a militant segment of the committee that wrestling oppressed all gay men who were not into wrestling and that the macho gay men coming to the centre every week to wrestle would make all the other gays there feel inferior.

Well!! I was even *more* than surprised!! I was taken aback!! I had never in my wildest dreams thought I would *oppress* anyone!!

It had crossed my mind that the sight of an occasional vision of muscle might lure some of the more faint hearts on to the wrestling mat. I had only seen that as a good thing. They might actually find they enjoyed it once they got involved!! But *oppress* them? Who, *me*?

I had thought my arms were open and welcoming. In fact, I had to have it explained to me that a lot of gay men feel oppressed by society. They feel oppressed, of course, because their anger has been stifled and, with it, their ability to be aggressive or to compete. Unable to use their anger they are unable to stand up for themselves, to prevent themselves being pushed around, being put upon, being manipulated or being exploited.

No wonder they feel oppressed. But they are not actually being oppressed by society that puts the same pressures on other (heterosexual) men who manage in spite of it. They are being oppressed by their *own* inability to express their anger. What causes that? Why can they not express their anger? Why is it repressed?

As we have already seen, many gay men feel that wrestling is "something they should not do". What makes them feel like that? Why should they not wrestle if they want to? Is it tied up with not being able to express their anger? Not being able to compete?

We shall see. It is all part of the straitjacket that stifles us and makes us helpless.

DEPRESSION

Research has shown that some people are more liable to become depressed than others. Alcohol can cause depression leading to a worsening of self-esteem (Cabaj 1996) If you are sober and depressed, this is usually caused by being angry with someone and not being able to tell them (Malan 1979, p.3). This usually raises the questions: Whom are you angry with? Why are you angry with them? and Why can you not tell them? Strange how unexpressed anger keeps popping up, isn't it?

Typical situations where one cannot express one's anger are with people who provide you with something: One's parents provide one with love and care (and a home for much of one's life). One's boss provides one with a job and money. And one's lover provides one with love and care and sexual fulfilment.

You may be frightened that, if you tell them you are angry with them, they will be hurt, offended, or will not like you any more and will take away those things they provide which you need. Many people feel that nice people do not express anger.

If you were frightened by the anger of your parents when you were a child then it is natural to feel that others would feel the same way about you if you showed your anger to them. Children express lots of emotions, particularly the ones that they do not know how to deal with, by crying, and anger is one of them.

I can remember my father telling me as a child when I was crying that, if I did not stop crying, he would give me something to cry about. This helped to stifle my anger (which was already repressed) even further and made it difficult for me, for the rest of my life, to be able to express it.

Why is it then that depression sometimes rears its head after a bereavement?

The remaining partner is angry with the deceased because he/she feels that their partner has abandoned them. Of course the dead partner cannot be told how angry the surviving partner is with him/her, and the anger that cannot be expressed results in depression.

PERPETUAL ANGER

Some people who have not expressed anger since they were born have bottled up so much anger that they cannot help it oozing out of their ears. (My friend Andy is an example of this, as I mentioned earlier.) Everything seems to annoy them. And it is significant that it is usually *things* and not people that irritate them.

People might retaliate or become aggressive. Usually their anger is out of proportion to the cause because all the bottled-up anger from the past cannot help coming out too. This becomes very tiring for their friends, if they have any.

A friend of mine hates cats and gets very angry at the sight of one. In the play about the romance between Robert Browning and Elizabeth Barrett, when the lovers elope to escape Elizabeth's tyrant of a father, her father searches for her pet dog to wreak his anger and vengeance on. Fortunately, Elizabeth has taken her dog with her to Italy. Enlightened by the plot of the play, I suspected my friend's anger with cats was displaced from a person. It didn't take much research to discover that he hated his sister who had a cat and to draw the conclusion that instead of confronting his sister with his anger he vented it on cats who, for him, represent his sister's cat. It is surprising the ravelled way the mind can work.

ACTING OUT

It is a coincidence that Winifred Rushforth described putting anger out of one's mind as like locking the children in the cellar where they are able to turn the water, heating and power off, because when I was a child I did just that when I was punished by my father and had no other way of expressing my anger.

I simply switched the electricity off at the mains when my mother was cooking Sunday lunch and my revenge was complete when they phoned the electricity company to report the power failure and never thought to check the mains switch. The electricity company sent a truck with several workmen from Cape Town fourteen miles to our smallholding in Kuils River to try to find the fault.

When people are frightened of expressing their anger they sometimes do something to "get back" at the person without having to confront him/her with the anger that they caused. Of course, if pressed, the person will deny that there was anything intended by whatever they did. This does not help the anger to go away.

A more virulent strain is when people bottle up their anger and are unable, for whatever reason, even to contend with the person who caused the anger. They then find someone else who reminds them in some way of the real person they are angry with to unload all their anger on to instead.

Sometimes they may even set the person up so as to have an excuse to be angry with them for in the first place. They feel unable to tell the person who caused the anger in the first place that they are angry with them usually, like people who become depressed, because they need something from that person or because that person is someone they love, used to love or ought to love.

Psychologists call this "acting out". This is a problem psychiatrists often have to deal with and it causes them headaches as there can be no resolution of the problem unless the perpetrator admits that he is angry and that that is why he acted in the way that he did.

If the person is so frightened of expressing his anger in the first place that he has to act out instead, he is most unlikely to admit to being angry in the second place and so the situation becomes deadlocked causing headaches for the psychiatrist, the patient and the patient's victim.

All acting out achieves is to poison relationships. As one relationship is poisoned and the victim bows off the scene the perpetrator then has to find another victim to take his place in order to be able to act out on instead, so that he can continue "acting out" his anger. The perpetrator ends up being a lonely person.

Anger can be directed at things, as we saw in the previous section, **Perpetual Anger**, but "acting out" is directed at people. The problem is that when anger is "acted out" it is not dissipated and does not go away or evaporate. This makes the problem particularly difficult to deal with as one cannot reason with a person who is "acting out" his anger.

One can recognise this when it happens as the anger being expressed will be out of all proportion to whatever the second person (the victim) is supposed to have done to provoke it. Psychiatrists' waiting rooms and the law courts are full of people in this unhappy state. We will examine the problems caused by repressing anger more closely when we look at the benefits one can get from expressing one's anger safely.

PASSIVE-AGGRESSIVE BEHAVIOUR

Dentemaro and Krantz give a wonderful example of passive-aggressive behaviour in their book *A Straight Talk About Anger*.

Mother says to her daughter, "Could you babysit your little sister this weekend?"

Daughter replies, "Oh, mother, I'm going to Mary's party on Saturday night and Louise and I are going ice-skating on Sunday!"

Mother responds, "Your father and I wanted to go to a hotel for the weekend to give your father a break."

Daughter says, "It'll spoil my arrangements for the weekend. Can't you go to the hotel some other time?"

Mother then says, "Yes, we'll just have to go some other time. Your father hasn't been feeling well and I thought a break would do him good. The hotel was making a half-price offer for this weekend only, but we can go some other time."

Mother could, of course, have been direct and said, "Look, my dear, your father hasn't been feeling well and I think a break would do him good. There's this hotel that has a half-price offer for this weekend only. I know you have made arrangements for this weekend already, but could you make a big sacrifice for your father and stay home and babysit your little sister so that we can get away? I'm sure your father would appreciate it very much."

Passive-aggressive behaviour can appear to be kind or complimentary but ends up being hurtful as with these further examples:

"Oh, I see you've had your hair cut! Did you cut it yourself?"

"Did you have a nice holiday? Couldn't you afford to go away?"

The person will deny that he is angry or that there is a sub-text. He will use the excuse, "I was only joking! Can't you take a joke?"

But passive-aggressive behaviour leaves a sour taste in people's mouths and will sour a relationship or, at worst, poison it completely. People feel that they do not need this kind of sentiment and can probably do without it, so why should they endure it?

THE DESTRUCTIVE POWER OF ANGER

People may be frightened of expressing their anger because of painful childhood memories of seeing the destructive power of anger: especially of an adult who was inebriated or completely drunk. This may have become the *proof* for them that anger is only destructive and that expressing their anger would bring dangers. They did not like what happened (they may have actually been terrified) and this may have left them also with the feeling that, in turn, nobody would like *them* if they expressed their anger and behaved in that kind of way.

But, of course, expressing one's anger does not necessarily mean breaking the place up or starting a fight. I have already shown how Andy was able to express his anger with me in a very calm and relaxed way (page 22) and shown the different levels that one can use to express anger (page 9).

People put their anger out of their minds, hoping or believing that it will go away. What happens is that they end up with an enormous amount of anger bottled up inside them and then, suddenly, if they let go or, worse, *lose control* of their anger over some small point (as with the camel it may only be a straw), the flood-gates are opened and it all pours out in a way that is quite out of proportion to the event. It may be very destructive if a great deal of anger has been repressed and been festering inside the person for a long time.

Losing control of one's anger is not the same thing as using one's anger in a controlled way. Losing control of one's anger occurs because people are unable to express their anger calmly when it first occurs and they bottle it up instead. If people have a lot of anger bottled up inside them it may need very little provocation for them simply to lose control of it completely and unexpectedly, and for it to burst out uncontrollably at a time when they would most like to keep it under control and when such a display of anger is most inappropriate.

JUST GOOD FRIENDS

As unpalatable as it may be to many people, the fact is that submissive, repressed men are not sexually attractive to most people except, of course, to sadists. And their own mothers.

The type of men that most people find sexually attractive are ones who are in charge of their lives, who know what they want and who get what they want. This means men who are able to express their anger so that they are not put upon, pushed around, manipulated or exploited – especially not by their mothers.

Gay men have cottoned on to this in so far as they have realised what key unlocks many gay guys' sexual feelings and so they dress up like these sorts of people: hard hats, leather motorbike gear, gym vests, cycling shorts, or whatever. This is also undoubtedly the reason that gay men are going to the gym in droves as Brian Pronger attests in his book *The Arena of Masculinity*.

Does this work? You bet it does! It helps them score. After they have scored the only problem is that once the new conquest discovers, or realises, that the sexually-attractive muscular guy in the hard hat or whatever is really a mother's boy, the sexual attraction fades and they end up being just good friends.

Of course there are many men on the gay scene who have long-lasting affairs, but for most gay men, by the age of thirty, they have begun to realise they are not going to find Mr Right.

One needs to remember that, while there are a lot of gay men on the scene, there are also a lot who never go on it at all. Perhaps they have already come to two frightening conclusions. They know that they stand very little chance of picking anyone up. Or they do not *want* to pick up any of those on the scene. They can see they are just wearing fancy dress, and are not taken in by it.

This will change for you if you come out of your straitjacket because, if you use your anger to take control of your life, you will become sexually attractive.

LOCKED IN THE CLOSET

On the subject of alcohol abuse we looked briefly at gay men who are prevented from going on the gay scene by homophobic families, who never let them out of their sight. Let us look at this group a little more closely. These men dare not come out because they know they would be despised by their families and ostracised by them. They live in the pockets of their families (or the families manage to keep them under surveillance though the families would see this merely as "being close") and for these gay men being "themselves" is simply impossible. They dare not have phone calls from gay friends because they would not be able to explain them to their families. They dare not buy gay magazines or accept gay "freebies" because they have nowhere at home where they could hide them. As a result they find it difficult to find out about gay pubs and clubs and other gay associations that might be of interest to them. Even if they manage to find out, they are never able to go to any gay establishment because they would never be able to explain to their families where they had been or make an excuse.

A gay man I knew about six years ago fell into this category. He was an alcoholic, and did his drinking at a local straight pub/bar and at home. His parents had treated him badly, which made him despise himself, but he would not go to Alcoholics Anonymous or his doctor for help.

We have been talking about people who repress their anger being manipulated. These are extreme examples of people being manipulated, and not being able to stand up for themselves. I have no idea what percentage of gay men fall into this category but they are living in virtual prisons and will stay there until their parents die, by which time their youth will have passed, and probably all their chances of finding happiness with a mate. By that time they will be so used to living in a prison that they will not know how to behave in the outside world. The freedom of the outside world will seem dangerous to them and leave them feeling exposed. They will probably create a new prison for themselves as the only way they can feel comfortable because, as they will see it, their new prison will protect them from the dangers of the outside world.

CONCLUSION

This chapter suggests that repressed anger is the cause and mechanism of the gay straitjacket and that there are many consequences of repressing anger which one would rather be without, especially if you value your happiness.

Psychology is a very young discipline which may be the reason that, in the face of these classic symptoms of repressed anger that are so prevalent in 90% of gay men, it seems that most psychiatrists have not recognised that gay men repress their anger. Books such as *Textbook of Homosexuality and Mental Health* (edited by Robert Cabaj and Terry Stein), *Male Ho-*

mosexuality: a Contemporary Psychoanalytic Perspective by Richard Friedman and the *Psychology of Sexual Orientation* (edited by Louis Diamant and Richard McAnulty) do not address what is, for most gay men, a simple neurosis that has become a major problem for them in distorting their lives. Because the neurosis occurs so early in life they seem to have accepted that "that is the way it is".

If that was indeed the case, gay men would be frightened of playing body-contact sports and that would be the end of it. There would not be in addition all the mechanisms I have been describing in the above pages for dealing with internal anger that is becoming uncontrollable that are symptomatic of repressed anger.

After publication of this book I am sure that we will see a change in the attitude of psychiatrists unless there is a reason of which I am not aware.

How long do you want to go on spending your life in a straitjacket? Not all gay men suffer from all the consequences that have been described, but the price of having to endure even one or two of them is a high one.

As you can see, it is very important to be able to express one's anger and you are therefore quite justified in being very angry with your parents for not encouraging you to express yours. Other (straight) boys are encouraged by *their* parents to express their anger, so you must be very angry with your parents that they prevented you from expressing your anger and did not encourage you to express it. We will discover in Chapter 2 why there is this difference between how pre-gay and straight boys are treated.

Understanding ourselves is so important to our happiness that it is a crime that psychology is not taught in schools. I spent a great part of my life on the verge of suicide, subject to depressive moods that I was unable to understand and unable to do many things that other "integrated" people seemed to find so easy. It has taken me most of my life to understand why I was the way I was, and in doing so I have learned why it is that other people are the way *they* are. Without this knowledge I would never have found happiness with Andy.

I hope you will be able to learn from my experience and find happiness too. The implication so far may have been that all the gay man has to do to escape his straitjacket is to engage in some anger-release therapy. Unfortunately, it is not as simple as that. I will of course explain how you can rid yourself of the "fear of violence" neurosis (see Glossary) that I have alluded to. This is overlaid by complicating factors as we shall see in the next chapter.

You may, however, also be wondering why this gay straitjacket (or anger-repression neurosis) occurs in as many as 90% of gay men but not in the other 10%. Let us start by looking at the nature of homosexuality and bisexuality which will help us to understand also why the repression of anger is so common amongst gay and bisexual men.

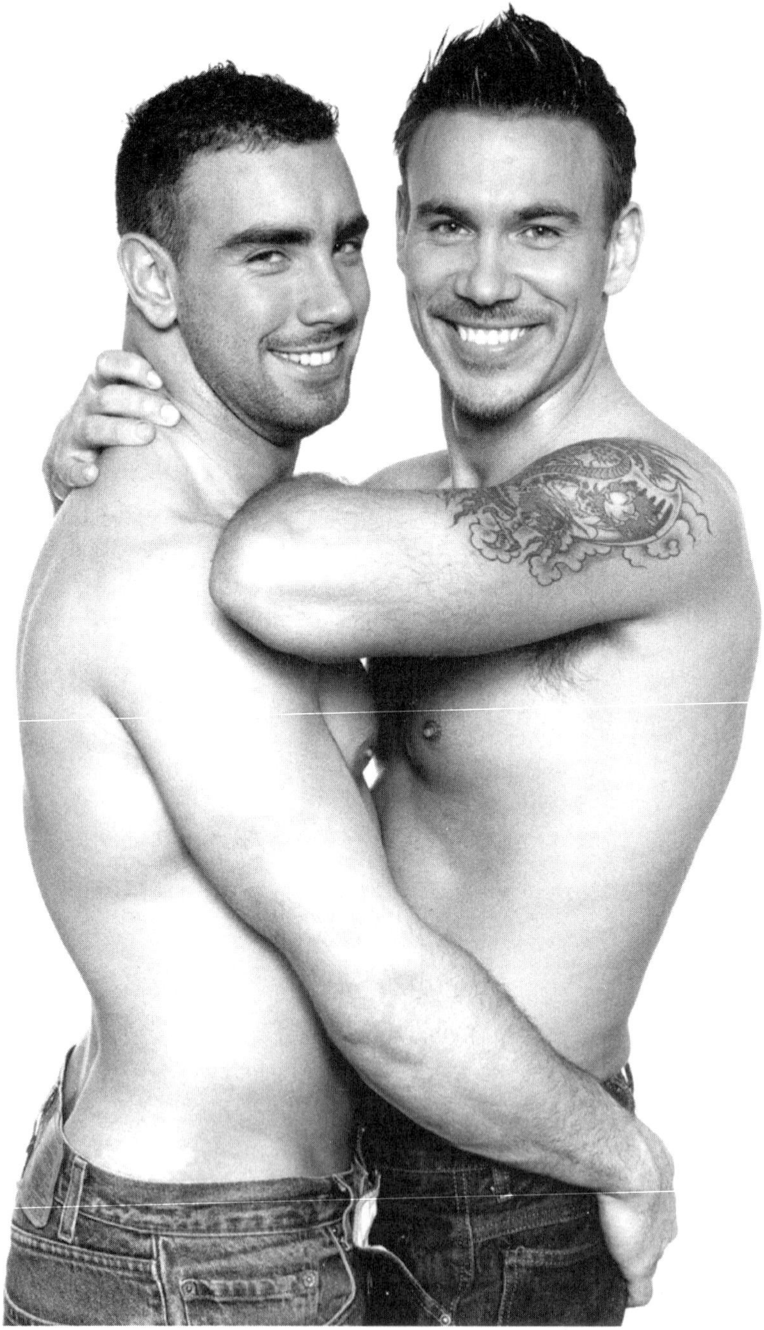

THE NATURE OF HOMOSEXUALITY AND BISEXUALITY

TO help us understand the nature of the gay straitjacket better, and in particular what the gay man can do to escape it, we need to look first at the nature of homosexuality.

You may have noticed that in the very first paragraph of this book I hinted (in an anecdote) at how one mother treated her young son. What if you had been that son? How would you have felt about your mother?

They say that what freaked Oedipus out was not the discovery that he had killed his own father and married his mother, but the discovery that when he was a baby his parents had tried to kill him by leaving him in the woods where the wolves would kill him. They did that because they had been given a prophecy that he would murder his father and marry his mother and they hoped that, by killing him, they would prevent the prophecy from coming true. (In writing that last sentence I very nearly wrote ". . . murder his father and kill his mother" which would have been a Freudian slip revealing how I feel about my own mother.)

Of course I am not suggesting that your mother and father wanted to kill you as a child.

But you must be very angry with your parents that they prevented you from expressing your anger and did not encourage you to express it as is the case with other (straight) boys.

Children will do anything to be loved and we automatically feel (perhaps because we *want* to feel) that our parents will act in our best interests. What if you suddenly discover that they did *not* act always in your best interests? A wave of anger might sweep through you at such a discovery but, because you are so skilled as you have been all your life in putting your anger out of your mind, you will not even be aware of this wave of anger sweeping through you. Would it leave you feeling betrayed? Can you be angry with someone you love? Can you love someone you are angry with?

We have seen in Chapter 1 how many problems can be caused by repressing one's anger.

Well, of course, one *can* both love and hate the same person but for people who repress their anger, as *you* do, it can be a very difficult feat to achieve. Malan explains this in his book *Individual Psychotherapy and the Science of Psychodynamics*. He describes with great sensitivity the crisis that this can cause:

> What the therapist needs to reach, by every means in his power, is *hidden anger against someone whom the patient needs or loves* – or in Freud's words, *has* loved or *ought* to love . . . this mixture of love and hate for the same person is one of the deepest and most painful conflicts that human beings suffer from, and depressive patients will do everything in their power to avoid it.
>
> The forces in the individual opposing the acknowledgment of this anger or hate are of many different kinds. There is first of all simply the *pain of conflict*; there is *guilt*, already mentioned many times; and there are all the offshoots of love, which include *sadness* and *grief, concern, tenderness, remorse, protectiveness, compassion*, and the *need for reparation*; and in the end these may lead to the ultimate sacrifice, the feeling that one will kill oneself rather than acknowledge, or bear the pain of, or give expression to, the impulse to harm the other person.
>
> (Copyright: Butterworth-Heinemann Ltd. Used with permission.)

In exploring the nature of homosexuality we are going to find the role played by some parents; and I must warn you that you may find these revelations difficult, painful, or even impossible to bear.

If you find that the passage leaves you feeling suicidal then, without doubt, it is caused as Malan suggests by the difficulty of facing how angry you feel with someone who has been so good to you and whom you love so much.

You may not feel angry, you may feel only suicidal. You may not feel your anger because you have repressed your anger throughout your life (that is what this whole book is about). The fact that you do not feel your anger does not mean it is not there. It means that your anger is residing in your subconscious where you are not aware of it.

How do I know that? Well, if you took the anger out of the equation you would only feel disappointed with your parents. You would feel regret at what had happened. You would not feel suicidal. If you feel suicidal it shows that there must be anger there (whether you feel it or not) which you cannot bear to feel for your parents, so the anger rebounds from your parents whom you are really quite right to feel angry with. It rebounds to yourself and you feel angry with yourself because you have dared to feel angry with your loving parents; and because you feel that you must be a terrible person to feel angry with your parents who love you and who have given you so much. You may feel that suicide is all that you deserve. However, if you went through with it your parents would be absolutely distraught and beside themselves with grief. Do you really want to cause them so much pain?

Whether your parents behaved in the way they did intentionally or whether it was wholly unintentional on their part, is immaterial. You are quite right to feel angry with them. They will love you none the less. That is really the important thing.

If the rest of the chapter is so dangerous, is it worth risking reading it at all? It may be a baptism of fire but it will help you to come out a better and happier person in the end. I say that as one who has already travelled the path. At present you are labouring under a misapprehension and knowing the truth always gives you power, painful as it may be to acquire that knowledge.

The nature of homosexuality has been studied for decades by sociologists, psychologists and biologists who have tried to discover the cause of homosexuality, and in doing so have revealed its real nature.

Strangely enough, the cause has been attributed to different things by sociologists, psychologists and biologists but if you accept one set of findings that does not mean that the others must be wrong. It simply means that each of the disciplines has looked at the subject from only one viewpoint and seen only one facet of it. It is not surprising to discover that homosexuality is a multi-faceted state.

What I have attempted to do is to try to put all the facets or findings together and then suggest a model of homosexuality that is logical and demonstrates how each facet is linked to the others to form a whole that cannot exist without the evidence from all the disciplines. It is necessary that the model is consistent with our everyday experience of homosexuals and homosexuality. If it did not reflect homosexuals as we know ourselves and as others know us, then the model would be suspect.

Very often gay men (and especially militant ones) reject research evidence because they do not like what it says about them or about their parents, and they therefore reject it out of hand, labelling it as "academic", implying that it has no relevance to everyday homosexuals. (You will see later why I hesitate to use the phrase "normal homosexuals".)

One psychologist (no less) who had read my book *Wrestling for Gay*

Guys (and should have known better) suggested that I should rewrite the book as the research evidence I quoted was "dated". The findings of Galileo, Newton and Darwin are also dated but that does not make them invalid. Had he presented me with alternative research (that he approved of) I might have paid more attention to him. Many more readers have told me how similar the research findings were to their own life experiences.

Dr Irving Bieber (whom we shall discuss later) suggested that homosexuals had a "close-binding-intimate" relationship with their mothers and a bad relationship with their fathers who were often absent. Militant homosexuals rejected these findings out of hand because Bieber and his associates (who were all psychiatrists) had come to these conclusions by examining their patients. What applied to "mentally-ill homosexuals", cried the militant homosexuals, could not apply to homosexuals who were well.

However, many other researchers came to the same conclusions from studying homosexuals who were "mentally well" as Bieber did from studying homosexuals who were "mentally ill" so it seems that they *do* apply to all homosexuals, and dodging the truth will not bring home the bacon.

For this reason I have occasionally included anecdotes in order to illustrate what researchers have found by offering their message freed from technical jargon. Hopefully, the anecdotes will ring bells for some of my readers where the clinical facts may not.

I am not really concerned with the cause or causes of homosexuality, but with the *nature* of homosexuality. In exploring this we may well find ourselves looking at the cause, if there is any, too.

CROSS-DRESSING

Many sociologists exploring the nature of homosexuality have found that persistent cross-dressing (that is, dressing in clothes of the opposite sex) in male children was a good (80%) indicator that the child would grow up into a homosexual adult (the other 20% grew up heterosexual).

Frederick Whitam and Robin Mathy, who researched *Male Homosexuality in Four Societies* (Brazil, Guatemala, the Philippines and the United States), found that 90% of their homosexual sample had exhibited cross-gender behaviour (playing with girls' toys, cross-dressing, etc.) as children.

The relevance of these figures here is that, probably, 90% of adult male homosexuals have displayed a strong feminine need as children, while 10% have not displayed such a need. You may think that the latter 10% grow up more straight-appearing (and perhaps more closeted) than the former 90% and this is indeed what Whitam and Mathy found in their sample.

I have already alluded to these figures of 90% and 10%. This is where they come from and they will crop up again and again in this book as they mark a fundamental difference between these two groups of gay men which carry over into different aspects of their lives. They have been confirmed by many other researchers, as we will see in the next section.

What these figures tell us is not only that there is a range of homosexual types, but that the great majority have shown a strong feminine need as children. As adults this need may remain the same, it may have decreased, or it may have increased.

THREE GROUPS OF HOMOSEXUALS

Whitam and Mathy found that the male homosexuals they studied in the four societies fell into three broad groupings: In 10% there was no early cross-gender behaviour. As adults this group were quite masculine in appearance and had occupations such as engineer or electrician. The second group consisted of 65% of their sample. These were cross-gendered to varying degrees as children but this behaviour diminished or disappeared at puberty. As adults they chose traditional masculine occupations including physician and stockbroker, but also arts or interior design. The remaining group of 25% exhibited extensive cross-gender behaviour as children and remained more or less effeminate as adults with some cross-gender behaviour. The occupations they chose included interior design, florist and hairdresser.

What is remarkable is that the 10% group of homosexuals in their sample does not show any femininity at any stage during their lives. In this way they stand quite apart from the other 90% of gay men who have shown varying degrees of femininity. We shall learn more about them later in this chapter.

These percentages applied to all four societies Whitam and Mathy studied and are generally confirmed in varying degrees by the other researchers in the field.

Whitam and Mathy report that cross-gender behaviour (including cross-dressing) and the relationship with adult sexuality had been studied and established by Bieber *et al.* (1962), Zuger (1966, 1970, 1978), Stoller (1968), Evans (1969), Kleeman (1971), Lebovitz (1972), Saghir and Robins (1973), Paluszny *et al.* (1973), Thompson *et al* (1975), Money and Tucker (1975), Green (1976, 1979, 1986), Whitam (1977, 1980), and Money and Russo (1978).

Richard Green (whom we will meet in the next section) reports that Joseph Harry (1982) studied fifteen hundred homosexuals of whom 36% remembered cross-dressing as children, and that Alan Bell and his colleagues in a study of 600 homosexual men found that 37% had cross-dressed and pretended to be female as children (Bell *et al.*, 1981).

What all these researchers have clearly identified is a spectrum of femininity in their samples of male children who grew up into homosexual adults that stretches over about 90% of their samples with 25% to 37% having cross-dressed as children and the remainder showing lesser cross-gender behaviour such as avoiding boys' games, playing with girls, playing house, playing with dolls, and being called "sissy". (Being called "sissy", short for "sister", may not in itself seem to make a child effeminate but one has to realise that it represents behaviour which the boy's peers see as sufficiently unmasculine to be worthy of the epithet.)

PARENTS AND HOMOSEXUALITY

The best, longest and most thorough study of gay men and their parents was done by Richard Green, a Los Angeles psychiatrist (now professor of psychiatry and professor of law in residence at the University of California at Los Angeles), who repeatedly interviewed straight sons as well as gay sons before and after puberty in his study *as well as their parents* over a *15-year* period.

Compared to most of the previous studies, this was a mammoth task. He undertook his study because earlier researchers had shown the importance of persistent cross-dressing by children as an indicator of adult homosexuality. Green hoped to clarify why 80% *did* become homosexual and why 20% did *not*.

He took as his sample boys who cross-dressed persistently and, as a control group, boys who did *not* cross-dress. He hoped to establish why some boys exhibit cross-gender behaviour and some do not, and to find out how these childhood behaviours affect the sexuality of the adult.

He interviewed his sample of boys before puberty and after puberty. He also interviewed their parents several times over the years. Much of his subsequent report, *The "Sissy Boy Syndrome" and the Development of Homosexuality*, is taken up with verbatim transcriptions of his interviews so that the reader can judge the quality of the respondents' statements directly.

If I refer repeatedly to his findings, you should not assume it is because Green is alone in research in this field. The reason rather is that he has studied the development of the boys' personalities as well as their relationships with their parents at different times over a 15-year period and he has studied their parents *as well*. He also used a technique known as "depth interviewing". That means that subjects are allowed to talk and associate freely on the given topic rather than reply to a set of formal questions, some of which may, at best, be restrictive or, at worst, loaded.

This has resulted in a far clearer understanding of these relationships than other, smaller studies were capable of. The other studies play an important part in confirming the validity of Green's work and, indeed, in making it possible in the first place. I have also found in his results explanations for phenomena that I have observed around me. In fact, the boys in my Gay Wrestling Group unwittingly corroborated his findings as I shall explain later.

What he found was that the majority of the parents of the gay men had wanted girls during the pregnancy and that, after a boy was born, the fathers showed a loss of interest that resulted in their absence (compared to the fathers of the sons who grew up to be straight) at the crucial time of their son's life between the second and fifth years. Disappointed fathers who were not absent when the to-become-gay son was aged 2 to 5 years can still make the child feel abandoned, which is much the same thing.

Green was not alone in this finding. Researchers who had found evidence before him of hostile or absent fathers and close or overprotective mothers included Irving Bieber *et al.* (1963) and, as reported by Whitam and Mathy in *Male Homosexuality in Four Societies*, Miller (1958), West (1959), Brown (1963), O'Connor (1964), Evans (1969), Thompson *et al.* (1973), Stephan (1973) and Saghir and Robins (1973).

Some friends of mine have tried to contradict these findings by assuring me that they had had good relationships with their fathers. In fact the time they had a good relationship with their fathers was during their teen years and this is in stark contrast to straight sons who, during their teen years, form alliances ("gangs") with their peers and tend to rebel against their fathers. It is during the period of 2 to 5 years that the damage of a bad or distant relationship with their fathers is done in the case of gay men. It should be pointed out that most of us do not have a very clear memory of that time of our lives apart from isolated incidences and so it is really of little use asking gay men whether they had a distant relationship with their father, though evidence of this bad relationship may persist into later years at a time that is easily remembered.

Amongst my friends one gay man (at the time about 27 years old) told me that he had not spoken to his father since he was 7 years old. Another gay man I knew shared his mother's bed with her as a child when his father went to fight in the Second World War, presumably for mutual comfort, but when his father returned my acquaintance refused to give up his place in his mother's bed and his father was forced to sleep in another bedroom until the marriage eventually broke up.

Of the gay sons in Green's study 6% had been dressed in female clothes from *before* their *first* birthday, 35% from before their second birthday, and (when the child was able to choose for himself, let it be said) 55% from before their third birthday when the parents indulged this cross-dressing, whereas the parents of the straight sons actively discouraged it. On the other hand, there were a few children in the study who cross-dressed in spite of their parents' attempts to stop them.

After I had written about Green's findings in my book *Wrestling for Gay Guys* one gay man that I had wrestled with admitted to me that he could remember being taken to the doctor by his mother and the doctor saying to her, "Why do you dress him like this? You must stop dressing him in girls' clothes!" He could not remember what age he was at the time.

In the first paragraph of Chapter 1 of this book I described the boy in the pram whose ringlets made him look like a girl.

I should confess here that when I came of age at 21 I had two parties: one for my family and family friends, but another (drag) party for my gay friends at which I wore a strapless, white ballgown that I had had specially made for the occasion. Although I thought at the time that that was the thing to do and was what I wanted, I realised later that I felt claustrophobic when I wore women's clothes so I stopped doing it. The fact that it felt claustrophobic indicates to me now that it is more evidence of the constricting effect of the gay straitjacket.

Now before you jump to the conclusion that your mother (or both your parents) manipulated you, you need to appreciate that we *all* would have the world behave the way we want it to and so we are all guilty of attempting to manipulate others at some time or other.

We have seen (page 9) that anger prevents people from being manipulated so if you were manipulated the fault lies just as much with you because, had you been able to express your anger, you would have been able to say, "Sorry, mom, but I want to learn judo to be able to prevent myself being bullied at school". Or, "Mom, if I don't kick a ball around with the other boys they'll all think I'm a sissy and I'll lose them as friends!"

Since Green's study it has allegedly been shown that a gene in the DNA can have an influence in causing homosexuality, though two independent subsequent studies were unable to find any link. This will be looked at in the section **The Gay Gene**.

In his study Green acknowledged that children are born different: he points out that a (then East) German scientist Günter Dörner, has also claimed that wrong hormones supplied to the foetus before birth can cause homosexuality. We will also look at this in the section **Wrong Hormones in the Womb**.

However, I want to emphasise that I am discussing here not the cause of homosexuality (if there is one) but the environment that children grew up in who became homosexual adults.

DISCOVERIES THROUGH WRESTLING

I ran the first wrestling club for gay men in Britain between 1976 and 1980. As the stereotype of the gay man portrays him so much as lacking in masculine aggressive qualities, you would think that if a gay man learned to wrestle this would be a great source of pride for him, and that he would want to tell everyone to gain their admiration and praise for his courage and determination and also to earn their encouragement.

To my surprise this was not the case. When I asked the members of my gay wrestling club if they had told their parents that they were learning to wrestle (an honourable achievement to know how to defend oneself from muggers in the street, I would have thought, especially for a group who are notorious for lacking aggression), almost all said that they had *not*.

Asked why they had not told their parents the men seemed unsure of their reasons, but they seemed to think their parents would not approve of wrestling for them. They mostly admitted they would tell their parents if they joined a club to learn to play tennis.

If their parents, like those in Green's study, had wanted a daughter

The Nature of Homosexuality and Bisexuality

before the birth of their gay son and still persisted in seeing him in terms of the longed-for daughter, this would certainly explain why wrestling, in their eyes, would be inappropriate for this child and why the sons felt unable to tell their parents that they were learning to wrestle, although tennis would be acceptable.

The parents of straight men are usually pleased to be given evidence that their sons can "stand up for themselves". As most gay men (the 90%), consciously or subconsciously, feel that wrestling is "something they shouldn't really be doing" it can be expected that *their* parents still see them, their (homosexual) sons, as the daughters that they had longed for; and consequently the parents' unfulfilled longing for a daughter expresses itself in tacitly expecting the son to behave as a daughter would, tacitly (or not so tacitly as the case may be) discouraging behaviour, interests and pastimes (even friends) that do not agree with their expectations of a daughter.

The gay men, being unable to express their anger, are powerless to prevent themselves being manipulated in this way. If they are turned into "pansies" by their parents they will doubtless be very angry with their parents for not encouraging them to express their anger as other little boys do. They may also partly have themselves to blame.

The gay men need to get away from their parents' repressive attitudes before they can assert their own desire should this lead them towards participating in football, rugby, judo, wrestling or (Heaven forbid!) boxing!

Parents who are loving and understanding can still be repressive. When the first psychiatrist I consulted asked me what my parents were like, I said they were "nice people" and they *were*, but that did not stop them subtly keeping me from body-contact sports or manipulating me into a polite, inoffensive, ineffectual, "nice" boy.

Your parents might accept your being gay but this is likely to be because you are colluding with them in playing the role of the longed-for daughter (whether you are feminine or even if you are *not* physically feminine) and because you are not virile or aggressive which would completely shatter their fantasy (see Glossary).

I need to emphasise here that manipulation of the gay son to play the role of the longed-for daughter seems to occur only with the 90% of gay men, those who have shown some femininity at some point in their lives. The other 10% do not show any femininity at any point in their lives and neither do they seem to be manipulated by their parents to be feminine in any way either. They are able to participate in body-contact sports without let or hindrance and without the consequent hang-ups and problems of guilt that other gay men (the 90%) seem to suffer from as indeed *I* did. We will look at those later in The Classic Guilt Complex .

Because the other 10% of gay men are able to participate in body-contact sports like wrestling *without* any feelings that that is "something that they should not do", they find it hard to understand why the 90% of gay men have problems when trying to participate in wrestling or in any other body-contact sport.

That in itself makes it quite clear that they (the 10%) are completely different from the other 90% of gay men who have hang-ups and problems when wanting to wrestle. While helping the 90% to cure their repressed anger this book will enlighten the other10% so that they can see the problems that most gay men suffer from and can appreciate the right way to help them to participate in sports if they feel they want to.

My mother did not like the idea of my wrestling, though her brother wrestled. I found out how much she disapproved when I came back from a wrestling session one day with mat burns (when the skin is grazed on wrestling mats covered with canvas) and far from offering me any sympathy she retorted, "Serves you right!"

MISSING THE BOAT

A gay man who wants to take up a sport like wrestling is therefore likely to be in his (often late) twenties before he can make the decision to join a club.

You may think that it is no big deal if you only start to learn to wrestle in your late twenties. Better late than never. But this creates unnecessary, and often insurmountable, problems for the son.

It has generally been accepted in sports that the earlier children begin a sport the better they will become at it, and wrestling is no exception. Controlling bodies of amateur sports usually try to catch them young.

Straight men may start learning to wrestle when they are between 7 and 14 years old and may give it up when they leave school (at 16) or when they start courting, and only the really keen will continue wrestling when they have partners or families.

A gay man who joins a straight wrestling club when he is in his late twenties, will thus find that most straight guys of the same age are on the point of giving it up. In any event, they are unlikely to have the patience at that point to wrestle with a beginner (unless the beginner is their own son); and may, in any event, regard someone (even a straight beginner) wanting to learn to wrestle at such a late age, rather dubiously.

It may seem that the gay man has missed the boat (and all because of his parents!). But, wait a minute!

GAY WRESTLING CLUBS

What about joining a *gay* wrestling club?

Gay wrestling clubs are, more than likely, run by gay wrestlers who form part of the 10% of gay men who have had no coercion from their parents to avoid body-contact sports in order to play the role of the longed-for daughter and have gained sufficient experience by the time they are in their twenties to be able to run a club and to coach. Such men, as I have already pointed out, will not have experienced and will be unaware of the hang-ups or problems that the other 90% of gay men will experience described in this book and in more detail in my book *Wrestling for Gay Guys*. Like straight wrestlers they may actually have been wrestling since they were 7 years old! The feeling you will get from them is that, if you want to wrestle, why don't you just get on the mat and wrestle?

But, as this book is trying to explain, for 90% of gay men it is not as simple as that. We have already realised that 90% of gay men repress their anger, but wrestling (like most sports) requires participants to use aggression which is an offshoot or physical expression of anger.

If you cannot express anger you will not be able to be aggressive and this is, of course, why the 90% of gay men avoid sports. They do not have the wherewithal to compete against other men who have no problems with being aggressive. That is the first problem they will have.

The result for the gay man in his twenties wanting to learn to wrestle is that, while he will be made most welcome in a gay wrestling club, he will not be offered any understanding or psychological help with his problems other than he can glean for himself from my books. It is for that reason that there is a Problem Page on the Power Books website at
http://www.pb.clara.net/WresFGG/help.htm

THE FOOTBALL FAN

When I was running the Gay Wrestling Group my phone number was publicised in the gay press and I used to have many enquiries. One such enquiry was from a gay man in his forties who was turned on by footballers and regretted that he was then too old to take up the sport.

"What should I do?" he wanted to know.

"Get where the action is!" was my advice. "If you are too old to start learning football that should not stop you joining a football club. They probably need people in organisational and administrative posts. They also have linesmen and you are not too old for that. Get where the action is and you will be nearer to the men you are attracted to!"

Some months later he phoned me again to tell me that he was a linesman for a football club and was over the moon about it. He just regretted that he had not had the courage to do it earlier.

Well, you do not need me to tell you that it was his parents who held him back from enjoying his life the way he wanted to and needed to in order to be happy. When I was in my late twenties and living at home I used to feel that even going to *watch* wrestling, professional or amateur, was something I should not be doing. My gay friends at the time thought I was very daring even to do *that*!

THE OTHER BOYS ARE TOO ROUGH FOR MY LITTLE JOHNNY

Richard Green found that many of the sons who grew up to be gay adults had had a serious illness or even been hospitalised early in life. In his study some of the mothers kept their sons away from other boys once they were out of their prams because "the other boys are too rough for my little Johnny". Perhaps they had not only desired a daughter but were actually afraid, for whatever reason, of having to cope with a son who was masculine in all senses of the word, virile and aggressive.

From the mother's point of view she may believe that little harm can come from protecting her child in this way by keeping him away from other boys of his own age but this manoeuvre can actually have far-reaching repercussions for her child later in life, as we shall see.

The Nature of Homosexuality and Bisexuality

In my own case I was an extremely difficult birth for my mother as I had a congenital curved spine. I learned about it only when a gym master in high school pointed it out to me, but it was certainly the reason why I was over-protected.

My parents must clearly have given my school strict instructions that I was not to be made to play football or rugby. This was why, when a sports-master tried to involve me, for my own good, in playing rugby (pages 5–6) my parents did not know what to say to me when I reported playing my first game. They did not know what to say to me because I had never been told that I had a curved spine or that, as a consequence, I was being prevented from participating in body-contact sports. They were manipulating me behind my back.

I eventually only realised what the explanation for their behaviour was when I was in my fifties.

Hank Trout, founder and president of both the Windy City Wrestling Club in Chicago (1977–1980), and the Iron City Wrestling Club in Pittsburgh, Pennsylvania (1989–1991) until he moved to San Francisco, gave me an interview for the British alternative wrestling magazine *The Grapevine* when he visited London in 1998.

He told me he had been very sickly during the first five years of his life. In photos of the period he appears with spindly limbs and distended stomach. Finally the doctors diagnosed congenital heart defects. The heart valves were allowing too much blood into the heart and not letting enough out so that the heart swelled and rubbed against other organs.

The solution was open-heart surgery which was revolutionary for the time (late 1950s) and extremely risky as they gave him a less than 50% chance of surviving the operation and no idea of the prognosis. Without the operation they believed he would die before the age of ten. As it turned out, two days after the surgery he was out of bed, and running around with no need of therapy or medication but that did not stop his parents pampering him for the next five or six years, he told me. Physical education and rough-house were forbidden, he said, until a doctor eventually lost patience with his parents and exclaimed, "Goddammit, Anne, he's healthier than you are!! Leave him alone and let him be a boy!!"

Being kept away from one's peers as a child gives the gay man little chance of engaging in any rough-and-tumble which would help him to build his strength, and his knowledge of how to handle himself or to acquire the consequent self-confidence.

CRUSHING YOUR FATHER

Green found in his study of homosexuals and their parents that the fathers were mostly not very sporting themselves, which is why they had not encouraged their sons in the first place in ball-kicking skills that most fathers take for granted.

Apart from not wanting their "hoped-for-daughter" sons to display traditionally masculine skills, the fathers may actually feel humiliated if their sons show sporting abilities in excess of what they themselves are capable of. This may simply remind them of their own inadequacies and leave the fathers feeling totally crushed by their son's sporting abilities (if the son were to display such skills).

This has terrible consequences for the son who, frightened that he will lose his father's love (or, more likely, frightened that he will never get his father's love) will be completely crippled with regard to any sporting ability that he may up to that point have shown.

Crushing my own father, unintentional as it was, had terrible consequences for me in my own life.

When I was aged 9 or 10 my father helped me to build model theatres out of fruit boxes. They were invariably called Drury Lane at my father's suggestion after the Theatre Royal, Drury Lane in London. It never occurred to me that my father might have had aspirations in this direction. He had been in London during the First World War and I presumed he was simply drawing on his own experience.

When I was fifteen years old and in my second last year at high school, *The Squirrel Club*, the children's section of our local newspaper, *The Cape Times*, announced a play-producing competition for its young readers. I saw this as being the start of my theatrical career taking off. I was ecstatic. I entered.

I had decided to produce and direct *The Miracle Merchant* a one-act play from a short story by Saki (H.H. Munro) the British humorist, and that I would play the lead. The rest of the cast was drawn from schoolfriends. Come the day of the competition we discovered that another friend, Bill Smuts, was entering the competition. My parents lectured me repeatedly on not to forget to congratulate Bill if he should win the competition.

In the event, my production tied in first place. Neither my mother nor my father thought to congratulate me. My father, who was normally the life and soul of parties that we threw at home and who enjoyed telling my mother's lady friends jokes, sat as if he had suddenly become catatonic. After the performance he simply sat solemnly in the hall as though lost in thought and said nothing. At the time I thought nothing of it.

After that, I had difficulty in learning my lines. At dress rehearsals I would practically have a nervous breakdown as I could not remember which scene came next and panic would ensue. Acting became a terrible ordeal for me.

When I came to London my friends all thought I would try to go into the professional theatre but at that time most of the provincial theatres were doing two-weekly or, in some cases, one-weekly repertory and I knew I could never learn a part in two weeks never mind one week so a career in the theatre was a non-starter.

It was only about the age of 36 – when I was in group psychotherapy and, whenever I talked about my acting I always recalled the scene of my father sitting in the hall as though he had become catatonic – that I began to realise that that must have some significance for me in connection with my acting failure. With the help of the psychiatrist who led the group, I came to realise I had crushed my father at the time and that that had had a devastating effect on me for the rest of my life. By then it was really too late for me as far as an acting career went. The damage had been done.

CRUSHING YOUR MOTHER

If that was not enough, I actually managed to crush my mother as well though, I should emphasise, that is rather exceptional.

My mother played the piano and, I thought, quite well. She had in her repertoire pieces like Grieg's *Wedding Day at Troldhaugen*, Liszt's *Liebestraum (Nocturne No. 3)*, and *Gardens in the Rain* by Debussy which require considerable technical ability. I wanted to learn to play too and was sent to a nearby teacher, Joyce Kadish, who was a South African concert pianist of repute when I was 7 or 8 years old. She later persuaded me to take music as a subject in high school and about that time people would remark that I played with a beautiful "touch".

My mother had learned to play the piano in a small country town in the Orange Free State, a farming province of South Africa. She felt that her own playing lacked expression and she admired the touch that I had been taught. I offered to teach her how to put expression into her playing.

She was devastated, although I did not realise how devastated till much later when my father told me that when I offered to help her she had sworn she would never play the piano again! I had crushed my mother too!

When I related this to a psychiatrist much later he asked me why she had reacted in that way. I had been hoping *he* would be able to explain it to *me*.

Whenever I asked her to come and play a piece that was too difficult for me she now refused, and I found that I could no longer play any piece without making mistakes compulsively. If I managed to play one line of music without making a mistake I would be overcome by panic that rapidly increased until I ended up making a mistake. Perhaps by making mistakes I was psychologically trying to show her that I needed her help or that I was not a better pianist than she was.

I explained my problem to another psychiatrist later when I was feeling suicidal but his advice was only to practise more! This problem was later cured for me when I was in group psychotherapy at the Tavistock Clinic in London but by that time I was in my mid-thirties and again the damage had been done. I had gone to university with music as one of my subjects, but I could not keep up with the set pieces I was given to play and memorise in an attempt to cure my stumbling playing. I could neither play the pieces without mistakes nor memorise them. I dropped out of university after only three months.

In case you, like the psychiatrist, are wondering why my mother was devastated by my offer of help, I think that having a baby made her feel extremely important as she could supply all the baby's needs. She therefore wanted to retain this situation in order to retain her own importance. My asking her to play pieces that were too difficult for me maintained this importance in her eyes, but when I offered to help her it switched the relationship making *me* the important one and herself the student, and shattered her illusions of importance.

GAY MEN AND STRAIGHT MEN

In his study Green compared gay males with straight men of the same age and height and found that the former were on average 2.27 kg/5 lb lighter than the latter. However, he was dealing with boys around puberty. Another study that compared homosexual adults with heterosexual adults found that the straight men of equal height to the gay men were on average 6.25 kg/13¾ lb heavier (Weinrich 1976, p.129).

This is hardly surprising, as it is well known that gay men tend to participate less in sports than straight men do and can, therefore, expect their muscles to be less developed. Since, to be stronger, a muscle has to grow bigger, a smaller muscle is a weaker muscle. We can therefore conclude that those gay men who are lighter than their straight counterparts of the same age and height are also weaker than them.

Therefore, should a gay man decide to play a sport in his late twenties, or learn to wrestle, he is going to be up against men who are heavier and stronger than he is if he goes to a straight club. This will put him at a distinct disadvantage – a second problem for him. His third problem will be finding himself at a further disadvantage if he is learning to wrestle even with other straight beginners of the same age (late twenties) who have picked up basic wrestling strategies from rough-and-tumble during their childhood. Having been kept away from his peers as a child means he will have little knowledge of how to handle himself in rough-and-tumble, whereas his straight counterparts will have had this experience and gained this knowledge. Trying to learn some holds from books will not be sufficient to put him on an even footing with the straight beginners.

Because most gay men see wrestling as "something one shouldn't really do" they need to get away from their homes and parental control before they can decide it is something they really *do* want to do. This means that these gay men are often well into their twenties before they *begin* to learn to wrestle which is, as we have seen, *after* most straight men have given it up.

The actual problem is, as I say, that gay men need to get away from their homes and parental control, and this underlines the point that the parents do not appear to like their gay sons participating in masculine sports. The findings of the research studies about the attitudes of parents of gay sons cannot be dismissed as being purely academic and not relevant to the general public. The evidence in the general public simply corroborates the research evidence that I have quoted above.

The attitudes of parents who repress their gay son's masculine qualities in this way produce more problems for him which we will look at further in Chapter 3.

FEAR OF VIOLENCE

Guys with a lack of aggression are not usually aware of it, as *I* was not when I wrestled, and so it is not usually seen by them to be a problem. Other wrestlers complained that I was "holding back", by which they meant that I waited to be attacked before retaliating, instead of being able to initiate an attack myself.

Once when I was wrestling at the Central YMCA in London I was invited by another member to wrestle with him. He was about my height but had the most muscular thighs. In view of the episode I had suffered being trapped in the thighs of my father's friend (page 4), this made the present wrestler the most desirable guy for me to wrestle with. However, he waited for me, being a novice, to make the first move and waited, but as I was hamstrung by this "fear of violence" I was not able to do anything. I felt whatever move I made would simply play into his hands and I would be trapped again. The result was that, after five minutes of squaring up, we never even came to grips and so I never had the pleasure of wrestling with the guy with whom I most wanted to wrestle.

This is how the gay straitjacket makes us helpless and prevents us from enjoying ourselves and being able to be proud of how we acquit ourselves. Instead, we end up being ashamed of ourselves and humiliated as a result.

You do not *have* to be this way. You can change. How? Read on!

In my Gay Wrestling Group when I pointed out to one member that he was "holding back" he refused to accept my criticism so strongly that he arrived at the next workout armed with a video camera and recording e-quipment (this was the 1970s) he had borrowed so that he could see himself wrestling and so see for himself whether or not he was holding back as I claimed. I think he really believed he was going to prove me wrong. It was only when he saw himself wrestling that he could see what I was alluding to.

This "fear of violence" was cured for me by the psychiatrist at the Tavistock Clinic and serves as the central core around which this whole book has been developed. We will discover what it is in Chapter 4.

GAY POLITICS REARS ITS HEAD

I mentioned above (page 45) that homosexuality has been studied by sociologists, psychologists and biologists, and that by the 1970s the cause of homosexuality was attributed to different things depending on whether you asked a biologist, a sociologist or a psychiatrist as their research projects seemed to lead them in different directions.

The psychology school said that children were turned into homosexuals by their parents: the absent or distant father and the close-binding-intimate relationship with a dominating mother.

A little learning is a dangerous thing and, fuelled by the misconception that children could be turned into homosexuals by the adults around them, a campaign of hate and persecution against homosexual teachers led by Anita Bryant, the "Orange Juice Queen", spread across the United States of America in 1977–1978. This drove many gay teachers from their jobs and some to suicide while others were attacked and killed by angry mobs.

Militant homosexuals felt that to combat this campaign what was needed was the proof that homosexuality was not due to the environment but was inherent. Whether or not this could be borne out by facts did not seem to enter into it.

THE GAY GENE

Fortunately for them, in July 1993 the news broke that scientists had discovered new evidence that homosexuality may have a genetic basis and that scientists might soon be able to identify a gay gene that is passed to men by their mothers.

Dean Hamer, a geneticist at the Laboratory of Biochemistry of the (American) National Cancer Institute, had in fact discovered what he described as "a marker for a gay gene". Dr Richard Pillard of the Fuller Mental Health Center and Michael Bailey had done a study of twins in which they found that among identical (monozygotic) twins if one was gay there was a 50% chance of the other being gay (Bailey and Pillard, 1991). With fraternal, that is non-identical (dizygotic) twins, they were both gay about the same percentage as non-twin brothers. And non-twin brothers were gay more often than adopted brothers who had no relation to the family. They believed this to be a classic genetic finding suggesting that a trait has a genetic component.

By extending the study to more distant relatives it was possible for Hamer to trace how the trait was passed on in families. If a pattern emerged, it might be a clue as to which chromosome was involved.

As soon as he saw that homosexuality was running down the mother's side of the family Hamer began to get pretty excited because to a geneticist that can only mean one thing: x-chromosome inheritance. I will explain below in **Alternate Explanations** how this pattern in families could be caused by psychological inheritance.

They needed to look at the DNA and by examining it under ultra-violet light they found an orange band occurring in the same place (in Xq28) for all the gay men but not for the straight men in their study. What they were able to claim was that they had found that there was "a genetic locus that was correlated to sexual orientation in a certain population of gay men".

Hamer admitted that sometimes in shorthand people say there is a gay gene, but that is not exactly right because there are probably many different genes involved, not just one gene, and according to him there are certainly not any genes that determine for sure a person's sexual orientation – "there's a lot of other environmental and other non-genetic factors that are involved" to quote his own words (Paul Manners, 1997).

Chandler Burr, author of *A Separate Creation*, lectured the Human Rights Campaign in the USA that "we have *almost certainly* found a gay gene" (*ibid.*) and that was about the way that the media saw it too.

Unfortunately for Hamer no one has to date (December 2001) been able to replicate his findings, which would have conferred scientific acceptance on his work. Two attempts to replicate the linkage analysis aspect of his work failed to find any evidence of X-linked transmission (Bailey *et al*. forthcoming, and Rice *et al*. 1999).

In his book *The Mismeasure of Desire* Edward Stein explains exactly what properties a gene in the DNA is able to confer. He says that genes in themselves cannot directly specify any behaviour or psychological phenomenon. What actually happens, he says, is that a gene directs a particular pattern of RNA synthesis which, in turn, specifies the production of a particular protein which, in turn, may influence the development of psychological dispositions and the expression of behaviours.

WRONG HORMONES IN THE WOMB

Green acknowledged that children are born different: he points out that

Günter Dörner has claimed that wrong hormones supplied to the foetus before birth can cause homosexuality. This is not as unlikely as it may at first seem: the body secretes saliva in anticipation of a meal, it secretes adrenalin in anticipation of a sports competition, and so it would really not be at all surprising if a pregnant woman secreted extra female hormones in anticipation of a daughter being born even if, in fact, she was carrying a male foetus.

In fact for conception to occur at all and an egg to become fertilised in the womb delicate changes in a woman's hormones need to occur at different stages to allow the process to proceed to the next stage. Situated in the centre of the brain is the thalamus and under it is the hypothalamus which is responsible for maintaining our body temperature, the right fluid level in our body and levels of glucose in the blood. It is where our "body clock" is situated and it is also responsible for sexual activity in adulthood. For instance, when testosterone is produced in the Leydig cells in the testes it is secreted into the blood and then carried around the body. When the testosterone reaches the brain our hypothalamus turns our mind to sexual matters. In the human foetus the hypothalamus is fully developed by the fourteenth week of gestation.

Dörner administered the extra female hormones to the rats he used in his experiments and showed that the extra hormones caused different effects depending on which part of the hypothalamus was developing in the foetus at the time, but the principal effect was to make the foetus homosexual when adult.

The fact that he noted there were "different effects" partly explains why there is a whole range of degrees from completely heterosexual, through bisexual to completely homosexual as Kinsey, Pomeroy and Martin described in their book *Sexual Behavior in the Human Male*. Clearly environmental factors must also play a role and it would be impossible to discover what proportion of the effect should be ascribed to each of these two causes. One could say that these biological factors create a silhouette of the people we are sexually attracted to and environmental factors and experience fills in the detail.

In their study Kinsey, Pomeroy and Martin found a spectrum of stages between homosexual and heterosexual and drew up a scale of seven degrees known as the Kinsey scale:

    0   completely heterosexual with no homosexual

    1   mostly heterosexual, only slightly homosexual

2 mostly heterosexual, but more than slightly homosexual

3 equally heterosexual and homosexual

4 mostly homosexual, but more than slightly heterosexual

5 mostly homosexual, but slightly heterosexual

6 completely homosexual.

Dörner administered the female hormone by injecting the rats but he warned that the imbalance could also be produced by an illness (pathology).

Dörner's work has been discounted by some researchers because the homosexual behaviour that occurred in his experimental male rats was to arch their backs (called lordosis) in the way that female rats do when they are sexually ripe for copulation. They felt that, because normal (heterosexual) male rats mounted the (homosexual) male rats that arched their backs, this, the researchers claim, made the heterosexual rats homosexual as well as the experimental rats and therefore made a nonsense of Dörner's work. Anyone who ascribes to this criticism is expecting rats to behave sexually the way humans do. Sexual behaviour in male rats is triggered by the sight of another rat arching its back, which behaviour is normally performed only by female rats on heat. A male rat will therefore be duped by a male rat behaving in this way: it does not compromise the heterosexuality of the male rat that mounts another male rat that is arching its back. The mounting rat is responding normally to the stimulus. Even though it is a deception, he is sexually aroused by the *female* behaviour of the other rat, not by its masculinity. These researchers need to look at Dörner's work again.

In the section above on the different groups that homosexuals fall into (page 47) we saw that Whitam and Mathy found that 90% of homosexuals showed cross-gender behaviour at some time in their lives but 10% did not show any cross-gender behaviour at any time. We also noted in Green's work (page 49) that some parents longed for a daughter when the wife was in fact carrying a male foetus and that in many cases the parents actually dressed the male infant in girls' clothes or condoned cross-dressing in the child even when the son was old enough to decide for himself. There was also the male baby with Shirley-Temple ringlets described in the first paragraph of this book (page 1), and my wrestling friend who told me that he remembered the family doctor telling his mother to stop dressing him in girls' clothes.

What these facts seem to suggest when you put them together is that in 90% of homosexuals the mother wanted a daughter before the birth (during the pregnancy), that this must have disturbed her delicate hormonal balance causing the hypothalamus to make the child homosexually orientated and that this behaviour in the son was later reinforced by the parents after the birth because they had wanted a girl in the first place and gave vent to their wishes even when they were confronted with a child that was male.

On the other hand 10% of homosexuals showed no cross-gender behaviour at any time in their lives, which can be explained if at no time during the pregnancy did the parents want to have a daughter but were content to have a child of either sex. In their case the delicate balance of hormones in the womb that caused the hypothalamus in the foetus to become homosexually orientated must have been upset by an illness as Dörner predicted was possible. As the parents did not, at any time, prefer a daughter the son was free to take part in football, rugby, boxing, wrestling or any other masculine sport without any influence being put on him by the parents to desist or to behave like a longed-for daughter.

This revelation may come as a shock to many gay men as well as to their parents. Their first reaction may be to deny it. This is not scientifically proven fact (as yet). It is only a model that I am suggesting based on the current knowledge, but I challenge anyone to put all the facts that have been established by research together and explain them in any other coherent way. What other explanation can there be?

I suggested this model in my earlier book *Wrestling for Gay Guys* and the feedback from that book was that it rang many bells for the people who read it.

Almost every time parents of gay sons are interviewed on television about how they felt when they discovered their son was gay their answer almost without fail is that their first reaction was to say, "Where did we go wrong?" I feel it is no accident that this was their first reaction.

As most of the gay men that I have come across who, like myself, are interested in wrestling tend to feel, consciously or subconsciously, that wrestling, for instance, is "something they shouldn't really be doing", it can be expected that their parents, too, still see them, their (homosexual) sons, as the daughters that they had wanted. Consequently the parents' unfulfilled longing for a daughter expresses itself in tacitly expecting the son to behave as a daughter would, tacitly (or not so tacitly as is often the case) discouraging behaviour, interests and pastimes, even friends that do not agree with their expectations of a daughter.

As I have already mentioned, Dörner explained that pathology (illness) can cause wrong hormones during pregnancy and in such a case one would not expect the parents to have a longing for a daughter during the pregnancy or, after the birth, to be disappointed with a son or to try to influence him in any way to be like a daughter.

This would explain why 10% of the gay men in Whitam and Mathy's study showed no cross-gender behaviour as children and would also neatly explain why some gay men are able to wrestle without any problems while the other 90% whose parents longed for a daughter run into all kinds of problems if they want to learn to wrestle or take up any other "masculine" sport.

As I have explained (page 64), the hypothalamus gives the child a silhouette of the person that he will be sexually attracted to (rather like the silhouettes one sees on public toilet/restroom doors) so that he knows that it is a man or a woman but not much more. Many animals react to silhouettes or, as they are called, *key stimuli* (Russell and Russell 1961, pp. 70–71, 96). Then the environment and life experience (as we will see in Chapter 3) fills in the full picture of the type of person that is sexually attractive to the individual.

For gay men who will get a kick out of not only running their hands all over other men, but also of controlling those men they are presently afraid of, wrestling must be the ideal pastime for them to participate in as it will encourage them to use their anger to become aggressive. Aggression is an offshoot of anger and is an excellent way of expressing your anger safely.

I think one can also safely assume that the same goes for those gay men who seem to be able to box, play judo, rugby or football without the problems (with their parents) that affects the other 90% of gay men except, of course, for the problems they encounter if they come out to straight players of their sport.

ALTERNATIVE EXPLANATIONS

If Dean Hamer was wrong, how can one explain the fact that homosexuality tends to run in families?

Here we need to turn to Eric Berne. Berne (1910–1970) was a Canadian psychiatrist who practised in California most of his life and developed what he called *Transactional Analysis*. His book *Games People Play* explaining his beliefs became a best-seller.

According to him people behave in life according to the dictates of their parents, grandparents, guardians or foster parents. That is, parents tell their children what to say and do in certain circumstances or, in other words, *how to behave* in life's different circumstances. Most of the time the instruction is by example. Berne said parents give their children what he called "scripts". The implication is that these are neurotic and not usually the most sensible way of dealing with a particular situation.

One can observe families where, when a woman of the family is expecting, the others will demand to know, "Do you want a boy or a girl? Yes, but which would you *prefer*?" By which means the pregnant woman is perhaps persuaded to believe that she actually has a choice or, by wishing, can influence the outcome.

This ritual can be handed down from generation to generation in that family and it is not surprising that it occurs on the female side of the family as it is the women who traditionally have more to do with the new baby than the men will.

By contrast, in other families if such a question were asked the question would be summarily dealt with by a "I really don't care as long as it is a healthy baby" response.

In the former family one can observe Berne's neurotic "script" at work while in the latter family a much healthier outlook exists.

It could be this kind of psychological baggage that obtains in some families to cause homosexuality to run in the family rather than being due to genetic causes.

In Bailey and Pillard's work with monozygotic twins (page 62) about 50% of the twins were both gay when one twin was gay. This was taken to be proof of a genetic factor. But, in the monozygotic pairs where only one twin was gay (the other 50% of the cases), this could not have been caused by genetic factors, so what caused the one twin to be gay? I prefer one explanation that accounts for both outcomes: why only one twin of the monozygotic pairs was gay as well as why both the monozygotic twins were gay. This would happen if the androgens (the hormones required to masculinise the hypothalamus of the foetus in the womb) dropped to borderline quantities when there may be sufficient androgen to service only one of the twins but not both. One of the monozygotic twins would then become heterosexual but his brother would become homosexual. If the level of androgens dropped even lower so as to be insufficient to service even one twin then both twins would be gay. This is in line with Dörner's dictum.

A REPLY TO MY CRITICS

I realise that many gay men who are concerned about gay rights (page 62), gay equality etc., will be upset that I have dug up research which highlights the importance of the environment, especially the effects of the parents, research that they have hoped would simply be forgotten about. I would that it could be so. If the research into a gay gene had been substantiated by being replicated it would still not cancel out all the research into the effects of the environment which has been replicated and substantiated again and again by many different researchers. As I have said, I have needed to use that research which explains why most gay men's anger has been repressed in order that we can cure this neurosis. This is far more important especially since, once gay men are able to express their anger and use it constructively, they will have a much more powerful weapon with which to fight for gay rights and equality than they have at present.

THE MALE ANIMAL PACK

What gay men who have been kept away from their peers as children never learn to understand is the way a group of straight men compete all the time with each other in order to test each other's weaknesses and to find each other's position in the hierarchy of the group and so, ultimately, who will be leader of the group. This is usually done by continually putting each other down, usually in a jocular way, in an attempt to discover each other's weaknesses.

Faced with a put-down most gay men will feel hurt and attacked and, since they have repressed their anger all their lives, they will not feel able to defend themselves or to reply to the put-down, as most straight men do, by expressing their own anger in return with a riposte. The gay men are reposing in their gay straitjackets, remember, and are helpless because of it.

Of course, the pack need to get rid of weaknesses in order to make the pack stronger so if you reveal a weakness you will be doomed to be persecuted until you are eliminated from the pack. This does not happen only with humans but is repeated in the animal and bird kingdoms too.

When we get to Chapter 4 we will deal with how to handle put-downs and so help you to make a place for yourself in the male pack.

LOVING YOURSELF

A psychiatrist once said to me that you need to love yourself before you can love anyone else. That came as a surprise.

Reaching an orgasm (and therefore the concept of "love") for me, up to that time, had meant fighting with another man to escape the submission hold he was trying to put on me or trying to apply a hold on him that would make him admit I had beaten him. And before that point was reached I needed him to punish me to some extent (to arouse my anger) and I also wanted the pleasure and satisfaction of seeing him writhe helplessly in pain in the grip I had locked him in.

Love, therefore, seemed to me to have to do with punishment, revenge and power. And later, as I will describe in Chapter 3, my expression of "love" became a lot more violent, and, yes, sado-masochistic. What did loving oneself have to do with it?

Yes, I loved myself when I won. And I loved it when I paid others back for the pain and humiliation they had inflicted on me.

How could I love myself? I had been humiliated as a child in my first wrestling encounters. I was prevented from playing with my peers (for example, in rugby, page 5–6) so that I saw myself as inferior as I had not learned the skills to beat them and was prevented even from competing with them. I had failed as a pianist owing to my compulsive mistakes that prevented me from performing publicly and made me drop out of university. I had failed as an actor owing to the anxiety that that provoked. I had never built my muscles up as big as I wanted them to be. I felt (at that time) that I was unlovable. I had periods of depression that made everything seem futile and the only way I could endure all that was to punish myself for my inadequacies and failures. How could I love myself?

Many other men on the gay scene are involved in sadism, masochism, flagellation, bondage, humiliation to name but a few. How much do *they* love themselves? Not a lot, I would guess.

I would also know that my guess was absolutely correct. Of course, the psychiatrist was perfectly right. You need to feel that you are valued and that you therefore have something of value to give to other people so that they will want to love you in the sense that loving has to do with tender feelings of caring for someone and nurturing their good qualities. You need to feel that they will want to care for you because of your value. That is what love should be about.

It is surprising that there is so much sadism, masochism, etc., on the gay scene. One cannot help wondering whether this is linked to the gay straitjacket or whether all these people each have a collection of other problems as I did that promote their low self-esteem to the point of self-loathing which then drives people to punish themselves. Or am I unique in having such a catalogue of failure? A word that has recurred several times already in this section is humiliation.

David Malan has shown in his book *Murder, Anorexia and Suicide* that humiliation is an extremely potent force in driving people to murder and it may also be a potent force with gay men because, trapped as they are in their straitjackets, they are very helpless. This helplessness makes us prone to feeling humiliated (by our own poor performance) as well as *being* humiliated (by other people) which, again, can end up in the individual as self-loathing driving people to sadism, masochism, etc. There is another incident concerning humiliation and my father that I need to explain about myself to illustrate my humiliation.

I have already described (pages 3–4) the incident when we were picnicking on the beach and my father's friend trapped me between his legs and prevented me from escaping no matter how hard I tried. Many years later, after I had cured my manic depression, when I was fifty-nine years old and had had to give up wrestling and body-building owing to high blood pressure, I was lying at the side of the Tooting Lido swimming pool in London.

A very attractive young man came by in swimbriefs. He was so handsome and his physique was so beautifully developed that I felt my self-confidence draining away, running out of my body as though it was a liquid and was spilling on to the ground under me. About a minute later I felt so lacking in self-confidence and ashamed of myself that I doubted that I would have the confidence to be able to walk back to my motorbike to go home as all my strength seemed to have drained away. It was that bad. I really thought they would have to summon an ambulance to get me home.

I did manage to get home but this feeling stayed with me. The next day the feeling was still there. It was not depression. Then I realised what it was! It was humiliation!

The young man at the swimming pool was so handsome and so muscular that he made me feel humiliated with my own body to the point where all my self-confidence had drained away. I kept remembering being trapped between the legs of my father's friend as a child (page 4). Why did I keep remembering that? Was there a connection?

Then the penny dropped. My father's friend had taken my place in my father's affections and, by trapping me between his legs, showed me how helpless I was and that there was nothing I could do about it to get back my position in my father's affections. All my life I had needed to build up my muscles and succeed at wrestling so that I could see off anyone who tried to take my place in my father's affections. All this when my father had died when I was eighteen!

The man at the swimming pool was so much more handsome and muscular than *I* was at that time that he left me feeling totally threatened by him, that he would be able to take my place in my father's affections and there would be nothing I could do about it. This brought me back to the position of feeling that I was not good enough to get my father's love. That there was something about me that made me unlovable. Hence the sensation that my self-confidence was draining away.

SADISM AND MASOCHISM

The helplessness that one is subject to when trapped in the gay straitjacket means one is a sitting duck to feel humiliated or even to *be* humiliated because (straight) men around you are continually doing things that you are unable to do.

David Malan (1997) had found that humiliation by a woman had driven a man to want to commit (and nearly succeed in committing) murder. With me it was my *own* helplessness that humiliated me and drove me to masochism. I guess this is the case with other gay men otherwise there would be no accounting for the large S & M subculture on the gay scene.

Not being able to play the piano, not being able to act, not being muscular enough: all these problems of mine humiliated me. Other gay men may suffer other problems that are different from mine but if they are humiliated enough their self-loathing will turn to sadism, masochism, etc.

too. There is plenty of evidence on the gay scene that this is happening, also, to too many gay men. By escaping the gay straitjacket you will empower yourself to stop being humiliated and so start an upward spiral of becoming proud of yourself instead.

Some psychiatrists believe that there is not really such a thing as masochism. They see it as sadism to other people or sadism to oneself. It has been established that there are many more masochists than there are sadists. What causes some people to become sadists rather than masochists and vice versa?

If you feel that you are inferior to someone there are two ways you can correct the situation. Either you can improve yourself until you are better or you can make yourself superior by pulling the other person down.

This principle applies to people who have been humiliated by themselves to unbearable depths. They feel the need either simply to punish themselves for their inadequacies (becoming masochistic) or to make themselves feel superior by dragging the other person down by humiliating him and being sadistic to him. This is why, given the right circumstances sadists can be turned into masochists and vice versa. It may be that sadists have more pent-up anger and need to vent this anger on someone, whereas masochists simply feel they deserve the punishment.

It may be that masochists want to punish themselves for the humiliation they feel responsible for inflicting on themselves. Sadists, perhaps, have been humiliated by other people and therefore feel they have someone else to blame. They therefore need to "act out" their anger and revenge on a willing (masochistic) victim.

Since many gay men are trapped in a straitjacket, they are unable to reduce the humiliation they feel by improving themselves (unless they follow the advice in this book or undergo psychotherapy). The only way open to them then to deal with the humiliation is either to deal with the inferiority they feel by punishing themselves for the humiliation they have experienced, or to tear other people down (by being sadistic to them).

What these gay men on the S & M scene need to do at all costs is to escape their straitjacket. They need to be able to express their anger so that they are not so helpless. By not being so helpless they will suffer less humiliation. Less humiliation equals less inferiority and less self-hatred. This slows down the downward spiral of self-loathing. As the humiliation vanishes and turns to pride in themselves instead, they will at last be on an upward spiral.

This book will not be able to cure problems like making compulsive mistakes when playing the piano but, once they have become more self-reliant and able to express their anger they will have less helplessness to be ashamed of or humiliated by.

Their remaining problems may then become more easily identifiable and therefore more easily treatable if they take the trouble to speak to their doctors about them. Clearly, at present any humiliation caused by these more individual problems is lost in a jumble with the humiliation caused by the helplessness of the gay straitjacket.

But worse, there is S & M on a conscious level such as bondage, whippings, burning with candles, and so on. There is also masochism that our unconscious mind engineers us into without our realising. If you are suffering anxiety caused by guilt, the anxiety is caused because you are worried that you will be punished for whatever it is you feel guilty about. Once you are punished the anxiety abates (for a while) so your unconscious mind can engineer that you punish yourself to cure the anxiety. This all happens on an unconscious level and you will not be aware of these thought processes. How does this happen? As there are more masochists than sadists it can be difficult for a masochist to find someone to satisfy his masochistic needs.

George L. Engel in *Psychological Development in Health and Disease* points out that patients who suffer from guilt invite self-punishment through a predilection for painful, disagreeable, humiliating and defeating situations, a proneness to accidents, injury or surgery. Dr Richard Friedman in *Male Homosexuality: a Contemporary Psychoanalytic Perspective* warns that "coming out" to the wrong people may be a way of satisfying masochistic needs. In these cases, he says, the sadistic aspects of homophobic society prove impossible for the masochistic person to resist. He goes on to say that, for a sub-group of masochistic gay men, the motivation to engage in so-called opportunistic sexual activity in order possibly to contract AIDS (Flavin, Franklin and Frances 1986) derives from a masochistic fantasy tantamount to playing Russian roulette.

In the 1960s a friend of mine contracted gonorrhoea and saw a doctor who put him on a course of antibiotics. At the end of the course he had to go back to the doctor for the usual check-up to confirm that he was clear of the disease, but by the time he saw the doctor again he had become reinfected with gonorrhoea. As he had become infected once, one would have thought that this would have been a wake-up call to warn him that he needed to ensure that the other persons used condoms. Becoming reinfected in such a short space of time cannot be explained by simple negligence. Friedman also says that the "relentless pursuit of heterosexuality" by some gay psychoanalytic patients is a masochistic ploy that clinicians should avoid responding to. Since the patient's aim is unattainable, such treatment would be long and costly, with the only result for the patient being an enormous financial burden.

There is another problem with overt sadism and masochism. That is, when the body suffers an injury (as it does with masochism) it builds up scar tissue under the skin to protect the body from being hurt in that place in future. This means that the first time sadistic pain is inflicted it is really extremely painful. But with each subsequent occurrence it will feel less and less painful as the body adapts to the injury that is being inflicted.

In order to produce the same amount of pain on subsequent occasions, the amount of injury has to be increased and will, probably, never again be as painful as it was on the first occasion. The subject who needs to be punished for the humiliation he has suffered will need greater and greater punishment to be inflicted on him as time passes, and this has the effect of making him feel that, as the punishment increases, it must be because he is becoming a worse and worse person who deserves so much more punishment. Thus a spiral is created which, unfortunately, is going downwards.

This is not a healthy situation to be in and, as the subject has more and more pain inflicted on him his self-loathing increases, he gets further and further away from loving himself, and it becomes more and more impossible for him to experience real tender love with another person and the enriching happiness that that can bestow.

What do you want for yourself for the rest of your life?

NEED FOR LOVE

We all need to be loved. Children will do anything to obtain their parent's love. We have seen that with 90% of gay men this will extend to repressing their anger as children in order to allow themselves to be manipulated by their parents so that the parents will be able as far as possible to fulfil their desire for a daughter and the children will get their parents' love (but at the expense of becoming emasculated). There may be other reasons that cause gay men to repress their anger.

Now that you are grown up it is time for you to find your own mate. Your parents will not always be there for you but, in any case, you need your own mate to fulfil your sexual life and be a life companion to you.

Running to your local gay pub/bar for a quick sexual fix may seem satisfying and relieving at the time but that is all that it is, a quick fix.

The kind of men who make good mates are men who are in control of their lives. This means that they are, as far as is necessary, able to control other people, too, who may try to push them around, manipulate them, or exploit them and so on. They are able to assert themselves. They do not back away from or avoid people or businesses that treat them badly, because they can obtain satisfaction when it is necessary as when they are treated badly.

People who are unable both to stand up for themselves and to obtain satisfaction, cut themselves off from those people or businesses who treat them badly. That means they are slowly reducing their circle of friends and businesses whom they can deal with. They gradually retreat from the world until they end up living solitary lives. They do not make good mates. People instinctively know this because they carry this aura of failure around with them.

If you are colluding with your parents in playing the role of a daughter for them you may find that you do not fit the requirements of men who make good mates or whom you are attracted to. Are you going to remain single for life? Do you want to?

Can you make the adjustment necessary to become more like the kind of man who will make a good mate? It may not have been possible for you to make any adjustment in the past, even if you knew then what kind of adjustment was needed, but by the time you have finished reading this book all the knowledge and all the tools will be at your fingertips.

Will that compromise the love you still want to get from your parents? Which is more important to you? Perhaps you should think a while before you answer that question.

Your parents were important to you when you were a child and you needed them to do things for you. At your present age you do not need them to do so much for you, though you still love them and want them to love you, whereas you may want a mate who can do things for you as an adult that your parents cannot do for you . . . who can be a companion and share your life with you and fulfil you sexually.

THE TOURIST GUIDE

I stumbled across an interesting example of how a mother's unintentional coercion made her son behave in a particular way and resulted in making his life hell for him in the world outside his home.

I was touring South Africa on my motorbike when I stopped at a tourist spot and went into the toilets. (It had been a long ride.) I found a good-looking young man standing at the stalls. I was wearing my motorcycle leathers with the emblem of a gay motorcycle club on my jacket and, perhaps seeing this, the young man engaged me in conversation.

"Are you here on your motorbike?" he asked.

"Yes", I replied.

"I am a guide with a coachful of tourists", he told me.

"That must be nice – being paid to visit different parts of the country."

"Yes, I like it", he continued, "but I have these terrible people on my coach. They want me to do *everything* for them. It really gets me down. It's very exhausting."

"What sort of things?" I asked.

"I have to go to fetch their medicines and sun-tan lotions and buy their stamps. It never ends."

"Oh", I replied, "Would you happen to know where the public library is?"

"Yes", he said, "I've got a street map of the town for my tourists. I'll give you one and show you where the library is."

"I need to do some research on the locality", I went on, "as I want to write an article on the African arts and crafts in the area."

"That's no problem", he replied, "I'll do the research for you and write your article for you. Just give me your address and I'll post it on to you."

"No, I'm not asking you to write the article . . . "

"That's no problem. How soon do you want it?"

"No, wait a minute", I said, "I don't want you to write the article for me. That's not what I'm asking. I just want to know where the library is so that I can go and read up about the district."

Then the penny dropped.

"Is that what happens with the people on your coach?" I asked, "They ask you where the chemist or the post office is and you offer to get all their stuff for them?"

"Yes."

"When did you first start doing this?"

The Nature of Homosexuality and Bisexuality

He looked at me for a moment before replying.

"My mother is an invalid and she can't do things for herself. She says she wants to do something and then I know I need to do it for her."

"Oh, I'm sorry to hear that," I said, "But I'm not an invalid and the people on your coach are not invalids. I enjoy reading up in the public library on topics that interest me and then I enjoy writing about them, and the people on your coach probably enjoy shopping and posting their letters and postcards home. You need to let us do these things for ourselves that we enjoy doing and just help us by telling us where the places we ask about are."

"Oh", he replied, "I never thought of it in that way before."

I do not know if the young man was gay or not and that does not matter. The lesson that can be learned from this example is that he had learned to behave at home the way his mother wanted him to and needed him to as she was an invalid.

What was not all right was that he behaved in the same way with the outside world and this made his life a misery for him.

This "tourist guide" syndrome works on different levels with gay men. It works, as I suggest, in a general way but it also works on a more specific level as the following illustration shows. I invited a gay friend to go to the theatre with me. He accepted and I booked two seats but on the night he did not turn up. When I questioned him about this later he accused me of "pressuring" him into going although I had simply given him an invitation which, I felt, he could quite easily have refused. I think he was so used to his mother manipulating and "pressuring" him that, like the tourist guide, when people made a straightforward request he felt obligated to agree or to do more than was actually being asked of him. This may also be why people feel oppressed by society – they are so used to being manipulated or "pressurised" by their mothers that they cannot get out of their straitjackets and stand up for themselves by saying "no". In Chapter 4 I will show you how to overcome this problem.

For the 90% of gay men it may be much the same. They behave as their mothers want them to – as the longed-for daughter, but when they behave in this way in the outside world it makes their lives a misery for them.

THE WAGES OF REPRESSED ANGER

We saw at the beginning that 90% of gay men find it difficult to express their anger. It is important to be able to express one's anger not by shouting or screaming but in a range of ways according to the particular need of the moment.

If one is unable to use one's anger it leaves one helpless as far as protecting oneself from manipulation, exploitation, being pushed around or being put upon, goes. But, worse, anger that is not expressed is stored in the unconscious mind where it festers, builds up and finally becomes uncontrollable, seeping out to poison relationships or bursting out when it is least appropriate and, even worse, exploding uncontrollably in a very destructive and frightening way as well as affecting your behaviour in all kinds of ways.

Being unable to use your anger means that you are liable to be subject to any of the following: being unable to stand up for yourself, being bullied, being unable to compete with other men, unable to reach a sexual orgasm with other men, needing to use drugs to achieve an orgasm, needing to be tied up (or mummified) to be able to reach an orgasm, constantly "bitching" and driving friends away as a consequence, needing alcohol to obliterate your problems, your low self-esteem and unhappiness, competing in an unattractive veiled way, feeling that society is oppressing you, feeling depressed, perpetually angry, unloading your anger on to people who are not responsible for it, unable to establish a long-term sexual relationship or being locked in the closet by your family not allowing you any freedom.

As though that were not enough we are going to find in Chapter 3 that by **Digging Deeper** there are other features that, because of the nature of homosexuality, lower our self-esteem to the point of self-loathing. These are all features of the gay straitjacket that make you helpless and ineffective. So much for Gay Pride. But do not despair. When we reach Chapter 4, **Escaping the Gay Straitjacket**, you will find that life can be a lot easier, a lot simpler and a lot happier. And a lot, a lot more rewarding! Once you know how!!

FURTHER RESEARCH

Before we leave the **Nature of Homosexuality** I need to say that what I have described above is what I feel one needs to know in order to understand how anger is repressed in so many gay men but not in others. I need also to put the research that I have quoted in perspective.

I did say earlier that I was interested in the *nature* of homosexuality and not really in the cause or causes of it. Nevertheless, in fairness, I think I should say there have been other developments in the search for a cause of homosexuality since then.

I have come to the conclusions that I have regarding a model of homosexuality because I observed certain phenomena – e.g. the mother dressing her son's hair in ringlets (page 1), the fact that most gay men feel that wrestling is something they should not do (with psychological consequences)(as we shall see) whereas some gay men wrestle without any psychological problems at all (page 53) and have then discovered in the research reasons that would explain these phenomena.

Although I have mentioned the "gay gene" (page 62), I do not see how this could have caused or be in any way responsible for the phenomena that I have just alluded to, but that does not mean that the result of Hamer's research is incorrect. It only means that I can see no direct connection between a "gay gene" and the phenomena that I have observed. A direct or indirect link may in time and with further research become apparent later. The same applies to other more recent research.

Following on Dörner's work showing that wrong hormones during pregnancy could affect the embryo's hypothalamus (page 64) some researchers looked for a difference in the hypothalamuses of gay men compared to heterosexual men (Simon LeVay 1991; Simon LeVay and Dean Hamer 1994). Unfortunately, LeVay used the brains of gay men who had died of AIDS in his comparison with brains of heterosexual men which meant it was not really clear whether the difference was caused by the man being gay or by AIDS.

Some researchers have looked to see if homosexuality runs in families (Bailey and Pillard 1991; Bailey, Pillard and Agyei 1993; Pillard 1990 and Pillard and Weinrich 1986). This could be caused by genes or it could be caused by an imbalance in the hormones in the womb or it could be caused by psychological inheritance. Others examined identical (monozygotic) twins to see if there were signs of homosexuality being inherited (Bailey and Pillard 1991; Bailey, Pillard and Agyei 1993). They found that, amongst twins that had been separated at birth, when one twin was gay 50% of the other twins were gay as well (see page 62) although back in the 1950s Franz Kallman had found 100% concordance: when one monozygotic twin was gay so was his twin brother (Kallman 1952a, 1952b, 1963).

Others researched genetic linkage (Hamer *et al.* 1993; Hu *et al.* 1995; Pattatucci and Hamer 1995).

Some have tried to formulate an evolutionary model of sexual orientation (Buss 1994) while others see evolutionary theory as having an important influence (Hamer and Copeland 1994, pp.180–186; LeVay 1996 pp.188–193; McKnight 1997; Posner 1992, pp.85–110; Ruse 1988, pp.130–149). Many biologists looked at animals and found that almost every genus shows signs of homosexual behaviour (Ferveur *et al.* 1995; Baum *et al.* 1990; Adkins-Regan and Ascenzi 1987; Nadler 1990; Vasey 1995). An encyclopaedic review was written by Bruce Bagemihl (1999). This would agree with Dörner's findings of an imbalance of hormones in the womb due to illness (pathology) whereas humans have the added tool of language and can thus use coercion on the children.

Other researchers admit that their work may help gay rights to succeed [including LeVay (1996, pp.231–254), Bailey and Pillard (1991a)] or benefit social or political goals [including Bawer (1993) and Sullivan (1995)].

Edward Stein reviewed this, what he termed, "emerging research programme" into the cause of homosexuality in his book *The Mismeasure of Desire*. He felt that much of the research into human sexual orientation did not meet the usual requirements demanded of scientific research as far as methodology and selecting samples was concerned. Several bold hypotheses are made, he says, but the evidence to support these hypotheses is quite weak.

Milton Diamond (1995) explains that each scholarly discipline has developed certain standards by which presented arguments or data are usually evaluated. These tests of validity, he goes on, might involve double-blind studies, the use of suitable controls, statistical analysis, peer review and critique, suitable comparison with available models, consistency with established theories within the particular field as well as other disciplines, and so on. Finally he says that the explanation that best links the majority of findings and depends on the fewest assumptions is to be most credited. Accordingly, Stein concludes that the mere fact that there are reasons to consider the emerging research programme does not show that its central claims are true or that the results are valid (p.226). He goes on to say that in a decade or so from now, the emerging research programme may turn out to have been a false start in the search for an account of how human sexual desires develop (p.228)

A BAROMETER OF BISEXUALITY

Following on The Nature of Homosexuality I would have liked, at this point, to explain how these neuroses affect bisexuals, if at all. Sadly, the research has concentrated on (chiefly effeminate) homosexuals, very little on bisexuality and even less on heterosexuality, so that leaves us knowing even less about the nature of bisexuality than we do about homosexuality.

The research, as far as it goes, hardly scratches the surface. It is reminiscent of the wit who described a barometer as a scientific instrument that tells us what kind of weather we are having (as though we could not look out of the window to see for ourselves). M.W. Ross in *Bisexuality and HIV/AIDS* (1991) describes various types of bisexuality: *Defence bisexuality* is when a person is concealing his/her homosexuality or may be on the way to coming out as gay or lesbian; *married bisexuality* is when a married man or woman takes part in homosexual behaviour; *ritual bisexuality* is when homosexual behaviour is prescribed, as it is in Melanesia, as part of the process of becoming a man; *equal bisexuality* is when a person is not bothered about the sex of the person he/she is attracted to; *"Latin" bisexuality* is when men in some countries who consider themselves to be heterosexual take the active role in anal intercourse with another man; *circumstantial bisexuality* can be *experimental bisexuality* when it happens only once or twice, or *secondary bisexuality* when it takes place because there are no heterosexual contacts as, for instance, in prison, or it can be *technical bisexuality* when it takes place as part of prostitution.

Some bisexuals are fearful of admitting their homosexual side and first come out as heterosexual before moving to bisexuality, others come out as gay and then later move to bisexuality (Bem 1996; Blumstein and Schwartz 1976a, 1976b, 1977; Fox 1995; Golden 1987; Rust 1992, 1993; Weinberg, Williams and Pryor 1994). Bisexuals feel, not that they want either a man or a woman, but rather that they want both (Matteson 1987), as each fulfils different needs (Weinberg *et al*. 1994).

In spite of these needs the sexual relationships that bisexuals have seem to depend on who is available at the time, to put it a little bluntly. By this I mean that a bisexual man may have a relationship lasting five years with a man but when this ends, because he has to move to another town for career reasons, he may then participate in a long relationship with a woman, or vice versa.

Given that there is a greater range of bisexuality (page 65) in the Kinsey scale (2–4) than either homosexuals (5–6) or heterosexuals (0–1) one would expect there to be more bisexuals than, at least, homosexuals but this is not the case. According to different research homosexuals outnumber bisexuals by 2.5–1 or 3–1 (Laumann *et al.* 1994; Wellings 1994).

Most of the bisexual men that I know have clearly repressed their anger so this book is bound to have meaning for them. Whether they have repressed their anger in the same way that most gay men have or whether it has become repressed because they have tried to repress the gay side of their personalities so as to pass for straight or for other reasons, I do not know. You will recall that, if you repress one emotion, you will repress them all as one cannot usually be selective in which emotions you repress and which you do not repress (page 14). Some bisexual men, apparently, do try to repress their gay emotions, if only at first, to pass for straight and this would, of course, more than likely result in them repressing their anger too.

We will return to bisexuality after we have dug a little deeper.

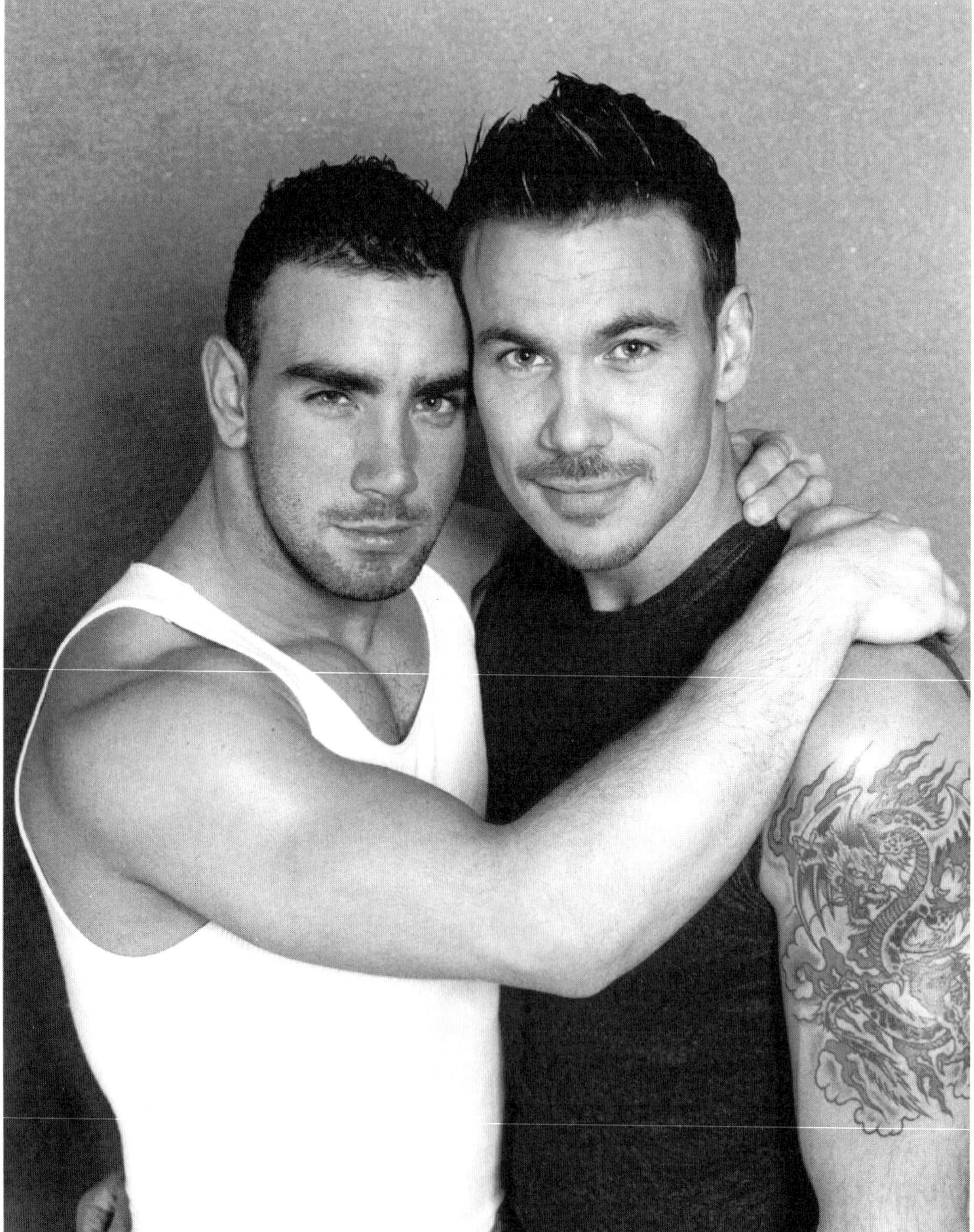

DIGGING

DEEPER

SOME of the topics we have already discussed will be re-examined because there is more than one facet to them that needs to be understood or because they may have other offshoots that embroil us in still more problems all of which you need to be aware of before the whole problem can be seen in perspective and resolved.

PARENTAL DISAPPROVAL

The problems with parents who do not approve of your following a masculine or virile way of life is that they never tell you that that is not what they want you to do. This leaves you with the impression that your upbringing is quite normal. It is the way everyone is brought up. Instead they try to influence you by making you feel bad when you do what you want to do, or making you feel stupid. Remember how upset I was when I reported my first attempt at playing rugby at the dinner table and it was greeted by silence (page 5)?

While you were growing up you have been kept away, not only from the other boys who were said to be too rough for you, but from everything that masculine boys do. Remember my first day at junior school when I was surprised at seeing my peers running around playing football and I was amazed how they all knew what to do (page 5)?

When this manipulation is tacit and never mentioned it is the worst kind because you never know that there is even a problem. Or you think that the problem is somewhere else: as with society oppressing you (page 13). When it is really your parents who have oppressed you all your life.

Jeff, an acquaintance of mine who tried to learn to wrestle when he was about forty years old, took the advice in my book to tell his mother that he was learning to wrestle.

She replied that he was "being silly" because he was too old.

At the Gay Games (see Glossary) at Amsterdam one of the American wrestlers was a woman of fifty-three who won a bronze medal in spite of having only started wrestling five years before. Nowadays women of eighty are learning to scuba-dive for the first time. This is all because people now understand that exercise keeps you young and active.

So what was Jeff's mother on about? Obviously he was not being silly at all but his mother hoped, by making him feel laughable and stupid, that he would give up wrestling which she did not approve of (because he was a longed-for daughter?).

The whole problem of your parents' disapproval of the (masculine) way you may prefer to run your life runs through your life as a sub-text and is never brought out into the open. Until now. Should you perhaps try to ignore it and not even tell them that you want to take up a pastime that they may disapprove of for you? We consider this in the next section.

THE CLASSIC GUILT COMPLEX

As wrestling coach in my club to teach gay men to wrestle I was surprised to learn that the members had not told their parents that they were learning to wrestle (page 51). I felt it was my duty to persuade them to inform their parents.

You might think, as my members did, that it was up to the sons to decide whether or not to tell their parents and, if they decided not to, that would be their own business and that would be the end of the matter, and was not the coach's concern. Unfortunately, you would be wrong.

If you do something that, at the back of your mind, you think would not be approved of, it follows that you think that what you are doing must be wrong, and this sets up a classic guilt complex. This is what all the members in my club were doing to themselves.

This is how it works: Because you feel you are doing something that is not approved of, or wrong, you begin to worry that you might be found out and this brings on anxiety because, if you are found out, you are frightened you will be punished. This reasoning is going on in your unconscious mind, you understand, you may not be aware of it.

If the anxiety becomes unbearable your subconscious mind might arrange for you to get punished in some way as, once you have been punished for doing what you thought would not be approved of, the anxiety evaporates, since the anxiety you felt was caused by the fear of being punished (for doing what was not allowed).

The punishment your subconscious is capable of engineering might also be double-edged. For example, missing your step and spraining an ankle while wrestling would not only punish you for doing what is not allowed but would actually also prevent you from doing what you imagine is wrong, that is, wrestling.

While, (since you have so much anxiety brought on about wrestling) if you injure yourself slightly on the wrestling mat, this might simply seem to you the *proof* that wrestling is dangerous and you will injure yourself more seriously if you continue wrestling. So you have punished yourself in some way and the anxiety has evaporated.

However, if you have *still* not told your parents, the fear that you might be found out may return followed by *more* anxiety and a cycle of events is set in motion.

What is not always clear to the person with something as vague as anxiety is that, in this case, it is caused by the worry of being found out (by your parents) and not really by the dangers of wrestling. In fact, sports doctors have stated that wrestling is one of the sports with fewest injuries owing to the way it is run and managed by the governing bodies.

The result is that you give up wrestling simply because you were unable to tell your parents in the first place what you were doing.

This is what I realised would happen to the members of my Gay Wrestling Group and why I felt it was my duty to persuade them to tell their parents that they were learning to wrestle so that they did not get trapped in a guilt complex which would have ended in them giving up wrestling for good.

Now that you are an adult perhaps it is time to consider whether what your parents want for you is the right thing for you, or whether perhaps you know better now what will give you pleasure and make you happy in the future. What will help to fulfil you as a person and give you the things you desire for yourself?

The best attitude to adopt to avoid getting into this kind of guilt complex, and the self-induced punishment which might result from it, is to say to your parents, quietly but firmly, "I'm sorry if you don't like the idea, but I feel it would be good for me to learn to stand up for myself, and so I am learning to wrestle". It does not matter if you never discuss the matter with them again. By telling them, you will have avoided getting into a guilt complex and will be able to continue wrestling without anxiety or without injuring yourself intentionally by accident either.

Of course, the same principle applies not just to wrestling but to any other sport or pastime that you feel your parents may disapprove of for you.

IF PEOPLE KNEW WHAT I AM REALLY LIKE

Fathers who spend less time at home after the birth of the to-become-gay son cause problems for the son without realising it. The son feels, though it may not register in his conscious mind, that his father does not love him because there must be something wrong with him that prevents him from being loved and that is why his father is spending less time at home with him.

If this reasoning was ever in the child's conscious mind or if it was ever only in his subconscious mind, by the time he has grown up he has totally forgotten everything except that there must be something wrong with him that makes him unlovable and that, therefore, he would not be liked "if people knew what I am really like".

When I confronted one gay friend who believed this about himself and asked him what he thought this thing might be that people would not like about him "if they knew what he was really like" he was quite at a loss.

After some prodding he confessed he might tell people what he really thought about them.

"And what might that be?" I persisted.

"Oh, if I didn't like the colour of a girl's dress I might tell her so", he confessed.

I told him most people would consider it his personal taste and not be very upset whether he liked the colour or not.

Another friend was an extremely good-looking guy and he was so sure that people were so dazzled by his good looks and did not notice what he "was really like" that he took a razor blade to his face to destroy his good looks in the hope that people would no longer be dazzled by his good looks and would then be able to see "what he was really like". Fortunately the cuts he made were not very deep and healed quickly.

This is the legacy their fathers have left them.

Escape the Gay Straitjacket

CHIPS

I have already mentioned how crushing my father (page 57) and crushing my mother (page 58) resulted in tremendous guilt that prevented me from functioning properly and following the careers I had wanted to pursue.

I grew up with dogs in the family and at the time that my father died we had a Skipperke (a small black Belgian breed that were kept as watchdogs on barges on the canals) and a cross between a Dobermann and a Collie whose parentage was not apparent as he resembled a short-haired German Shepherd more but with a timid, affectionate temperament. He had a little black along his back but mainly his colouring was light brown to tan with a white underbelly. We called him *Chips* and he was my favourite.

In fact, I had told many psychiatrists that I loved our dogs more than my parents. I was very close to Chips. For a lot of the time in my early teens he was my only playmate. Adolescence is a difficult time and whenever I retired to my bedroom to lie on my bed and cry Chips would come looking for me, snuggle up to me and lick the tears off my face, much in the same way that, when I was younger my mother had covered me in kisses when I had hurt myself to "kiss it better".

A year after my father had died my mother realised my sister wanted to return to England to get married and as I was away during the daytime and most evenings she became frightened of staying on our smallholding alone and so decided to sell it. She wanted to go and live with a friend and I needed to be in the centre of Cape Town. That meant our dogs would have to be put down.

This was a terrible blow for me. It would have been nice to be able to come home to the dogs but my mother was stubborn and sometimes stupid. I decided I would just have to bite the bullet and say a big goodbye to Chips when the time came.

Dogs seem to know that something is afoot when people start packing cases: they become restless and forlorn. The day before I was to leave home I went to give Chips a cuddle but he evaded me. That had never ever happened before. Was he sick? I ran after him but he seemed irritable and ill at ease. He could not bear for me to touch him. All I got was a reproachful look before he loped off into the dark recesses of the chicken shed where I could not reach him.

I never saw him again. I felt I had destroyed the thing I loved. The guilt I felt was overwhelming.

I had finally managed to leave home but at what a price! I had killed

Digging Deeper

my father and the dog that I loved more than anything. How can you not hate yourself for that? I felt it was my mother's way of revenging herself. That reproachful look that Chips gave me before he ran away from me said it all.

LOW SELF-ESTEEM

There is undoubtedly a lot of low self-esteem amongst gay men.

This is self-evident from the sadism and masochism subculture that exists, from the number of master-slave relationships, and from, even in "normal" gay relationships, the amount of domination or humiliation that takes place within the sex act between gay men. It is not often like a heterosexual sex act where the two people bring each other to a climax at the same time. Or where the cries of the woman and an increase in the fluids in the vagina physiologically promote the ejaculation of the man.

There are different feelings that can contribute to this. People can feel that they are so awful that they need to punish themselves. People who feel really bad about themselves can want to punish others to make them feel just as bad just to square things or, better, to make others feel a lot worse. People who feel others are responsible for the bad way they feel may simply want to punish others to revenge themselves.

You may not, at first, think that low self-esteem is caused by repressing one's anger, but it is. Psychiatrists say that people need to feel accepted by their peers in childhood and in adolescence. Not being able to express one's anger means one cannot participate in rough-and-tumble, football/soccer or other masculine-oriented activities. This results in being rejected by one's peers, being ostracised, scapegoated, and feeling inadequate and ashamed, with a consequent loss of self-esteem all as a result of not being able to express one's anger as other boys can.

When I was thirty-two years old I was working full-time as an instructor in a gymnasium. We had a manageress called Wendy whose boyfriend used to hang around with her in her office. He was, apparently, extremely jealous and imagined that she was being seduced by most of our members, which I knew was not true.

One evening we heard his demented voice screaming from her office, "I'll *kill* you, Wendy, *I'll . . . KILL . . . you!*" I was the only other member of staff present so it was really up to me to take the matter in hand but, as

I could not express my anger and had simply never had to confront another man or deal with this kind of crisis before, I did not know what to do or where to start. I was hamstrung. One of the gym members who had been exercising went into her office and told her boyfriend to leave the premises at once which he then did.

I was in my straitjacket and unable to express my anger so there was nothing I could do. I felt humiliated that a customer had had to deal with the situation instead of myself, a member of staff.

My relationship with Ken taught me a lot about myself and enabled me to let all my anger out. Yes, *all* of it. It also allowed me (and him) to be punished for our bad feelings about ourselves, not to mention guilt. We had a wonderful time!

THE STORY OF THESEUS

Before I tell you about my friendship with Ken I need to explain why it was that I became friends with many ex-convicts. I believed that I befriended them because they were usually rough and tough and prepared to indulge in wrestling with me (prior to having sex). The ones that I got to know had been treated appallingly by their fathers and consequently had oceans of anger bottled up inside them that they needed to express. They were raring for a fight. So I also felt we were birds of a feather . . . but it was not as simple as that.

Eric Berne whom we have already met (page 67), maintained that people live their lives according to the scripts that their parents give them. He also believed that many people act out their favourite fairy story in real life.

For instance, some women believe that, if they act as a skivvy for the rest of their family, then, like Cinderella, they will get to go to the ball and marry the Prince and live happily ever after. So they spend their lives acting as skivvies.

Psychiatrists' waiting rooms are full of people acting out their favourite fairy stories, according to Dr Berne, because the tragedy of acting out fairy stories is that in real life the happy ending never, or hardly ever, occurs.

Instead, people get eaten by the wolf in the case of Red Riding Hood, they remain asleep for a hundred years (or the rest of their lives, whichever is the shorter) in the case of Sleeping Beauty, or they get killed by the giant in the case of Jack and the Beanstalk or the bean that they invested their

Digging Deeper

life's savings in to buy, turns out to be worthless and have no magical properties. And so on.

When I was nine or ten years old I was given a book of stories for boys that included Charles Kingsley's story of Theseus. It was undoubtedly my favourite, interested as I was in wrestling.

Even after I read Dr Berne's books it took me several years to realise that I was trying to act out this story in my life, as for a long time I did not consider the story of Theseus to be a fairy story. I thought it did not qualify.

But, of course, as the gods of ancient Greece were not real, that is just what it is . . . a fairy story.

As Theseus grew up his mother took him to a great stone every year and, eventually, when he was big and strong enough to lift the stone he found a pair of golden sandals and a sword underneath it.

His mother told him it was time for him to go to Athens where he would find that his father was the king there. He set off and met a series of thieves and robbers on the way.

There was Periphetes, who wore only the skin of a bear and wielded a large club with which he killed his victims. Theseus wrested the club from him and killed him with his own club.

There was Scyron, who made travellers wash his feet and, as they did so, he would kick them over the top of the cliff to their deaths below so that he was able to keep their money and possessions. Theseus made Scyron wash *his* feet and kicked him over the cliff.

There was Procrustes, who welcomed travellers into his home to spend the night in a bed there. If they were too long for the bed he chopped their feet off and if they were too short for the bed he stretched their bodies until they fitted. Either way they died. Theseus made Procrustes lie on his own bed.

But, best of all, there was Kerkuon, with whom travellers had to wrestle and if they lost he killed them. They dined together the night before they wrestled and Theseus looked across the table at Kerkuon and thought, "He has broad shoulders, but I trust mine are as broad as his."

The next day they wrestled. Kerkuon lost the fall and Theseus killed him.

When Theseus arrived in Athens he found his father and discovered that he was indeed king.

In real-life all my childhood wrestling encounters had ended badly for me but if I imagined I was Theseus I would win them all and when I arrived in Athens I would discover that my father was the king there.

Or so my subconscious mind must have thought.

What happened in truth was, I have to confess, I was robbed several times. On the plus side, I met Ken. He changed my life.

KEN

After I had to stop wrestling owing to high blood pressure I started visiting a public house/bar in Soho in the West End of London that was frequented by gays, ex-convicts and a few members of the army who wanted to make some money out of the gays who went there.

It was there that I met a small-time villain, drug-dealer and contract killer who had been trained in the Paratroop Regiment of the army (it is probably the toughest, and, like the SAS [Special Airborne Service], they say you have to be slightly mad to stick it) where he was taught to kill with his bare hands. He left the paratroops after robbing the till in the canteen. He wore a glass eye (he had lost an eye by being kicked in a fight), worked as an agent for MI5 too and been in and out of prison.

This may all sound rather far-fetched but, after he died, his wife told me her version of some of the events that Ken had told me about himself, and even how she had prevented a killing that Ken had contracted to perform.

Ken taught me a lot about myself and, if it were not for him, I would never have written this book or my previous book *Wrestling for Gay Guys*.

When Ken turned up in the pub straight out of prison I was warned by some of the other ex-cons (ex-convicts) that I had become friendly with, to beware of him because he would easily go berserk, smash his glass on the counter and ram the broken end into your face if you upset him. I gave him a wide berth.

However, Ken found out that the 750cc Triumph Trident motorbike parked outside opposite the pub was mine and he chatted me up. It turned out he was interested in my bike in more ways than one. Soon I had agreed to take him for a ride to Brighton and to Telscombe Cliffs further along the south coast.

We walked down to the foot of the cliffs and sat down on the mounds of pebbles. He was rolling a cigarette when he turned to me and said, "When I've finished smoking this joint I'll give you a fight." It was the nicest thing that anybody had ever said to me!

I have thought a lot about why that should be, and can only conclude that all my life I had wanted someone to treat me like a man, not like a daughter (though I had never been able to put the feeling into words until then), and that this was the first time it had actually happened. I had always been overprotected and automatically sidelined as a result.

"Boxing or wrestling?" I asked.

"You box, don't you?"

"Yes", I replied, "But we don't have any boxing gloves here."

"What do you want boxing gloves for?" he retorted.

He explained that gloves were only to protect the face. Neither of us wanted to be punched in the face. He because he was wary of losing the one eye he had left and I, because being short-sighted, I am predisposed to suffering a detached retina from a heavy blow to the head, although at the time I was wearing hard (scleral) contact lenses, which are suitable for wrestling and swimming in as they would not wash out. We therefore proceeded without gloves.

It was difficult slipping and sliding on the mounds of pebbles but we had a great time punching to the body and not to the face. Ken's upper body was rather skinny and tattooed but his legs were impressively muscular from all the army pack-drills he had done. He must have gone easy on me as it was quite even.

That was the first of many fights we indulged in together: boxing, wrestling, and macho combat in the nude or with belts as Ken was game to try anything, and some of the subsequent fights we had were not so even.

He warned me that his problem with going berserk, putting people in hospital and ending up in prison for GBH (Grievous Bodily Harm) himself, was that he would never give in. This meant sometimes that his opponent would then twist his arm (or whatever) harder to try to make him submit, and harder, and harder, till Ken was so frightened that his arm was on the point of breaking that he would go berserk and not know what he was doing, and at such times he was capable of anything, using the skills he had learned in the army, to try to get free.

He said that as long as I realised that he would never submit and stopped, when he told me he could not take any more, everything would be O.K. and I would have nothing to fear from him.

This did prove to be the case and was how we managed to enjoy punishing each other quite seriously on many occasions without any unfortunate consequences.

LEARNING THE HARD WAY

The next time Ken and I boxed it was at the squat where he was living – the unoccupied premises that he had taken unauthorised possession of.

An Irish friend had punched me continually in the *solar plexus* on one occasion to test my powerful abdominal muscles. He wanted to see how many punches I could take before the muscles became so tired that eventually they were unable to resist the blows and he would wind me. He had started off with ten punches, then given me another ten, then twenty, and twenty again and I think it was during the third twenty that I fell to the floor winded and he had to revive me (see Appendix page 225).

I thought that, if I punched Ken continually in the *solar plexus* I would tire his abdominal muscles and wind him, and have this feared villain doubled up on the floor at my feet so I suggested to him that we take it in turns to punch each other twice. (The first punch would tire the muscles so the second punch would have greater effect, I calculated.)

It was understood that we would not block or dodge punches. (We both wanted to get hurt and each of us wanted to pay the other back for the hurt he had inflicted, so there was no point in our punches not landing.) If one of us delayed throwing his punches (if he was writhing in agony, for instance) he would lose his turn after ten seconds. If one of us went down to the ground he would enjoy a count of twenty seconds after which the fight could continue on the ground.

Ken agreed, and I thought I had him.

We squared up in front of each other in a square, empty room that rather resembled a boxing ring. He returned my punches to his stomach by punching me on the side of the upper arm. I thought that was rather stupid. That was not going to hurt.

I kept punching him in the *solar plexus*. He never flinched.

The punches to my arm started stinging.

Then they started hurting.

I tried to ensure that my punches were hitting exactly the right spot.

Then every time he threw a punch it was like being stabbed with a knife. Sometimes, without my dodging, he hit my forearm by mistake or did not hit my upper arm where it really hurt.

When his knuckles hit the bones in my forearm it was excruciatingly painful but fortunately he was not actually aiming at my forearm. I remembered that in junior school the boys used to have a competition hitting each other on the side of the upper arm to see who would surrender first but I had never been involved in it.

I realised that it was too late for me to change to hitting his upper arm because it would take time before his upper arm was hurting as much as mine already was and by that time he would have won.

I would never be able to catch up. My tactic had backfired.

Ken called the end of the first round.

I needed a break.

The second round was more of the same.

I was in agony and it was not long before I just collapsed on to the floor where I could nurse my pain.

He started counting.

I realised that if I stayed down for ten I would lose my turn. I could stay down till twenty to have a longer break. If I stayed down for longer than twenty I would have him on top of me. I would be trapped under him unable to pull my arm back to throw a punch properly and so I would miss all my turns while he just rained punches down on top of me at ten-second intervals.

That was what *I* had wanted to do to *him*. That was why I had suggested those rules.

I was on my feet before twenty.

I had lost my turn so he hit me first.

I fought back gamely but my punches to his *solar plexus* had no effect.

Was he bluffing?

Was he, like Andy, hiding his pain?

Would I still wind him suddenly?

My arms were so sore I was struggling just to hold them up.

He had me in the corner of the room.

As I was up against the wall I could not pull my arms back to swing my punches. I knew he had the advantage. That was wonderful. I had to get out of the corner.

I escaped but a few more turns and I went down to the floor again.

He was standing over me.

I knew that I would lose my turn, but twenty seconds was not long enough to recover.

He was standing over me waiting for me to get up.

I knew that he would start on me again as soon as I stood up.

It was wonderfully exciting. I was getting hammered.

When I stood up I would get hammered some more.

This was what I wanted. I do not know why. Perhaps it was because it showed he was a champion that I was fighting. Perhaps I needed to get punished. Perhaps it made it a *real* fight. That I might need to punish myself for my guilt and low self-esteem did not occur to me then.

I got up before twenty. I had to.

Ken punched me twice. He could see I was finished.

He turned his shoulder to me and pointed at his upper arm.

"Punch me there", he said. I hit him twice on the arm as he commanded.

"Hit me there again", he said, flouting the rules.

I knew I would be asking for it, and that was what he wanted, but his encouragement somehow renewed my desire to fight back and to win.

I punched him twice on his arm again.

He revenged himself on me with renewed vigour as I knew he would.

I returned his punches and then called the end of the second round.

"No", he replied, "It isn't the end of the round yet. I haven't finished with you."

This was glorious.

After a time the pain does not get any worse. Your arms become tired and do not want to respond to your commands no matter how hard you want them to punch. You can tell from the sound that your opponent's punches are hitting harder. That they are stinging more. Then your will to fight seems to fade away. And even the will to stand up.

I went down a couple more times to the floor before he called the end of the round. It turned out also to be the end of the fight.

I was so exhausted and sore that I thought I would not have the strength left to enjoy sex, let alone reach an orgasm but after a beer and a rest it was not a problem. For either of us.

I suffered more pain in those ten or fifteen minutes than I had at any other time in my life, but somehow what I really regretted about it was when it stopped.

Yes, when it *stopped*.

Why?

It was wonderful getting cornered. It was wonderful when I went down and he was standing over me and waiting. I knew that as soon as I stood up he would pile into me and give me more of the same.

Did I need to purge all my guilt by being punished for it? Is it exciting being pushed to your limits and finding out that you can survive it and come back from it? Is it exciting to develop your self-survival skills?

I do not know.

The unknown is very frightening. The fear of boxing is the fear of being knocked out. Once you have been knocked out and know what it

Digging Deeper

feels like, being knocked out no longer holds any terror over you.

Once you have been pushed to your limits, and know what it feels like, and know that you came back from it, it no longer holds any terror over you and you grow in stature as a man.

However, it is important to learn the skills first.

CAN YOU EXPRESS YOUR ANGER?

The next time we met to fight, Ken asked me, "Are you one of those people who can't express their anger?" I replied that I could, and set about showing him how much anger I could express in a punch just to reassure him. At the same time I realised that it was important that he asked me.

It was important because it made me want to show him that I *could* express my anger. It also made me realise (if I did not already know) that fighting is about expressing one's anger and the reason some people cannot fight or are afraid of fighting is that they are unable to express their anger. It was Ken's question that made me realise I had to write this book though the realisation came much later.

We know already the dire consequences of not being able to express one's anger.

I feel it is important therefore that I ask you the same question.

Are you one of those people who cannot express their anger?

MACHO COMBAT

Ken was quite adventurous and we were soon getting involved in other competitions to see who could stand more pain. I later termed these macho combat, and it begins with punching each other on the side of the upper arm as schoolchildren do, but it does not end there.

I had indulged in ball wrestling or Wrestlerball, as we called it, with another friend. You have to wrestle in the nude and try to grab the other guy's balls and squeeze them until he submits although any other submission hold is also permitted.

Ken thought it was a waste of time wrestling and struggling to grab hold of each other's balls. So he devised new rules. We both grabbed a handful of each other's balls and, on the command to start, we squeezed them to see who gave in first. (A handful was like a Queen Anne ball-and-claw only upside down. Not like the American cow-milking grip.)

We flicked each other with the end of towels, flicked in a stinging whiplash.

We beat each other with leather belts. (Ken's dad had beaten him repeatedly as a child with a bicycle chain. He had prayed every night that it would never happen again but his prayers were not answered. In spite of this he remained steadfastly religious.)

He beat me with the buckle end but, as the pain comes from the whiplash sting of the leather on skin, I always won as the buckle end prevents the whiplash effect from occurring.

We took hold of each other's balls with one hand and, on the command to start, squeezed with that hand and punched each other with the other hand on the side of the upper arm to see who would give in first. Sometimes I was surprised how long the contest lasted but Ken usually said he could not take any more, claiming that, owing to my weight-training, I had a more powerful grip.

I am recounting these combats not so that you can copy them, but rather so that you can appreciate the depths to which the self-esteem of both of us had sunk and the amount of guilt we needed to be punished for in order to expurgate it.

FIGHT OR FLIGHT

Once or twice in my life it has happened that I have been wrestling with someone whom I found exciting and sexy and with whom I was eager to wrestle and have sex with but, after my pain threshold had been exceeded or, usually, after my opponent had tried to execute a move which is fine for the professionals to fake but is too dangerous for amateurs, who are wrestling for real, to attempt, my enthusiasm to fight him had suddenly changed to a feeling that I had a lunatic on my hands who was out to maim me and whom I needed to escape from.

Instead of feeling lucky that I was tangling with such a sexy guy I would find I was asking myself how I had got myself into such a dangerous position and how quickly I could get shot of the guy without causing any ill-feeling which might only prolong the visit.

In other words, I would start off being "switched on" by my opponent and then suddenly I would feel he had caused me to "switch off". It is, of course, what biologists describe as the "fight or flight" mechanism.

WINDING ME UP

This happened on one occasion with Ken but presumably with his army experience he had learned how to deal with it.

Henceforth he made us body-box for two or three rounds to begin each session before we moved on to the sado-masochistic macho combat. During these rounds he would exhort me, "I'm asking for it. Let me have it!"

You will never know unless you experience it for yourself what a *thrill* it was, after years of being prevented from indulging in anything that might allow me to express my anger or aggression, finally, not merely to be *allowed* to express one's anger and aggression but to be actually *encouraged* to express them!

I can never thank Ken enough.

AROUSING ANGER

Although I was now being aggressive, Ken found my fighting still lacked something. He felt that I needed to get angry, as people fight three times harder, he said, when they are really angry with their opponent. "Needle" matches, those where the contestants are previously angry with each other and have a score to settle, tend to be more exciting to watch. Remember my schoolmates wrestling on the beach (page 2)? Besides, he loved "winding" people "up", meaning to arouse their emotions, especially angrily or sexually.

What I realised later was that what he wanted was for me to come on harder so that *he* would get punished more. Without perhaps realising it (or perhaps subconsciously he did) Ken succeeded in making me extremely angry with him. He would make an arrangement to meet me later in the week in the Soho pub where we had first met. I would look forward to our date and work myself up into a fever of anticipation and sexual excitement as the time approached. Then he would not turn up.

I would be left high and dry, randy as hell, feeling very frustrated and extremely angry with him for treating me in that way, and for being let down. Usually the reason was that he had been high on drugs and not been aware of the passage of time (or so he said).

When we next sparred I could not resist the temptation to pay him back for standing me up and to vent my anger on him, and that proved to be an extremely good and cathartic stimulus.

When I visited him at home, as soon as I had entered the front door Ken would shut the door behind me, make me put my bag down and then greet me by punching me a few times to get my blood up. I would also recall how angry I had been with him for standing me up, and when we had changed and did get to fight, it was a much better feeling because, by then, our anger had surfaced with each other and we really *wanted* to revenge ourselves, to express our anger and to pay each other back.

About this time his wife discreetly hinted to me that he was intending to steal my Triumph motorbike. While I took precautions to prevent this happening I could not be sure he would not be successful.

I stopped using it to go to our rendezvous on the pretext that there was something wrong with the engine. What his wife actually said to me was that he had found someone who could fix my bike. Ken never told me that. I concluded that that was because he wanted the person to fix the bike for him after he had stolen it, and not to fix it for *me*.

But I knew how furious I would feel if he *did* manage to steal it, and I used my anger to punish him there and then while we were fighting in case he did manage to steal it and I did not have the opportunity to punish him afterwards.

KEN'S GUILT

One time I told him he could beat me at boxing but that he would never beat me at wrestling. Immediately, he grabbed me in a side headlock and we were wrestling. That was what confirmed my suspicion that he wanted to lose and get worked over, and that he needed to purge his guilt too.

Also about this time whenever we met to fight, in one of his hands he would have six or seven stitches that had just been put in or were due to be taken out the next day, in knife wounds that he had acquired in pub/bar fights. He would rip off the bandages to show me the stitches so I knew he was telling the truth, before insisting he was still able to fight me.

He was about twenty-seven years old at that time and claimed to have tallied up all the stitches he had had throughout his life. I forget the exact figure now but it was certainly over one thousand and may even have been over two thousand!! I *said* one had to be slightly mad to join the Paratroop Regiment!

Of course, I realised that no one needs to get into knife fights that often, in fact it must be quite difficult to *find* that number of knife fights, so he must be doing it on purpose (subconsciously rather than consciously). He admitted that, sometimes, the fights had nothing to do with him until he jumped in, with his paratroop skills, and grabbed the knife with his bare hand to try to stop it being used on someone else, although on other occasions he may have been a party to the argument.

Eric Berne would have said it was "scripty" (page 68), but it could be something people do because their subconscious knows what the (bad) consequences will be and actually wants that to happen to them (usually as punishment for their feelings of low self-esteem or guilt. This is the reason why some psychologists say that there is no such thing as an "accident"!)

It seemed to me that Ken's behaviour in getting into knife fights was unnecessary unless his subconscious mind wanted him to punish himself in this way.

When I pointed this out to him he admitted that, as he was a devout Roman Catholic, he was very unhappy and feeling terribly guilty about the people he had had to kill. (If I was in any doubt that this was not true, after his death his wife confirmed how guilty he felt about the people he had had to kill and that was why, eventually, she stepped in on one occasion before the killing actually took place and made him give the money back to the man who had commissioned it.)

Apart from the killings he felt guilty about, I cannot help wondering, remembering that his father beat him regularly with a bicycle chain, how much he needed to punish himself for not being good enough for his father to have loved him.

I suggested to Ken that getting into knife fights was extremely dangerous even with his army skills, and if he wanted to punish himself he should rather allow *me* to punish him as that would be far safer.

From my point of view, I did not want to lose him as I did not think I would be able to find another person like him with whom I could participate in macho combats where we went to such extremes of knocking hell out of each other.

I think he understood the psychological sense of what I was saying because that was the last time I know of that he had to have a cut stitched until he died two years later.

LOVE AND HATE

On one occasion when I went to Ken's house for a fight I felt a strong need to be cuddled. I cannot remember now what brought this feeling on. I can, though, remember a previous occasion when someone asked me if I wanted to be cuddled and I had felt quite surprised at being asked and had replied, "No, I don't. Thanks all the same, anyway."

After we had finished our fighting session Ken and I were sitting on the carpet and I said I felt I needed to be cuddled and asked him if he would cuddle me. He folded his arms around me but then, entirely unexpectedly, he kissed me on the forehead.

At the moment that he did that I felt something change. I do not know what it was. All my life I had wanted to be a tough guy. This need may have originated from the humiliation I felt in my first three wrestling encounters as a child. I wanted to be accepted by tough guys.

All my efforts to become friends with tough guys were spurned and I was always rejected. They would not allow me to join their club. They had not been interested in me as I had just been a wimp. Now this tough guy that I had been beating hell out of had suddenly showed me some affection.

We have seen (page 44) how difficult it is for some people to admit anger for someone they love. And how they would rather even commit suicide than admit they are angry with someone they love. This experience with Ken is a clear indication that it is possible to be angry with and love the same person.

Ken contracted AIDS from sharing needles to inject drugs. As he was terrified of dying of AIDS he took a heavy dose of cocaine after he had been for some time on Methadone, which is a substitute given to wean junkies off hard drugs. His body was no longer accustomed to such quantities of cocaine, as I am sure he realised, and his wife woke up the next morning to find him dead next to her in the bed.

FEELING PURGED

Ken was responsible for drawing out of me not only my aggression but also my anger that I had stopped expressing from my early childhood.

I used to arrive at his house thinking I must be mad to be going to have a fight with a villain who had learned to kill with his bare hands in the army, who killed people to order and who might go berserk on me and do anything to me, whom I knew wanted to steal my Triumph motorbike from me.

And, if that was not enough, I was actually going to provoke him by punishing him as much as he could take! How could I even *think* about daring to do something so crazy? But I used to leave Ken's place in a state of inner peace, feeling cleansed, purged, pure and, yes, elated.

Now I want to help you to express *your* anger so that you too can feel cleansed, purged, pure and elated, and rid at last of the suffocating effects of the gay straitjacket that leaves you frightened and helpless. Fortunately for you, you will not have to undertake such a dangerous baptism of fire as I experienced with Ken. But, baptism of fire it may still be for you none the less.

MORE DISCOVERIES THROUGH WRESTLING

If I thought that I was unique in bottling up my anger and needing Ken to help me to express it I soon realised that this was not so.

I remembered that some of the boys in my gay wrestling club were excessively polite when wrestling. When I had shown them how to perform a new move and told them to practise it on each other, I would frequently hear questions like "Do you mind if I try this hold/throw on you?" I had never ever heard that in a straight wrestling club. What I had heard there as the equivalent had been, "Do you want to go first? Okay. I'll go first."

"Do you *mind* if I try this hold/throw on you?"!!!

When I thought about it I realised I heard this excessive kind of politeness in the pub in Soho where Ken and I had met, where it sounded equally out of place. It was the ex-cons there whom one expected to be very rough and ready but, surprisingly, they were excessively polite to each other.

When I thought about that, too, I realised that the reason for that was that many of them had been dreadfully treated by their fathers (as they had personally told me) and consequently they, too, had a lot of anger bottled up inside them. So much anger, in fact, that, like Ken, they were likely to explode and go berserk at any moment if someone accidentally bumped their elbow and made them spill their drink.

As they were so frightened of setting anyone off they ended up being excessively polite instead to try and avoid trouble. That made me realise that the boys in my wrestling club must also, under their polite exteriors, have a lot of anger that was liable to explode at any moment, that caused them to be so excessively polite.

I need to make clear that it is the people who are excessively polite who are also the ones with the bottled-up anger that is ready to explode. The reason one can come to this conclusion is that they cannot know how anyone else in the club feels unless that other person has told them how they feel. The people who feel they might explode assume (because they cannot know) that others are feeling the same way as they do, that is, ready to explode too, so they behave very politely to them so as not to provoke them, but it is the ones who are excessively polite who behave that way because their own anger is explosive though they may not be consciously aware of their own anger. They may vaguely sense it but they attribute it to the other people.

Because none of us can know what is in someone else's mind without being told, the person who says he knows what others are thinking is revealing more of himself than of the people whose minds he believes he can see into.

What this also shows is that wrestling is a very provoking sport. That is, it provokes anger in the opponent who does not want to have his shoulders pinned to the mat, but is pushed and pulled against his will by the other wrestler until he is forced by his opponent into that position.

This is what makes it such a good sport for gay men who may not be aware of the anger inside them because they have been bottling it up for so long and have become so expert at concealing it (even from themselves) or avoiding it.

LOVE, ATTRACTION AND REJECTION

We all need to be loved and children will do anything to be loved by their parents. Apparently they will stifle their anger and allow themselves to be manipulated. It is not easy for gay men to find love. They have to tread through a minefield. There is a very good reason for that.

Men are biological enemies. In other words they compete against each other to find a mate. This presents a particular problem for gay men, most of whom, as we have seen, have stifled their anger and aggression and are not able, for those reasons, to compete with other men. This is, after all, why they avoid body-contact sports.

This means that on the gay scene it is difficult to know whether you can trust your best friend not to suddenly become your enemy and steal your lover from you. This is one of the reasons why a lot of gay men cannot bear to go on the gay scene. They feel too threatened by everyone.

I was in a group psychotherapeutic session one day when I commented that I did not know what one of my friends saw in his lover. The psychiatrist commented that, perhaps, he just thought that he was a nice guy.

With my own experiences of wanting to wrestle with a man as a prelude to having sex with him, and with the amount of sadism and masochism, humiliation, master-and-slave relationships and bondage on the gay scene, the idea of loving someone because he was a *nice guy* just sounded rather unreal to me. That did not seem to be the way it was in the gay world.

Most gay men are extremely sensitive to rejection. This is probably because as we have seen (page 49) their fathers were absent during their critical age of two to five years leaving them feeling that they were not good enough for him to have loved them. And leaving them with the feelings that, if people discovered what they were really like, they would discover what it was that made them unlovable (page 90).

This means that if a lover drops them they have a triple shock. Not only have they lost their lover, they have gained a competitor (an enemy), and they have also been reminded (of their fantasy) that their fathers could not love them because there is something about them that makes them unlovable.

ATTRACTION OF OPPOSITES

Another time, another place, another psychiatrist. He said that if you repress any emotion you will automatically be attracted to someone who is able to express that emotion. As we have seen, this is known in common parlance as the attraction of opposites.

In heterosexual relationships this would benefit the offspring as they would learn to express the emotion each partner repressed whereas, if like were attracted to like that, if both repressed an emotion, the offspring would repress it too.

This would explain why on the gay scene where most gay men are repressing their anger there is such an attraction to sportsmen, footballers, labourers, construction workers, professional wrestlers (although many gay men are frightened to admit it), and (for older gay men) Hell's Angels, all of whom are characterised by their ability to express their anger, often as aggression.

It explains why so many gay men wear the clothes of these types the better to seduce other gay men who are attracted to them. Does it work? You bet it does! But only until the other person realises the guy in leather motorbike gear, or whatever, is a timid fairy underneath and then the attraction fades and they become just good friends. Their attraction for each other lasts only long enough for them to each obtain a "quick fix" sexually. Hopefully.

Attraction of opposites also works on a much broader canvas throughout heterosexuality. Daryl Bem (1998) explains that most cultures, including our own, polarise the sexes by dividing up work and power between the two sexes. This emphasises or exaggerates sex differences, he claims, and, in general, superimposes differences between men and women on almost every aspect of social life. This ensures that most boys and girls grow up feeling different from peers of the opposite sex so that they will, when grown up, be sexually attracted to each other. Bem chooses to call this "exotic becomes erotic" (Bem 1996) but what he is talking about is, of course, that when people repress an emotion they will automatically be attracted to people who express those emotions. This helps men and women to become attracted to each other, though the hypothalamus will already have generated a silhouette of that person as I have explained earlier (page 64), indicating their sex, in each person's sexual make-up. Thus, men repress their housekeeping, nurturing and caring feelings while women express these feelings; and women repress their competitive, combative, constructional and engineering feelings while men express these. This system helps the two sexes to become attracted to each other.

From this we can see that equality of the sexes is bad for heterosexuals as it defuses this powerful psychological attraction.

BISEXUALITY REVISITED

Where does that leave bisexuals? We have seen why gay men are attracted to aggressive men, why heterosexual men are attracted to housekeeping, nurturing and caring women, and why women are attracted to competitive, combative, constructional and engineering men. Where does that leave bisexuals?

Bisexuals are attracted to both men and women and must, therefore, repress their housekeeping, nurturing and caring feelings *as well as* their competitive, combative, constructional and engineering feelings. As well as this psychological attraction, their hypothalamuses must also be undecided, being caught betwixt and between, providing them with a silhouette which is both male and female, in order for them to be sexually attracted to both men *and* women.

Can this really be the case? Well . . . I know four bisexual men. One of these can be discounted as not being truly bisexual as I would say he was a Kinsey 5 (page 65) although he fathered a son he was predominantly gay. The remaining three I would describe as very repressed, which is what one would expect if they were repressing so many emotions. How would I know that? Because they lack spontaneity – a sure sign of repression. When you ask them a question they often have to think awhile before answering; and suggest to any of them to go to a restaurant or to see a show and you have to wait while they agonise over their soul-searching, before, probably, giving you a refusal. One of them has admitted to me that he has a "low sexual drive" and, barring physiological causes of which his doctor is not aware of any, this would most likely be caused by repression as we have seen (page 14) and underlines/underscores my hypothesis. Clearly, three examples do not go to proving a theory, but at least it *is* a hypothesis, which may suggest avenues for future research.

THE NATURE OF LOVE

Another time yet another psychiatrist. He said that love was to do with tender feelings of caring for someone. That quite surprised me, given my own experiences and direction (page 70).

I know, when I was in my teens I thought love would be lying between cool white sheets with someone one loved. Only the reality was that any gay guy I fancied I could not reach an orgasm with.

Are sadism, masochism, flagellation, bondage, humiliation, subservience and water sports really love? I am afraid I have to say that I do not think they are. People whose tender sexual feelings have become so entwined with their guilt, self-loathing, low self-esteem and repressed anger have to use all these kinky methods to try to get into touch with their sexual feelings.

In his book *Homosexuality* (p. 71) Charles Socarides claims that whenever homosexuals feel weakened, frightened, depleted, guilty, ashamed or in any way helpless or powerless they desperately need and seek a sexual contact. In the patients' words, he says, they want their "shot" of masculinity. He says they then feel miraculously well and strengthened. They instantly feel reintegrated upon achieving orgasm with a male partner.

For men who feel despised by most of the world, who feel self-hatred, who feel, as we have seen, helpless compared to other (heterosexual) men, inadequate and humiliated, sex becomes the one thing they can rely upon to make them feel fulfilled.

I had one friend to whom I was attracted because of his good looks, his Elvis-Presley hair-style and his muscular thighs glinting in his black-leather chaps but who was clearly a very unhappy person. It seemed to me that he needed sex once every hour, as I now realise, to boost his flagging morale and, if he happened to be riding pillion on my motorbike, I would feel the bike shaking as he masturbated once or twice during a journey (depending on how far we were going).

FEELING THREATENED

Besides wrestling, I have always been sexually aroused by men with muscular bodies. It was to emulate them that I spent so much time in gyms building up my own muscles.

One time I went to my doctor to see if he could help me or suggest a way I could build my muscles bigger.

"Why do you want to have big muscles?" he wanted to know.

I was at a loss. Doesn't *everybody* want to have big muscles?

Some years later I saw a photo of Mike Mentzer on the cover of a muscle magazine. I had never seen muscles like that before! I felt the adrenalin actually squirting into my stomach. It was not butterflies in my stomach, it was butterflies with fire-hoses! I had to get my muscles bigger. (Mentzer died in 2001. He was only 49 years old.)

I went back to my doctor and told him about the adrenalin squirting into my stomach.

"Do you feel threatened by men that have muscles that are bigger than yours?" he asked.

Yes! Yes, that was it, of course! They frightened me! And I feel threatened.

We have seen that men are biological enemies (page 108) and that this presents a special problem for gay men because they feel unable to compete with other men.

TWO SIDES OF A COIN

However, if someone you find threatening (because he is your biological enemy) becomes your lover then that proves he is no longer your enemy and immediately cancels out the threat that, previously, he was presenting to you.

It is like two sides of the same coin.

The problem has been resolved as far as one "enemy" goes but if another man comes by who is more handsome, younger or more muscular than your lover, he is likely to present another threat and it is easy to fall into the trap of resolving the new threat by, if possible, making him a lover so that he is no longer an "enemy".

This could account for much of the promiscuity that one finds on the gay scene. Gay men are not so much interested in finding lovers, one could deduce, than they are interested in diffusing the threat presented by other gay men who seem to have advantageous characteristics that they themselves lack.

The reason gay men feel so easily threatened by other men is that they are not allowed and not able to compete with them.

Being helpless inside the gay straitjacket, they are unable to compete so the sight of a younger, more handsome or more muscular man presents a frightening threat. As they are so helpless there is nothing they can *do* about it. That is what makes it really disturbing.

If gay men were able to come out of their straitjackets and compete they would realise that these other, though seemingly superior, men are not superior to themselves after all. They might realise that they themselves have qualities that the seemingly superior men do not have. They need to compete with these men for these equalities to become apparent or, in other words, to cancel out the threat they pose.

What competing with other men does for you is to show yourself how good *you* actually are. It shows you that you may actually be better than the younger, more handsome, more muscular guys because you have other qualities that make you better. It may come as a surprise to find that they are not such a threat after all!

However, you will never find this out until you come out of your straitjacket and find you are *allowed* to compete, as I discovered with Ken.

YOUNGER, MORE HANDSOME, MORE MUSCULAR

If you look through the personal small ads in a gay paper you cannot help but notice the number of men who are looking for younger, more handsome or more muscular partners.

Are they all really wanting to turn these people into lovers in order to diffuse the threat that they pose? Gay men tend to be very sensitive to feeling that others are superior or that they themselves feel inferior.

We have seen that, if you feel others are superior, there are two ways you can become superior to them: either you can tear them down, such as by bitching about them, or you can become superior to them by improving yourself.

Of course, if someone presents a threat because he is younger than you it may not seem that you can ever reverse your age to become younger again than the young man. That is not what I am suggesting. Age with maturity is a quality that is far preferable to young beauty and ignorance.

The trouble is that so many gay men are trapped in their straitjackets

Digging Deeper

and feel constantly that straight men are superior to them. That leaves them consistently feeling inferior, lowering their self-esteem, and thus leaving them feeling easily threatened by young men, or men who are more muscular or more handsome.

It is only by escaping their straitjacket that they can acquire the qualities and maturity in themselves that will allow them to admire themselves so much that their own self-confidence will not be eclipsed by youth, more muscular or more handsome men.

They have not been allowed to develop their own self-confidence by developing their own muscles. It is amazing how much beauty well-developed muscles can add to a face. They have not felt that that was allowed for them.

Like Hank Trout (page 56) they have not been "allowed to be boys" so straight boys have left them behind in developing their bodies by playing sports and their aggressiveness by playing sports, with the result that *of course* the gay men feel inferior. And a younger man or a more handsome man or a more muscular man simply *reminds* them how inferior they feel. Consequently the gay men feel even more threatened and need to try to neutralise the threat posed by younger men, more handsome or more muscular men by making them lovers.

I LOVE ANDY, ANDY LOVES ME

There is something that I have not yet mentioned about Andy. You may recall that I said that he never showed pain (page 18).

I have mentioned that if one represses one's anger one will very likely repress all one's other emotions including the tender sexual feelings.

You may have already realised that Andy was not only repressing his anger but, as he never showed any pain, he was repressing that emotion as well. What this has meant for him is that, yes, of course his sexual feelings were stifled, but so were his feelings of affection and indeed most of his other feelings.

This has meant that, even now after we have expressed our anger with each other in words and therefore no longer need to punch each other to release our sexual feelings together with our anger, he is still hardly able to show any affection although his self-confidence is improving.

Given what I know about him and about psychology I understand that this does not mean he does not love me but only that he has difficulty in showing it. A tentative hand on my back was about all he was able to manage some months ago, but that meant more to me than I can say. Over the recent months his confidence has improved, his touch and grasp have become more assured and the improved interaction has resulted in a more satisfying sexual experience for both of us which is constantly getting better and better.

Although he has had a string of girlfriends from the time when we first met it is only four years ago in 1997 that he was able to give his current girlfriend a child.

Given that I know he has had problems with his sexual feelings with me (as I have had with him) I imagine he has had the same problems with sex with his girlfriends and that may have, in part, been responsible for him having had so many girlfriends in the time that I have known him, perhaps because he was not able to give them the child that they longed for and so made them feel dissatisfied with him.

I mentioned above that most of his other feelings were stifled as well. By that I mean that if you offer him food and ask him what he would prefer he does not know what he would like. This creates a problem in a restaurant.

He never knows what he would like to do. This is all because he is not completely in touch yet with his own feelings. On the one hand he does not like being *made* to do anything but on the other hand he does not know what he would *like* to do. This makes it difficult for others to interact with him or to make a choice for him when he is unable to do it for himself..

FEAR OF REJECTION

As Andy's biological parents allowed him to be adopted he is frightened of revealing his love as when you give your love to someone you also give that person the power to cause you suffering. Giving your love to someone means you also give that person the power to hurt you by rejecting you.

In Andy's case he has the same fear of rejection that most gay men suffer from but with him it is caused not by his father being away from home but by his parents giving him away and abandoning him, putting him out for adoption.

Digging Deeper

He is convinced, and terrified, that people will find out what he is really like and then abandon him as his biological parents did because, he believes, there must be something "wrong" with him.

This, you recall, was the shock for Oedipus (page 43).

FEELING ANGRY

There are likely to be two types of the 90% of gay men among the readers of this book. Some will be completely unaware of ever feeling angry while others may feel that they are sitting on top of a volcano liable to explode at any minute.

If you are one of the latter I will show you in the next section the safest way for you to defuse your situation and start to let your anger out safely. If you are currently unaware of your anger, finding out that you can actually have any anger as you progress through Chapter 4 will be a new experience.

Do not be frightened by feeling angry. Remember that it is actually a good emotion (page 9). It is nature's way of protecting you from other people. It is a force that you can use constructively to improve your life, to stand up for yourself, to prevent yourself being manipulated, exploited or put upon or pushed around, that you can use to compete with other men and to be able to win!

It is a force that you can harness that will help you to do things you have been too frightened to do before. It is a force that can make you feel proud of yourself. That will make others proud of you, too.

That will make others admire you. And that will change your life.

ESCAPING

THE GAY

STRAITJACKET

Stage One - ENDING YOUR FEAR OF VIOLENCE

Now that we have looked at the gay straitjacket, all the problems that are caused by repressing one's anger, the nature of homosexuality and its ramifications which undoubtedly compound this repression of anger, we are ready to agree that we would be far better off without the gay straitjacket.

Indeed you are probably wondering why so many gay men seem to suffer from repressing their anger. This was all revealed to me by a psychiatrist at the Tavistock Clinic in London during the group psychotherapy that I undertook there from 1966 to 1971.

What brought the subject up at the group was that I had had a confrontation with a man at work. As I mentioned earlier, he had put me down, sent up me if you like, by saying rude things to me in front of other workers. He was asking for it but he knew he could get away with it as he knew I would not be able to do anything about it and, of course, he was right . . . I could not.

I thought he would stop teasing me if I punched him on the jaw (I had done some boxing with friends) but I was frightened I might break his jaw (an acquaintance in the gym had told me it had happened to him at work) and that there would be a court case, the police would probably come to interview us and I might get the sack. Or worse, if I tried to use my wrestling skills and tried a wrestling takedown on him so that I could put a submission hold on him to force him to apologise, he might fall badly, breaking a leg or banging his head against the wall and have to go to hospital with a fractured skull, and the ambulance would have to come to take him away, there would be a court case and I would get the sack, on so on . . . All the thoughts of what might happen just left me powerless to do anything.

This is typical of what many gay men would describe as their "fear of violence" that makes them helpless and frightened of expressing their anger. And makes them frightened of a confrontation with another man.

If you are one of those people who abhor psychology that explains someone's behaviour in terms of what happened when that person was a baby, I must beg your indulgence for a page or so, when I will have something important to say to you.

When I retold this incident in the psychotherapy group the psychiatrist spoke to me quietly and very slowly. What he said cured my fear of violence and will probably cure yours for you. He gave me time to take in each element and this is the way you should read it.

Try to visualise what he is saying.

"A baby is very helpless, but it gets warmth and love from its mother, its milk, and has its nappies changed by her to restore its comfort. These are things a baby can't do for itself. Because the mother cares for the baby in this way, it is quite normal for a baby to want to have its mother to itself.

"The father can appear as an intruder. And the baby may want to, somehow, get rid of him so that it can have its mother to itself.

"But the father is a giant compared to the baby and very powerful and he is also the breadwinner, whereas the baby is very weak and helpless.

"The baby imagines that, if it tried to do away with the father, the father might do something terrible to the baby in retaliation.

"The baby would have done away with the breadwinner, and would also have to cope with the anger of its mother who would have lost her husband.

"This is a truly frightening situation to be in. You can perhaps imagine for a moment what it must feel like from the baby's point of view, a situation that the baby remembers for the rest of its life: not as what would happen in a conflict with its father, but as what would happen if it got into conflict with any other man.

"Of course, this is only a fantasy in the baby's mind but if, as he grows up, he happens to be punched by another boy, or knocked heavily to the ground or perhaps threatened with a knife by another man, an event like that can become the *proof* for him that something terrible *will* happen to him, as in his fantasy, if he ever came into conflict with another man, and so he becomes even more frightened of other men."

Even though I had learned how to stand up for myself and wrestle, this frightening fantasy of what would happen if I, still as a baby, came into conflict with my father, was remembered in my subconscious mind, arousing all the frightening images and fantasies of what might happen that prevented me from jumping into action as straight men would.

What you need to realise is that the fantasy you had as a baby is now out of date as things have changed a lot since then and are very different now.

You are a grown man, as big as your father or perhaps even bigger. You are your own breadwinner. You are younger and more active then he is now and you are no longer a helpless baby, having to rely on your mother to change your nappies for you or to feed you.

This was what cured my "fear of violence" and my fear of other men and changed my life. I have no doubt that it will do the same for you. Therefore take your time to consider it carefully. Re-read it if you like.

After a psychiatrist makes an interpretation on the way the people in a psychotherapeutic group are behaving there is usually a long silence while the people think about this new way of looking at their own behaviour, the new aspects and how they affect each person, before the group can pick up the conversation again and continue with the discussion.

I therefore think this is a good place for you to put down this book for a few days so that you can be left with these extremely important remarks in your mind and have time to mull them over and consider them fully before continuing.

THE PAINFUL TRUTH

I know that a number of people discredit any psychological explanation that involves what happens to people when they are babies, and I am sure they have a good reason for doing this.

Why would people want to discredit the truth unless the truth was too painful for them? Perhaps because, for instance, they once did something to a baby that they now feel guilty about and do not want people like myself to lumber them with the responsibility that they cannot bear to accept for their past actions. They would prefer us to believe that you can do anything you like to a baby (especially if you are jealous of the baby) and it will make no difference to that baby in later life because babies do not have feelings yet.

This is, of course, patently untrue.

Unfortunately, I am not prepared to collude in their deception. I think this interpretation on the previous two pages and its significance for all gay men, either directly or indirectly (if lack of aggression is not a problem that you personally have), is far too important to allow it to be discredited by people who are out only to salve their own consciences.

For so long, male homosexuality has been associated in almost everybody's eyes with lack of aggression that it has almost been taken for granted that you cannot have one without the other.

AN UPWARD SPIRAL BEGINS

But now we can see that lack of aggression due to a fantasy of violence is not intrinsic to gayness, it is a completely separate entity, a neurosis, and it can be cured as it stems only from a fantasy that occurred in childhood, a fantasy that most gay guys have grown up with.

That it occurs to gay men more than to straight men may be connected with the fact that, as we have seen, the gay man's father was hoping for a daughter and was disappointed with a son. Researchers have shown that many mothers of gay sons, as we have also seen, devote more time to the baby than to their husbands after the birth, provoking jealousy in the husband/father. Thus the baby may become aware of this jealous conflict with the father (over them both wanting the mother for themselves) and also become sensitive to rejection (by the father originally) which is a sort of double-edged sword.

That is, the baby wants to get rid of the father but, when the father is got rid of, the baby feels that there is something about himself that must make him unlovable which must have driven the father away.

This can result only in guilt. Guilt means you feel you have done something wrong and this can result only in lower self-esteem.

By realising that the cause of this guilt is invalid, one removes this guilt (there may be other guilt due to other causes) at a stroke and also the associated low self-esteem. Similarly, there may still remain low self-esteem due to other causes which we shall look at and try to expunge also.

The interpretation concerning the baby's first imagined conflict with its father is the interpretation that I was given at the Tavistock Clinic and that cured my own fear of violence and consequent inability to be aggressive, that is, to be able to express my anger physically as aggression. After hearing it and assimilating its meaning I found I no longer had these frightening fantasies such as the one I described (page 6) that prevented me from doing what I wanted to do and what other (straight) men do without thinking about. Though I did not realise this immediately, it suddenly opened the doors to all kinds of behaviour that I previously avoided and I hope and trust that the same will happen for you.

I am sure that, if you are prepared to take it seriously, to think about it and consider for a moment how babies feel about the world around them, you will understand the truth of this explanation, its validity and its consequences. It could change how you feel – if, of course, fear of violence and lack of aggression are problems that you had in the first place.

If you *are* being taunted at work, as *I* was (and around the world this must happen to thousands of people every day and be settled without a single punch being thrown), if you are *frightened* of what might happen, your taunter will see it in your face and in your hesitance. But if you are *not* frightened to throw a punch your taunter will also be made aware of that when you fix him with your eyes as you say firmly, "That's enough of that!" or retaliate with your own riposte (which is probably the game your taunter wants you to play) and which I will show you later how to succeed ar.

That is the way I usually respond nowadays and we will look at how you should go about doing that in the section **Anger and Self-assertiveness**.

Most bullies will stop their taunts if you say, "That's enough of that!" – but only if you really mean it, and really know how to throw a punch, too, if you *have* to. They will *not* be convinced if you say it in a feminine

Escaping the Gay Straitjacket

way or while sashaying your hips. Why not? Because real sportsmen, as we will discover, have learned not to waste their energy on useless, ineffective movements. They save all their energy to put into movements that are effective and decisive.

Even if your "fear of violence" has now vanished that is not the end of the story. It is a new beginning. As a toddler you were kept from your peers or were too frightened of them to join them. This deprived you of all the physical development they achieved and the skills that they acquired from that time to the present. If you are no longer to see yourself, even subconsciously, as inferior to them, you will still need to catch up with them before you can feel as good as (or better than) them and so eliminate the low self-esteem that this provokes. We will look at how you should go about achieving this in the rest of the book.

JEALOUS FATHERS

There is yet another complication with regard to the fantasy that caused your "fear of violence". We saw in Chapter 2 that after the birth of the to-become-gay son the father lost interest in the child and spent less time at home (page 49). What very often happens is that, perhaps owing to the baby's frailty or illness (page 55), the mother spends so much time with the new baby that the father feels excluded and ignored by his wife. He then becomes jealous and angry. This may be the real reason why he spends less time at home.

For the baby who has the fantasy the psychiatrist described above, of wanting to get rid of his father, the father's anger with the baby may aggravate the baby's fantasising that conflict with his (angry) father would result in a disaster for him, thus making him even more terrified for the rest of his life of coming into a conflict with other men.

Let us look for a moment at this fantasy of "violence" from a psychiatric point of view. Freud believed that, between the ages of 3½ and 6, boys have to go through a phase in which they want to compete with their fathers and get rid of them to have their mothers to themselves. This he called the Oedipus complex. Professor George Engel describes what happens in the case of some men in his book *Psychological Development in Health and Disease* and says that excessively "harsh or punitive" attitudes of the father make the solution of this complex more difficult. (It seems

AFTER *Escape the Gay Straitjacket* went to press Donald Black realised that there is a certain set of circumstances not mentioned in the book that may come in the way of some gay men who fall into the 90% group and delay them from curing their "fear of violence" neurosis.

An example of the problem can be seen in what happened to a reader in Seattle.

He first wrote to Donald Black to say that he did not feel that what the psychiatrist said on pages 120–121 could apply to him as he had a very good relationship with his father.

He was remembering his teen years but for straight sons this is the time when they rebel against their fathers and form their own "gangs". A good relationship with the father during the teen years is characteristic of some gay son-father relationships that have started off badly as described in many places in this book.

The reader in Seattle was in fact unable to recall his years from 0 – 5 so to verify this he asked his mother how his father had reacted to his birth. She said he was away more of the time after the birth.

That clinched it for him. He realised that his mother's possessiveness must have made his father jealous and driven him away from the home as researchers have so often described. He had been unable to recall it as that was during his age 0 – 5 years, but it reflected exactly what the psychiatrist had described on pages 120–121.

As he reached this realisation his neurosis that made him frightened of "violence" just vanished into nothing. He e-mailed Donald immediately that his fears associated with wrestling, a sport that he participated in, were at an end and he was beginning a new era in his life.

Perhaps it would help you if you asked your mother (if she is still alive) how your father reacted to your birth.

How can you tell if your neurosis has been cured? Suddenly you will no longer feel intimidated by other men, and your fear of "violence" occurring will no longer be there. This major shift in the way you see the world can hardly go unnoticed by you and will signal it has been cured.

As your mother fed you, dressed you and changed your nappies when you were a baby it is quite normal to want to have her to yourself and to, somehow, do away with your father. When your father spends less time at home it is difficult not to believe that *you* did not *cause* this, and that your father will want to revenge himself on you. Actually, it is your mother that

P.T.O.

he was angry with, not you, because she gave too much attention to you and not enough to your father.

It is this fear of what your father will do to you that, Donald believes, causes you to be frightened of your father and also of other men, and results in this neurosis. Your fear is *misplaced* because it is not you he was angry with, but your *mother*! He had no intention of harming you.

Many people cannot believe that they had a bad relationship with their father when they were a baby. I am afraid that this is the *sine qua non* of the neurosis that 90% of gay men suffer from. Donald believes it is what causes the neurosis in the first place. In other words, if you are frightened of playing sports that proves you have the neurosis that causes a "fear of violence" and since you have this neurosis that proves your father spent less time at home after you were born and that you (**wrongly**) believed **it was your fault** and that he would take revenge on you.

This book comes with after-sales support. If, after reading pages 120 and 121 and this insert your neurosis has not been cured then **please write to Donald Black** at one of the addresses below explaining to him how you feel about what the psychiatrist said on pages 120 and 121. Donald will then help you to crack the problem.

If you have succeeded in curing your neurosis why not write to Donald anyway to tell him of your success?

Alternatively, you can consult the Problem Pages on our web-sites (see below) or discuss it with your family doctor.

If your neurosis is not cured there is very little point in trying to put into action the development that is suggested from Stage Two (page 137) onwards as one cannot "learn" to express one's anger or be assertive while your neurotic "fear of violence" is continually pulling you backwards. You need to be free of this fear before you can make progress. (Also see pages xiii and xiv.)

E-mail: donblack@gaystraitjacket.com
Postal: Donald Black, c/o Power Books, 54 Balham Park Road, London SW12 8DU United Kingdom
Web-sites:
Escape the Gay Straitjacket web-site (and Problem Page)
www.gaystraitjacket.com
Wrestling for Gay Guys web-site (including Problem Page and Directory of Wrestlers) www.wrestlingforgayguys.com

he is talking about gay men.) Such a father, he goes on, may seem to the boy so threatening that he may give up not only his mother but all women and treat the father in particular and all men in general with a passive, compliant attitude. Then, he says, the boy may see himself as the love object of the father (see page 112) and see the mother as his rival (the so-called negative Oedipus complex). The father's jealousy of the attention the child is receiving from its mother, must arise, as we have seen, within weeks of the birth but it is not clear at what point the child becomes aware of it. The child's first impression of his father will be of an angry, jealous man, causing the child to become frightened of his father so that, when the rivalry of the Oedipus complex arises, the child constructs the fantasy (see page 120) which makes competition with his father too frightening to contemplate and prevents the boy from working through the Oedipus complex. What Engel is saying, though he does not put it into words, is that, by becoming "passive" and "compliant", the child is burying his anger and that this will, as we have seen, have other disastrous results for him. Did Engel realise he was talking about repressing anger? The deleterious effects of repressing anger are so important that it is necessary for the link between passive/compliant and repressing anger to be spelled out.

This jealous attitude of the father may be what establishes this fear and fantasy in the minds of gay men and not in the minds of straight men who grow up completely unafraid of other men and able to express their anger so that they can compete against other men in body-contact sports. To demonstrate this further complication, I need to illustrate it with an anecdote.

Although my father helped me build model theatres when I was a child, as I grew older he became less and less helpful to me and more and more obstructive. I will give you some examples as these had further devastating effects on me.

When I started attending university he had to give me a lift in the car to get there but started out too late for me to arrive at lectures on time even though I told him one of the lecturers had warned us that he would not admit latecomers.

One evening I went to the theatre in Cape Town and missed the last two trains home. There was a station at Kuils River which was a mile from our smallholding and there was a later train to Bellville which was three miles from our home. I phoned home and told my mother I was at Cape Town station. She said my father had gone to Kuils River station to meet the last train to pick me up. As I was not on that train my father drove straight to Bellville to meet the last train there but as I was not on that train either he drove the eleven miles to Cape Town station where he presumed I would be. It was not a very big station as stations go (twelve or fourteen platforms) and after the last trains have gone it was pretty deserted so it is unbelievable that he could not find me there as he claimed. He drove home where my mother told him I had phoned and was waiting in Cape Town station.

He drove back to Cape Town, could still not find me at the station although it was deserted, and drove home again!

The next time both my mother and father drove in to Cape Town to fetch me and it was 2:45 a.m. by the time we all got home.

The further devastating effects that these events had on me came when I was eighteen and decided I should leave home to prevent more acrimony, but my father refused to let me leave. I wished he was dead. Within a month he had tried to push-start our large family car and suffered a massive brain haemorrhage. He was virtually in a coma. After a week in hospital he died.

I told myself I was not to blame for that but, if you wish someone would drop down dead and they *do*, it is very difficult not to feel that you did not have *some*thing to do with it.

Undoubtedly this guilt was another contribution to lowering my self-esteem.

If you wish someone would drop down dead and they only suffer a minor injury you can still feel responsible and suffer from enormous guilt, resulting in low self-esteem.

With most gay men the problem is more insidious. We have seen that, after the birth, the mothers of gay sons very often spend so much time with the new baby that the fathers feel neglected and excluded and then spend more time away from home.

For the baby who feels he would like to somehow get rid of his father so that he can have his mother to himself, when the father spends less time at home the baby is bound to feel that his wish has been granted (if only to some extent) and with that will come the associated guilt – insidious because it will never be stated or discussed.

The child will end up with a load of guilt for which he will never understand the reason. It will contribute to lowering his self-esteem for the rest of his life or until he realises how it has been caused and will then be able to see it was not *his* fault that his father spent less time at home, but his *mother's* fault.

TWO SETS OF FEELINGS

You may or may not have noticed that there appear to be two sets of contradictory feelings aroused by the father feeling his position has been usurped by the new baby and spending less time at home.

On the one hand the baby feels that, because he wanted to get rid of his father in order to have his mother to himself, he feels he is responsible for driving his father out of the home and consequently feels guilty because of it. On the other hand he feels there must be something about him that makes him unlovable (if people knew what he was really like) that caused his father to be away from home.

How can these contradictory situations both exist?

They exist in the subconscious mind but come into the conscious mind when it is in different moods (see Glossary) and so they are never both in the conscious mind at the same time.

It is the same mechanism that causes me, when I find I have some surplus money, to spend it on a coat but, the next day when I am in a different mood, I can remember I have some surplus money but am not able to remember that I have already spent it, so I spend the same amount a second time on another purchase. Another example would be that when you are in a happy mood you remember only other happy times and have difficulty in recalling unhappy times, but when you are depressed you remember nothing but loads of other unhappy events and cannot recall any happy ones.

THE OTHER BOYS ARE TOO ROUGH FOR MY LITTLE JOHNNY REVISITED

We have seen also that gay men often have early illnesses or sojourns in hospital that cause their mothers to over-protect them afterwards (page 55). This can leave the child feeling that he is too weak to compete against other men which would also exacerbate the fantasy in the child's mind as described by the psychiatrist above.

We have seen that some mothers of gay sons keep the child away from its peers as "the other boys are too rough for my little Johnny" (page 55).

Some psychiatrists and researchers (Friedman 1988; Isay 1989; Bell *et al*. 1981) question whether it is rather because the child is so frightened of rough-and-tumble and getting hurt by other boys that the mother keeps the child away from his peers. A question of which comes first: the chicken or the egg? These psychiatrists say that many gay men, later in life, complain about having been clumsy and maladroit as children at skills that other (heterosexual) boys take for granted. This is quite feasible. We have seen that the cause of the "fear of violence" is that gay men have wanted to have their mothers to themselves and fantasised about getting rid of their fathers to achieve this. They then become frightened of what the consequences of their action may be and what the father would do to them.

What people do when they have a fantasy is to look for proof that their fantasy is actually true and valid. At the same time it is known that one of the causes of getting injured in sport is if a person does not have their heart in it. We can just picture then the (pre-gay) child with a fantasy that other men are dangerous, encountering his peers for the first time. He is going to be frightened of them and wary of them. In this way he will not have his heart in it if the play turns to rough-and-tumble, and in that frame of mind, not having his heart in it, he is very likely to be injured. This immediately becomes the proof to him that he was looking for that his fantasy *is* true: men *are* dangerous and to be avoided: and reinforces his fear of other men.

Some psychiatrists wonder whether these gay men's brains are not correctly wired to make them clumsy and maladroit at masculine skills. I do not think we need worry about this possibility as we have such a good psychological reason for this behaviour: it is well known that being clumsy and maladroit is a defence against doing something one does not want to do. I knew a girl at work who said she never had to help with the washing-up/doing the dishes after a meal at home. This was because whenever she had helped in the past she always "accidentally" broke a plate or something and so was henceforth excused from this chore. When gay boys are so frightened of other boys do we need to look further for a reason for their clumsiness at masculine skills?

This may well be the scenario for many gay boys. On the other hand, when the gym-master at my high school divided our class into three sections according to our skills I was usually in the top (most agile) third. If I lacked ball-throwing skills it was rather because as a child I never had a football and the smaller ball that I did have at one time was usually commandeered by my father and my elder (adopted) sister so that I had to run back and forth trying desperately to catch it while they kept it out of my reach.

Dr Richard Friedman in *Male Homosexuality* says that some mothers' fear of male aggression leads them to confuse normal boyhood assertiveness and "rambunctiousness" such as rough-and-tumble with aggressiveness and destructive behaviour. In a study by Coates and Zucker (1988) many of the mothers commented on how nice, gentle and good their sons were compared to other boys whom they saw as mean, aggressive bullies.

Being kept away from his peers by his mother can serve only to make the child feel that other boys *must* be very dangerous if he has to be kept away from them, exacerbating the fantasy the psychiatrist described above that causes the "fear of violence" or providing the child with the proof that he has been looking for to substantiate his fantasy.

But it does not end there. Friedman points out that the child's self-esteem depends not only on feeling valued by his parents but also on being accepted by his peers. He needs to want to be like his peers and to be accepted by them. He needs them to want him to be like them. Heterosexual boys learn from their peers and from adult males how to behave in life's different situations. They become role models for heterosexual boys. When the gay child feels "different" and loses this interaction with his peers not only does his self-esteem suffer but he also loses contact with these role models who may value rough-and-tumble and body-contact sports that the gay child is frightened of. The result is that the gay boy has no role models apart from his mother. This is disastrous for him.

When I was on the point of leaving home my mother repeatedly said to me, "You don't know what the world is like", I suppose in response to some of the plans that I expressed.

By keeping me away from all but two or three (gay) friends my mother had ensured that I would not know how inter-relationships work or, in her words, what the world was like. In fact, when I was in nursery school I was always taken to play with girls!!

By being kept away from one's peers one never finds out how other boys stand up for themselves, how one can avoid getting into a fight without losing face, or what one has to do if one gets into a quarrel. One does not learn how other boys stand up to their parents. One never learns that it does not matter if one is quaking in one's boots when one has to stand up for oneself. The important thing is to appear unafraid.

Each of one's peers will have a different experience of life from oneself so there is an awful lot that one can learn from them about what the world is like and the best way of going about different situations you may be faced with. You have been denied access to this knowledge.

Another downside of being protected from your peers is that playing team games develops friendships and trust with other boys and men. Not having mixed with your peers or played team games with them means that you are left on the gay scene feeling that every other man is competing against you in finding a mate and that, therefore, other men are enemies and not to be trusted.

Many gay men cannot face going on the gay scene for this kind of reason, apart from their low self-esteem which only aggravates their fear of having to compete. They cannot stand the competition because they are in a straitjacket and helpless to compete or defend themselves and feel they cannot trust other men.

The mark of someone who is a failure in life is that they only have one plan. "When I win the lottery I am going to do this or that." The mark of a successful person is that they have more than one plan. When I was explaining this to a gay friend he remarked, "Oh, you mean they have a Plan B." And I replied, "Yes". It was only later that I realised they also have a Plan C if this should happen, a Plan D if that should happen, and so on. This is what a sport like wrestling teaches you. If you try to grab your opponent's leg to take him down to the mat, and you miss, you do not pack up and go home. You try some other tactic. Or you learn why the tactic you used failed and you try it again in an improved way.

It is only by having an exchange with your peers that you can learn about these different aspects of life, and the mother who thinks she is protecting her child is, actually, making insurmountable problems for him in later life.

The extreme of this is demonstrated by sons who have such close relationships with their mothers who do everything for them that, when their mothers die, the sons do not know what the world is like. The sons feel totally unable to cope with the world or with having to do things for themselves and often commit suicide as a consequence. Why do mothers do this?

It seems to me that they must be so lacking in purpose or fulfilment in their own lives that, when the opportunity occurs, the child gives them such a self-important purpose in life that they do not want to relinquish this mother/ baby relationship. In this case it is not Peter Pan who does not want to grow up but it is Peter Pan's *mother* who does not want him to grow up and become self-sufficient and no longer need her, depriving her of the self-importance he gives her while he is a baby and as long as he *remains* a baby.

A parallel exists with disabled children. The BBC used to have a radio programme for the disabled called *Does He Take Sugar?* which, as I understood it by the programme title, was trying to make able-bodied people aware that they ought not to ignore the disabled but treat them as people in their own right.

However, my experience was slightly different.

I was abroad on holiday and found there was a rather handsome young man who was in a wheelchair staying with his mother in the same hotel as myself. I greeted them when our paths crossed but the young man never spoke. His mother always spoke for both of them. One day, on returning from the beach I went to the lift in the hotel and when the doors opened the young man in the wheelchair was in the lift.

"Hello", I said, "Are you coming out?"

"No", he replied, "I want to go to our room but the doors closed suddenly and I found myself on my own in the lift."

I got into the lift with him and explained that in automatic lifts there is always a button to open the doors.

"Which floor do you want?" I asked.

"We're on the fourth."

"I'm on the third. I'll press the button for you. Can you get out on your own?"

"Yes", he responded, "The doors always open when we reach our floor."

The doors closed and the lift went up.

He was an attractive young man and I wondered if this chance encounter without his mother might be the start of a friendship.

"What did you do this morning?" I asked to make conversation.

"We went into the town as my mother wanted to do some shopping", he replied.

"Oh. I was on the beach."

"Yes, we went on to the beach yesterday. It's lovely down there."

The lift doors opened at the third floor.

"This is where I get out", I said, "I'll see you."

"Thanks for your help. I didn't know what to do", he called after me as the doors closed.

The next day I ran into him and his mother.

"Did you manage in the lift all right?" I asked the young man.

"Graham was trapped in the lift yesterday", his mother chimed in. "The doors closed before I could do anything, but he waited outside the lift on our floor until I caught up with him."

I then realised that it is not just that able-bodied people ignore the disabled; it is rather their *mothers* who want to live their lives *for* them that create the problem. They want to capitalise on the self-importance this

Escaping the Gay Straitjacket

gives them and maintain it.

With his mother present there was no chance of having a conversation with Graham. She always spoke for him.

If you are being shielded from the world by your mother as I was, you need to encourage her to find other interests in her life so that you can escape her tentacles even in adult life, and learn to speak for yourself.

This may not be easy, as it may be that your mother has problems relating to other people or lacks the confidence one needs to have an enquiring mind that enables one to discover other interests in life.

After my father died I became aware that my mother was trying to make me into a surrogate husband. When we gave up the smallholding in Kuils River we went our separate ways at first but after six months she decided to take a flat/apartment in Tamboerskloof on the slopes of Table Mountain which is within walking distance of the centre of Cape Town and so I joined her there.

Whenever she wanted to go out she needed me to accompany her as she had no one else to accompany her. When I wanted to be able to concentrate on doing some work at home I had to pin a sign up outside my bedroom door saying "Man at work" to keep her from interrupting me every ten minutes on various pretexts. "Would you like some coffee?" "What would you like for breakfast in the morning?" "What are you going to do tomorrow night?" "Did you phone Peter?" "Did you see this or that in the newspaper this morning?"

Within a week of my phoning a travel agent to enquire about the cost of travelling to England my mother fell down the stairs and shattered her knee. She was in hospital for six months.

This is not a loving motherly relationship. This is a straitjacket that my mother was trying to keep me in. A crutch she needed to support her.

I have not yet mentioned that the manic depression from which I suffered from my teens to the age of fifty-seven was apparently caused also, inadvertently, by my mother, but that is another story, another book.

I am amazed when I hear people who have lost their parents say that they look forward to being reunited with them when they themselves die. If I have to be reunited with my parents when I die, I would rather hope I never die!

Remember, I told the first psychiatrist who asked me what my parents were like (page 52) that they were "nice people".

Escaping your straitjacket will also help you to escape your mother, but if you cannot escape your mother you will never escape your gay straitjacket.

Escape the Gay Straitjacket

Will the price for you be as high as the price I had to pay? Will that be the excuse you use to stay in your straitjacket, helpless and ineffective for the rest of your life, but a nice pet for your mother? Or a nice daughter?

When your mother dies, as one day she must, will *you* want to commit suicide?

As loving as she is and has been, you need to be able to stand on your own feet for the many reasons that this book has highlighted. You need to become your own father for yourself and do for yourself what your father should have done but failed to do – help you to become a man.

You can do it. I give you permission to become a man. I will help you along the way.

ESCAPING LOW SELF-ESTEEM

In describing my relationship with Ken I have described the depths of masochism that we enjoyed together. We have talked about many gay men having low self-esteem and have looked, albeit briefly, at the gay S & M scene without specifically asking yet why so many gay men should be sadistic or masochistic though we have touched on some reasons.

With regard to Ken and his religious guilt over the people he had killed because he needed the money for drugs, I think it became crystal clear with regard to the knife-fights replaced by my punishing him that his masochism was clearly self-punishment or sadism to himself due to his religious guilt.

What makes so many people on the gay scene sadistic or masochistic? The first thing that springs to mind is wanting to punish oneself to atone for the guilt of having (supposedly) got rid of one's father as a baby so that one could have one's mother to oneself. This may be accompanied by feelings of self-loathing because you did not seem to be good enough for him to be able to love you "if people knew what I am really like".

We have seen that it is important for children and adolescents to be loved by their parents in order to feel self-worth. It is necessary also for children and adolescents to be accepted by their peers, not just their gay peers who form only a small percentage, but by *all* their peers to be able to feel self-worth.

There is also the constant feeling of inferiority when one is unable to do the things one sees (straight) men doing all the time around one, such as standing up for oneself, challenging other men if necessary, playing masculine sports, sweeping women off their feet, and making babies. This inferiority results in further self-loathing.

It is no use making the excuse that one does not *want* to do any of those things. That is simply sour grapes, plain and simple without any doubt. The fact remains that, even if one *does* want to, and there *are* many times when one would like to, and *needs* to, be able to stand up for oneself and to be able to challenge other men if necessary, one feels inferior because one is *unable* to do these things particularly while other (straight) men *can* do them.

If one is in a tender loving relationship that is satisfying, then any low self-esteem will be reduced because of the love that your partner will give you. If there is no satisfying tender loving relationship then the feelings of low self-esteem will be exacerbated. If there is a sado-masochistic sexual relationship then these feelings of low self-esteem will not merely be perpetuated, they will actually gradually get worse.

With regard to myself there were many other reasons for me to loathe myself that I have already described. There was my inability to play the piano due to my compulsive mistakes preventing me from being a performer and from completing my university course. There was my inability to perform as an actor (due to crushing my father). There was my failure (in my eyes) to achieve the physique I desperately desired. There was my inability (in my eyes) to become the masterful wrestler I wanted to be. There was my helplessness to understand or prevent the depressions that I was subject to while I was manic depressive, and there was the guilt for having been responsible for the death of my father and my favourite dog.

I cannot, from this distance, hope to dispense psychotherapy for all the kinds of personal reasons, such as those I have quoted for myself, that different gay men might be suffering from in addition to the reasons I have mentioned. What I *can* do is offer help for the reasons that seem to apply to most gay men. After that it may become more apparent to sado-masochistic gay men what other personal reasons remain to cause their residual low self-esteem, especially after reading about mine and those of other people that I have recounted in this book.

Up to this point this book has been full of examples of the low self-esteem and the humiliation that gay men suffer or have suffered. In case you have not been counting, the words "low self-esteem" have appeared 30 times and "humiliated" or "humiliation" have appeared 27 times.

We have seen that heterosexual boys have role models from whom they learn how to conduct themselves (page 129), but that gay men, because they had a neurotic fantasy in childhood, develop an unrealistic fear of "violence" that prevents them from getting on with their (heterosexual) peers from the toddler stage and means that they lack masculine role models from whom they can learn how to deal with all kinds of events du-ring life.

Stages One to Six of this book are designed to help you correct this deficit and to learn the skills that heterosexual men have so that you can feel on an equal footing with them, and no longer feel inferior compared to them or have anything to be ashamed of about yourself. Your new achievements will, rather, make you feel proud of yourself.

One of the things that little boys are taught is that they need to be strong, that they do not cry because they are tough. If you look at advertisements in gay magazines and papers it cannot escape your notice that they are full of models that represent these qualities. Clearly gay men hanker terribly after men who have the characteristics that they (the gay men) have repressed. The lesson to be learned from this is that if you admire muscular bodies (and feel threatened by people who have muscular bodies) the quickest way to improve your own self-esteem is to acquire a muscular body yourself. If you admire construction-workers then go to night school to learn bricklaying, carpentry, etc. If you admire swimmers, learn to swim or to dive. In this way you will *become* one of the people that you admire. This will improve your own self-esteem in great leaps and bounds, and you will also be meeting the people you admire and turning them into your friends. Now your self-esteem is on an upward spiral.

I will advise you on weight-training and bodybuilding in more detail in Chapter 5.

DOMINANT MOTHERS

Although you may feel guilty for having got rid of your father, you will now know that you were not as successful as you have supposed all your life that you were. For it was actually your *mother* who, by ignoring her husband and never giving him some of her attention after your birth, made your father feel unwanted and drove him away.

Nor was there anything about you that made you unlovable "if people only knew what I am really like" and prevented you from being loved by your father. It was your *mother* that prevented your father from loving you by denying her husband any wifely attention and not sharing the new baby with him.

It was also your mother who over-protected you, keeping you away from your peers because "the other boys are too rough for my little Johnny". This caused you to be frightened of the other boys (in addition to the fear you already had from your fantasy of "violence"), and to prevent you from learning how to stand up for yourself in rough-and-tumble or in other ways. It also prevented you from learning to express your anger safely with the other boys in rough-and-tumble or in simply kicking a ball around.

MOPPING UP

You may be wondering when I am going to tell you how to cure many of the problems that we ran into in Chapter 1, such as being late for appointments, bitching, causing accidents, being forgetful, suffering impotence, having bad relationships with friends and so on. These are all symptoms of anger – the anger that is repressed. As soon as you express your anger it will vanish and so will all these symptoms with it. Unbelievable it may be, but true. This is why I felt so clean, purged, pure, elated, and filled with inner peace after my body-boxing and macho-combat sessions with Ken (page 106). This is why repressing anger is so bad for you and why it is so important for your happiness that you learn to express the anger that has been bottled up inside of you for so long.

Well, of course, symptoms such as stomach ulcers and heart disease will not disappear overnight but I think they will stop getting worse and healing will begin though it may be slow.

This is why, now that you have lost your fear of other men, we need to help you on the path to expressing your anger so that you can finally escape the gay straitjacket and reap the full benefit of using anger as a positive force – the powerful force for good that it can be. This we will do in **Stage Two**.

Stage Two

Stage Two -
ANGER AND SELF-ASSERTIVENESS

We have seen that expressing anger does not necessarily mean shouting, screaming or demolishing the place. We have seen that there are different levels of anger and that anger can be expressed at any of the levels (page 9), not only in the most destructive way.

Aggression stems from anger, but a weaker form, asserting oneself, also stems from and is a way of expressing anger.

As you now are no longer frightened of coming into conflict with other men we can now begin to train you in behaviour that will be new to you and for which you will need to learn new skills. We need to train you in asserting yourself, expressing your anger and being able to use aggression in a way that will be beneficial to you.

MAKING A START

Many gay men who have been bottling up their anger all their lives are likely to have a seething cauldron inside them that will make them frightened to let any out in case, once the flood-gates are opened, they are overcome by the torrent that pours out. When anger is uncontrolled it can, of course, be very destructive so we need to avoid this.

If you feel that you are sitting on top of a volcano, the safest way for you to start letting out anger is to write it down. You can keep a diary, a journal, or turn all the events that make you angry into short stories, or whatever. You can write a letter to the person(s) who made you angry as long as you *never* post it – instead you should burn it. Describe in detail what caused you to feel or become angry and how you felt and what you wanted to do about it. One does not have to turn anger into only speech or action to express it. This is another valid way of expressing it. If you are an artist, turn it into a drawing, a painting or a sculpture, or a series of works of art. If you have a tape recorder you can narrate what happened and how it made you feel into the recorder and then play it back to yourself. On the other hand, people who let their anger out as soon as it occurs are likely to have only a small amount of anger inside them at any one time. They will therefore easily be able to control the amount of anger they want to let out.

Dr Kai Kermani, in his Autogenic Training (see Glossary) relaxation courses, teaches his pupils to express their anger in several different ways, as described in his book *Autogenic Training*. In one of these methods he asks his pupils to make a list of all the people, past and present, that they are angry with. They then have to imagine that each person is present so that they can then talk out loud to each person on the list, one by one, voicing all their anger with that person until they feel completely drained. Of course, to do this one has to find a lonely spot on a beach, on a hill or in a field, or even under the bed-clothes; or failing those, one has to turn the television or hifi up loud at home.

Other therapists suggest using a large cushion that you can imagine is the person with whom you are angry. In the privacy of your room, you can assault the cushion, punch it, kick it and do all the things to it that you would like to do to the person you are angry with.

If you are lucky enough to train at a gym that has a punch-bag you may have already put on the gloves and had a few sessions expressing your anger on it by trying to knock the stuffing out of it. If not, you might like to phone round your local gyms and enquire whether they have a punch-bag amongst the facilities they offer, so that you can go and use it. You need not feel self-conscious about it. If it is not a boxing gym the only reason they have a punch-bag is for their members to give vent to their anger on . . . so enjoy!

Failing that, try to encourage your local gym to invest in a punch-bag. Every gay gym should without doubt invest in one.

Twenty years ago punch-bags were made to hang from the ceiling but nowadays there are many models that stand on the floor. Once in position, the base needs to be filled with water or sand to stabilise it.

One particular type, called "BOB" (Body Opponent Bag) is modelled in plastic to look like a rather nasty tough guy and you can have lots of fun and pleasure punching him fearlessly right in the face and practising different types of punches on him. See Appendix B.

You will need a pair of special gloves (more like pads) when using a punch-bag to prevent grazing the skin of the fingers.

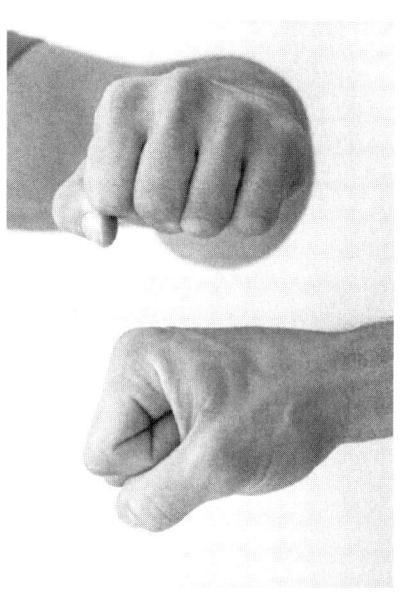

MAKING A FIST: two views showing the position of the thumb and the striking surface.

Escaping the Gay Straitjacket **139**

Remember that when you make a fist to punch the bag your thumb should remain on the outside. If you wrap your fingers around your thumb you will probably fracture your thumb when landing a punch. After the first session on the punch-bag you may find that your wrist feels a little tender. This is because it is unaccustomed to this treatment. Do not worry – after a few sessions the body will adapt till you no longer feel any tenderness when punching the bag. That is what training is for – to toughen up the body or to make it accustomed to performing certain tasks!

If you are a person who is unable to express your anger because you feel you are sitting on top of a volcano, it may be worth investing in your own punch-bag if you have a garage or spare room you can use it in. Then you can safely go berserk on it as there will be little else that can come to harm if you do lose complete control of your rage.

In Japan I am told that every town has an "anger" room where people can go to vent their anger safely.

If you do have facilities such as a spare room or garage with a punch-bag you might like to hire it out for a small fee to other gay men who want to be able to vent their seething anger safely. To facilitate this Power Books have a page on their website where you can advertise for free your anger room:

http://www.pb.clara.net/ETGS/angrooms.htm

Some psychotherapists (Kassinove 1995) believe that taking part in boxing does not get rid of anger at all but simply teaches one to express more and more anger. It would certainly be bad for people who are already expressing too much anger all the time. In your case, where people have *repressed* all their anger all their lives, increasing your anger is what we *want* to achieve so that you can actually become aware of it, so do not let people dissuade you from doing this.

ASSERTING YOURSELF

When you are served cold soup in a restaurant, do you say nothing but decide never to go there again? When the neighbours play their music too loudly all night, do you do nothing but have a sleepless night? Do you "not want to make a fuss"?

This is a script, in Eric Berne's sense, that has probably been handed down to you by your mother. It is a script that will make your life less and less enjoyable as you retreat from places and people that cause you distress. It is a script designed to make you helpless and put you in a straitjacket at the mercy of other people leaving you feeling oppressed by society.

Now that you are not afraid of expressing your anger you need to learn new skills that will help you to assert yourself and make others treat you with the respect you deserve. You have to promise me that you will never again say you "don't want to make a fuss".

It is not a question of making a "fuss", it is a question of what you are entitled to as a human being. For instance, you pay good money for a meal in a restaurant, you are therefore entitled to a good meal in return and you should not let yourself be short-changed. You deserve to be treated honestly.

In her book *Asserting Your Self* Cathy Birch suggests you draw up a list of your rights to help you establish in your mind what you are entitled to. She provides a sample bill of rights as a starting point to which you might want to add your own particular rights.

What you may have been frightened of in the past is starting an argument that would develop into a shouting match. There is a very simple way of preventing that.

One needs to view and state the situation objectively, sidestepping your rage. That is, present the facts as a barrister might argue the case for his client in court. "My client feels very aggrieved that the soup he was served was cold. He felt he could not enjoy it in that condition and therefore asked the waiter to have it re-heated." Well, not with the fancy formal language, but I think you will see my point. By distancing yourself from your own emotions you avoid falling into the trap of voicing acrimonious feelings such as, "At the prices you charge you should be bloody ashamed of yourselves for serving up rubbish as unpalatable as this! How do you think I can drink cold soup?!" and flying into a rage.

The best way to obtain satisfaction is, if at all possible, to *smile* – as it is harder to refuse a request from someone who is gracious than from someone who is frothing at the mouth. Do not worry if your smile appears phoney. With practice you will get better at it.

There are three things you should say. First of all, sympathise with the other person's point of view. "I can see you are very busy." "I know you do not give refunds on goods bought at sales." "I can see you are having a wonderful party."

Then state how you feel about the problem. This is your strong point because no one can argue with you about the way you feel. "I won't enjoy this soup if it's cold." "I feel very disappointed that the stitching on this

I have a right to be wrong
I have a right to speak
I have a right not to speak
I have a right to be listened to
I have a right to be me
I have the right not to be trivialised
I have the right to shut my door
I have the right to some free time
I have the right to choose what I do in my free time
I have the right to a lunch break
I have the right to proper nourishment
I have the right to be tired
I have the right to be disappointed and depressed
I have the right not to please everyone all of the time
I have the right to say no
I have the right to be consulted
I have the right to be kept in the picture
I have the right to forget
I have the right to change my mind
I have the right not to explain
I have the right not to feel guilty

Cathy Birch's Sample Bill of Rights
from Asserting Your Self *published by How To Books.*
copyright: Cathy Birch. Used with permission

suitcase is not up to your usual high standard." "I am unable to sleep as your music is so loud."

And, finally, say what you would like them to do about it. "Would you please re-heat the soup for me?" "I would like you to refund my money." "I would like you to make the music soft enough so that I can sleep."

Do NOT apologise! This makes it appear that you are in the wrong and sends the wrong signals to the other person. If you apologise they will not feel obliged to right the wrong they have done you.

Do not let them sidetrack you. "You need to ask the other waiter." "We never give refunds on goods bought in sales." "It's not my party." If they do not agree to your request then keep repeating the statements you have already made. Do not let yourself be drawn into discussing any subsidiary point. "I would like this soup to be re-heated. I would like this soup to be re-heated." "The stitching on this suitcase is not up to your usual standard. I would like to have my money refunded." "I would like the music to be turned down so that I can sleep. I would like the music to be turned down so that I can sleep."

Prepare what you are going to say beforehand and make sure it conforms to these three precepts to ensure your success.

Remember that, if any of your rights as expressed in Cathy Birch's Bill of Rights is contravened. that is when you *ought* to feel angry because that is how you can ensure that your rights are upheld. *That* is what your anger is for.

EXPRESSING AND REPRESSING ANGER

Expressing one's anger does not have to be destructive.

When people express their anger from time to time, there will only be a small amount of anger in them at any one of these times. They will find it easy to control and can express exactly how much or how little of it they want to express at any particular time.

It is, rather, the people who try *not* to express their anger, who bottle it up, who end up with so much repressed anger inside them that it becomes uncontrollable so that they vent more anger than is appropriate for the occasion or, when the flood-gates are opened, it bursts out of themselves and then anything can happen.

I can remember two occasions when I was younger when I became very angry indeed and expressed my feelings in very certain terms. Once it was to a shop assistant and the other it was to some students I was in charge of. The first occasion was when I was in my teens and the other was when I was in my twenties. I got butterflies in my stomach at the time (adrenalin pumping into the blood to prepare me for an emergency) and it took me several days to get over the fright of how I felt about the anger and the adrenalin that I was unused to experiencing.

If someone does something you do not like or approve of, you can say firmly, "That's enough of that!" to express your anger.

If someone tries to manipulate you you can even express your anger with a smile (it is called a "sardonic" smile) as you say, "I am afraid I won't do that! You will have to find some other sucker!"

Expressing anger with close friends or your family can often be a problem and end up in circular shouting matches. Words such as "never" and "always" are guaranteed to elicit a contradiction and inflame a situation, so avoid them at all costs!

The way to achieve this is to sidestep your first reaction, which may be to accuse the person of their wrong-doing. "You did this, you always do that!" will not solve the problem. Instead, simply express how the disagreement or the other person's behaviour makes you feel . You may have to think carefully about this to discover how it does really make you feel. "When you don't arrive on time for our appointment/date I feel frightened that our friendship has ended and that I am so unimportant that it was not necessary for you to tell me." "If I am not allowed to go to this party, I am frightened they may not invite me next time." The advantage of expressing how you feel is that other people cannot argue with how you feel. Instead, it gives them an opportunity to apologise or to change their behaviour in future to save you from feeling like that again. On the other hand, if it does not move them to make some reparation to you, it will give you a clearer picture of where you stand with them.

For any relationship to continue there needs to be communication between both parties, and if you can express your real feelings it is bound to improve the relationship and bring both parties closer together. However, this does not give you a licence to be rude and hurtful in the guise of "communicating" or being " honest". We have seen (page 13) that repressed anger can result in people being late for appointments/dates. When I was in my twenties I was sometimes as much as 45 minutes late for appointments (for this reason), but if someone kept me waiting for 10 minutes I wanted to break off the friendship. This may seem very unreasonable of me but there is a psychological reason for my inconsistency that I learnt about only many years later. People do not like to be reminded of aspects of themselves that they do not like or are ashamed of, and can be merciless in their condemnation of it in others. Clearly, I was so ashamed of my own lateness that I tended to overlook it but could not tolerate anyone reminding me of it in their own behaviour.

On the gay scene people meeting through contact ads often decide to meet in a "neutral" place. This is fine – there are good reasons for this, but how often do you hear of the other person not turning up? What actually happens is that the second person to arrive gives the first person the once over and, if he is not as Adonis-like, muscular or good-looking as the second person had hoped, he simply does not introduce himself but leaves the first person waiting – perhaps for another hour in case the other person is late – without anything to show for his wasted time. This saves the second person from having to say, "No, thank you" and it saves them from any anger the first person might want to express.

Gay men who have been manipulated by their mother (or parents) believe that this is the way to behave – that it is O.K. to manipulate other people – but other gay men are very sensitive to manipulation for this reason. Neither should you allow yourself to be manipulated in this way. What happens is that, because you cannot tell the other person how angry he has made you and how his behaviour has made you feel, you end up with depression (page 31).

If you are meeting someone for the first time and he has your phone number or address it is common courtesy for him to supply you with *his* phone number or address. If he makes some excuse such as, "I can't give you my phone number/address because I'm moving" he is not to be trusted. In other words, he wants to be able to manipulate you and does not want to give you the chance to reprimand him. In the event that he is moving he should give you *both* phone numbers or addresses, not decline to give you any way of reaching him. If he does not yet have the new phone number then you should postpone meeting him until such time as he can give it you. Do not allow yourself to be made into a sitting duck for manipulators.

PUT-DOWNS

If someone tries to put you down you can express and use your anger to retort, "You can call me a fart, but if I'm a fart you're a big shit!" and put them in their place.

If you are honest with yourself you will recognise that this retort is one you are more likely to hear from a straight guy, who has no qualms about expressing his anger, than from a gay guy. In fact, if a gay guy is called a "poof" or a "pansy" he is more likely to feel hurt than to be able to rebuff the put-down with a retaliatory put-down that expresses his anger and puts the other person in their place. (This is a sure sign that he is repressing his anger instead of being aware of it and using it to retaliate.) What straight men mean who use terms like "poof" or "pansy" about a gay man (or often even about another *straight* man), is someone who is unable to express their aggression (to stand up for themselves).

Never, on any account, reveal to anyone that you feel hurt by what they say to you, as this will only make them carry on taunting you in that way. Instead, you need to have lots of retorts ready to use to show them that their put-down does not worry you. If they call you "poof", "pansy", "fag" or "faggot" call them "scum", "turd", "wanker", "motherfucker", "fart" or "odious fart" in return. Other retorts that can come in handy are "You're a total jerk!" "Who's a bear with a sore head then?" "I won't start criticising you as I don't have all day." "What did your wife do to upset you?" "Oh dear, isn't your wife giving you any?" Memorise those and use them when necessary until you can invent more appropriate ones or copy ones that you hear others using.

We have seen that people can be merciless in their condemnation of others who remind them of aspects of themselves that they despise or are ashamed of (page 145). If someone calls you a "poof" or "fag" it may therefore tell you more about *them* than it tells you about yourself. This is something you need to bear in mind when people become very critical (meaning more than is necessary) of aspects of other people. Men who are certain of their own heterosexuality do not usually need to belittle others. There are two ways you can make yourself better than others. One way is to become better than others but, if you cannot do that, the second way is to drag other people down until you end up being better.

If someone puts you down, that leaves the score 1–0 in their favour and you are left humiliated. Gay men often feel unable to respond because the statement is true: because they have been "sussed"/found out. If, on the other hand as in the fart/shit example above, you have a retort, that leaves the score 2–1 in *your* favour: instead of feeling humiliated you will actually feel you have triumphed. You will feel good about yourself.

Therefore, if a put-down, or an exchange of put-downs, leaves you feeling humiliated it is *your own fault*. It is up to you to come away feeling you have triumphed. This is why it is important to *be able to use your anger* to your own advantage.

If someone puts you down when you have no reply, think about what you *should* have said and then have it ready for next time. There *will* be a next time. Once someone finds they can come off better by putting you down they will do it again, but next time it will be in front of other people. That will be your chance to humiliate them in return *and* in front of their friends.

MALE ANIMAL-PACK PSYCHOLOGY

We have already looked at this (page 69) and found that straight men are constantly putting each other down. This is the way they test each other's aggressiveness to find the position each one has in the male pack and ultimately who the leader of the pack will be. This is something women and gays do not understand.

The male and female elements of our society are constructed differently. Masculine society is a competitive pyramid, whereas female society tends to be a co-operative network. In her book *In a Different Voice* Carol Gilligan agrees but calls female society "a web of connectedness". Little boys are taught to be strong, not to cry, to stand up for themselves, they are given military toys, building/erector sets, they are taught to play competitive games (football/soccer) where winning is everything. Girls, on the other hand, are taught to be caring and gentle, to look after their dolls, to do housekeeping and cooking. It is not surprising that, when they grow up, they can work together in complementary ways but have difficulty working together as a team. As women and gays become part of what used to be a male-dominated group (the male-animal pack) in business generally and in the services (military, police, ambulance, etc.) they find they are being put down. As they do not understand the psychology of the pack, they feel humiliated and resent it. They then want to change the way the male-animal pack operates to suit themselves. Straight men need to learn that they can no longer function as a male-animal pack.

Or what women and gay men need, instead, is to understand the psychology of the male-animal pack and then use it to their own advantage. In that way they will become part of the pack and not intrude into it.

HOW TO SAY "NO"

I was in my late teens when my father died. My mother decided to sell up our house in Kuils River and to go and live with a friend while I went to live in the centre of Cape Town as I had a full-time job and was following a course in speech and drama in the evenings.

A friend of the family, Mrs Malmesbury, phoned me up to invite me to have dinner with her family. Her son Boetie was a close friend of mine. I declined as, I explained to her, I had a rehearsal for a play that evening.

"What time is the rehearsal?" she wanted to know. I told her it was at 8 p.m.

"Oh", she begged me, "Your mammy is going to be here and she hasn't seen you for some time. She is missing you and wants to know how you are getting on. Dinner will be at 6 so there will be plenty of time for Boetie to drive you to the station so you can catch a train to go to your rehearsal."

So I agreed to go. I felt I had no choice. However, dinner was served at 7 p.m. and I had just finished my dessert half an hour later when I announced that I would have to leave to go to my rehearsal. My mother was outraged.

"You can't get up from table as soon as you've had your meal. You can't be so rude to Mrs Malmesbury. I won't let you!"

I explained that I had initially declined the invitation but Mrs Malmesbury had insisted that, as dinner would be at 6, I would have plenty of time to go to my rehearsal afterwards. Mrs Malmesbury murmured that dinner had been delayed; but that, of course, did not solve the problem.

"Do you have to go to your rehearsal?" she wheedled, "You can phone them and say you can't come."

In theatre that is something you just do not do. If six or seven other people are taking the trouble to attend a rehearsal then you attend too if you are needed. If one person is absent that makes it no rehearsal as one will have to rehearse it all again when everyone is present, and if all the other actors behaved in the same way, one would never get everybody together at one time to be able to rehearse properly. I arrived at the rehearsal half an hour late and out of breath as I had to run the last stretch from the station.

You can invite anyone you like to a function, be it the President of the United States, the Queen of England or the Dalai Lama but, if they refuse, you should accept the refusal graciously and not try to coerce them into changing their mind to suit yourself. That would be manipulation and you should not be surprised if people resist it and even resent it.

Similarly, if you are invited to a function your host should accept your refusal graciously if you say you are unable to attend. If people want to know what the previous engagement is, or what time it is, or whether you can go another time instead, they are trying to manipulate you and you need to use your anger to stand firm.

It is nobody's business, not even your mother's, if you have a prior engagement, to know who it is with. You are entitled to your own private life and to keeping it private. (Add that to Cathy Birch's Bill of Rights.)

In the example above I should have told Mrs Malmesbury that I could not go as I had to prepare for my evening's rehearsal. I am quite sure I should have been learning my lines as this was a constant problem for me.

I have a friend who refuses an invitation by saying,"I'd *love* to come . . . but I *can't*." And one knows by the finality of his tone that there is no point in even thinking about him changing his prior engagement.

In the section **Asserting Yourself** (page 141) I gave you three things that you need to say. The same applies here. Sympathise with their viewpoint, say how you feel, and say what you want them to do. So, you need to say, "It's so kind of you to invite me. I'd love to come. Unfortunately I have a previous engagement" ("so you will have to excuse me" is understood and can be left unsaid).

If people do try to press you into revealing the details of your prior engagement you need to stand firm by simply repeating, "I have a prior engagement. I have a prior engagement", and not weakening into being sidetracked into revealing any details which will then give them the chance they want of manipulating you. Once you do that, you are telling them they can manipulate you, and then they will whether you like it or not. By repeating, "I have a prior engagement" when they ask you who it is with, they will eventually get the message that it is none of their business and you do not intend to divulge the information. It would be rude to state those facts bluntly.

Another time when you need to assert yourself is at a heterosexual dance when you are invited by a woman to dance with her when you do not want to. I am talking about ballroom (or old-time) dancing which still goes on in some places. The first thing you need to remember is that in our society the women traditionally wait for the men to invite them to dance, so any woman who invites a man to dance does so because she just cannot resist being manipulative. All the more reason for you to stand firm. You need to say the three things repeated above. "It is so kind of you to invite

Escaping the Gay Straitjacket

me to dance. I am not going on the dance floor. Why don't you sit down and chat with me?" as you find and offer her a seat. If she physically tries to coax you onto the dance floor repeat the last sentence again and again until she gives up. She ought to be aware of why you have not asked a woman to dance but is selfishly not considering your feelings, only her own. For myself, I enjoy dancing with men but do not enjoy dancing with women and manipulative women are especially difficult to dance with as they try to lead all the time instead of allowing the man to do the leading.

As we have seen, many gay men have been manipulated by their mothers and have learnt the "script" (page 68) from her. They then try to manipulate others in this way because they believe that this is the right way to behave. They need, of course, to realise that this is *not* the right way to behave as it will drive friends away. Other gay men, because they are so used to being manipulated in this way by their mothers feel "pressured" when other people make similar requests even though they may not, in fact, be pressured by the other people (pages 77 and 78). They need to separate in their minds the pressure their mothers put on them from similar requests by *other* people who do not mean to pressure them, and react differently to the two types of requests.

MAKING CONVERSATION

When I was running my Gay Wrestling Group in London in 1976–1980 we decided to have a party, and found that many members of the group did not want to come as they said they were "not good at parties". On questioning them we discovered that they meant they did not like having to make "small talk".

When one is angry with people one does not of course want to be bothered with pretending to be interested in them; while if one has low self-esteem one does not think that anyone would be interested in hearing about oneself; and these two factors combine to make one loath to make "small talk".

When I was twenty-one I was working for the University of Cape Town (on the administrative side) and at a party I was asked by the Head of the Speech and Drama Department what I thought of Shakespeare. I was actually quite surprised, even taken aback, that anyone would want to know what *I* thought of such an illustrious figure.

This is how the gay straitjacket limits what you are able to do. Making conversation is how one makes new friends and if you feel disinclined to make conversation you are limiting the number of friends you can make. Clearly, the more friends you can make the more chance you have of finding lasting friends or of finding Mr Right.

In their book *Don't Say "Yes" When You Want to Say "No"* Dr Herbert Fensterheim and his wife Jean Baer say that if you are at a party standing on your own you have two options: either you can go up to someone else who is standing on their own and make conversation with him or you can join a group.

Let us take the first possibility. This is what they suggest. You walk up to the guy and compliment him on something about his clothing that you like.

"That's a nice tie you're wearing." "I like your T-shirt."

Very likely he will tell you where he bought it or who gave it to him as a gift. You can then respond by telling him where you shop for clothes or you can mention gifts that you have received from friends, and before you know you are having a conversation.

Do not lie to him about his clothing. If there is nothing about what he is wearing that you like then say, "That is an unusual material your shirt is made out of." At first you may feel self-conscious about making an opening for conversation in this way but you will soon find that people welcome the opportunity you give them of talking about themselves.

If you decide to join a group in conversation, then stroll up to the group and listen to what they are talking about and wait for a moment when you can contribute an experience you had that is on the subject they are talking about.

If they ignore you it may be that your voice was too soft and got lost in the general hubbub. So try again when the opportunity presents itself and speak a little louder.

It may be useful to take a friend aside, not at the party but later, and ask him or her if they think you speak too softly as that will present problems for you on all kinds of occasions. It may well be that your voice is too low if you have low self-esteem and feel that others are not interested in what you have to say. Take the advice of your friend and adjust the level of your voice accordingly.

We all enjoy talking about ourselves as this makes us feel important when others express an interest in what we have to say or what we have done. The art of conversation is to give everyone, in turn, the opportunity or encouragement to talk about themselves.

If people are not talkative then you can ask them a question that gives them the chance to say how they feel about the topic the group is discussing. If, for instance, the group is talking about visiting Ottawa then you can ask, "Have you been to Ottawa?" If they say no, then ask, "Where do you usually go for your holidays?"

No one expects you to make earth-shattering statements in a conversation. In fact, if someone says, "Isn't that a beautiful sunset?" Then all they expect you to say by way of reply is, "Yes, that *is* a beautiful sunset!" When joining a group try not to begin by asking a question as that tends to sound like an interruption.

This technique, I have to admit, will not work in gay bars, where people may not want to talk to you unless they actually want to go to bed with you. They may be eyeing someone else they want to go to bed with and may be waiting for the opportunity or psychological moment to present themselves. So any attempt you make to strike up conversation may be rudely ignored. This is another reason why many people cannot abide the gay scene and avoid it.

In fact, someone once said that, when they stopped going to bars, they met a better type of person. They were not talking about gay bars but I am sure there is a lot of truth in their statement.

To make friends with someone you need to have a strong common interest and we will look at this in Chapter 5. For this reason Fensterheim and Baer suggest you go where the action is.

If you like swimmers then join a swimming club and learn to swim if you need to. If you like wrestlers then you will not meet any by watching the sport on television. Now that you are no longer frightened of expressing your anger and are not frightened of other men, go to a wrestling club and learn how to wrestle. You may remember the man in his forties who wanted to meet footballers (page 55).

Once you have learned these skills you can make as many or as few friends as you want at any time. It is up to you.

REVEALING YOURSELF IN A HANDSHAKE

When you shake hands with someone the other person can tell a lot about what kind of person you are from the way you grip his hand.

Most men take a firm or even strong grip of the other person's hand. A limp handshake gives the impression that you are weak, ineffectual, frightened of other men and not able to stand up for yourself.

You may remember that Weinrich found that straight men had 6.25 kg/13¾ lb more muscle on average than gay men of the same age and height (page 60). This means that gay men are proportionally weaker than straight men. This may be part of the reason that many gay men give limp handshakes. It is certainly the reason that some gay men resent having their hand shaken by someone with a strong grip. It hurts! Oh dear, that reminds you that you do not match up to other men, that you are weaker and therefore inferior. What we need to do is to make you physically stronger so that your grip can match that of any other man or, even better, hurt *his* hand when you shake hands so that he knows that you are someone to be reckoned with – not a wimp! You need to feel equal to all other men – as long as you are fearful that someone else's handshake will hurt you, you will remain feeling inferior.

If you reveal in your handshake that you are weak, other men will know they can push you around. Some may be too polite to do such a thing, but you are inviting trouble and it can come in many disguises. Knowing that you cannot stand up for yourself people can be extremely charming as they manipulate you, which makes it difficult to recognise. If you have a strong handshake they may think twice about it before even trying.

The gay friend who sold me his Triumph Trident (the one that Ken wanted to steal) found that the clutch lever on the handlebar was very difficult to pull; it was impossible for him to drive the bike around town where he continually had to change gear. On the other hand, as I had trained with weights for many years, I used to drive around town on the bike operating the clutch lever with one finger without thinking about it.

So the gay man who has not played sports or trained with weights will have to grip the other man's hand with much more effort than a straight man would in order for his grip not to feel limp in the hand of a straight man.

I would suggest that you practise shaking hands with your friends and ask what impression they get. What you need them to tell you is that your handshake feels firm as though you are decisive, strong and not frightened of the person you are greeting.

FINDING MR RIGHT

We have already looked at what kinds of men make attractive partners (page 35–36). We have also looked at the attraction of opposites and how gay men try to use this to their advantage (page 109). We have also seen why it fails. What we need to do now is to put all these points together and see what you need to do in order to find Mr Right.

The first and most important point is that gay men, because they repress their anger, will be attracted to men who are able to *express* their anger. That is why this whole book is aimed at encouraging you to learn how to express your anger. That is the type of man most gay men are looking for: ones who are able to express their anger (and also aggression, of course) because most gay men have repressed their own anger.

Playing the role of the longed-for daughter may make your parents happy but it is not going to please Mr Right. It is most important for you to realise that and to realise that you need to learn how to express your anger if you want to catch Mr Right.

For years gay men have been wearing the symbols of people who are able to express their anger in the hope of attracting Mr Right: leather, the leather motorcycle jacket, the hard hat, the gym vest. Gay men have even rushed to the gym to acquire a muscular body, but these symbols are not sufficient to create an attraction of opposites. Wearing the Olympic symbol (five interlinked circles) does not make you a sportsman. As soon as Mr Right finds out that really you are a longed-for daughter wearing fancy dress his ardour will cool and you will soon become "just good friends" (page 35). He may even deride your attempt as being an impostor, if he is not himself attempting to do the same. You need to show him that you *are* the opposite.

Mr Right, if he has read this book, may also be trying to express his anger. Will that nullify the attraction of opposites? No. Strangely enough it will not.

This is the reason. There is a difference between the way one feels inside and the way one appears to other people. I have often found that the guy in the gym who has the biggest arm muscles is often the guy who *believes* that his arms are still the smallest. He will be constantly doing arm exercises saying to himself, "I've got to get my arms *bigger*. My arms are so *small*. I've got to get my arms *bigger*." The reason that he believes this, is that the biceps is not a perfectly round muscle. It tends to have more height than girth. This means that if you look down at your own biceps they appear narrow (and therefore small), whereas if you look at their reflection in the mirror you can see their height and true size.

The same thing applies to one's body, which appears wider (at the shoulders) if seen from behind that it does when seen from the front. This is due to the way the back muscles (*latissimus dorsi*) spread out to the arms right from the bottom of the spine covering the ribs at the back whereas the chest muscles (*pectoralis major*) spread to the arms from the breast bone and do not cover and hide all the ribs as the *latissimus dorsi* do.

After spending years doing exercises in the gym that would widen my shoulders this was dramatically brought home to me when Andy happened to be walking in front of me one day. I saw how wide his shoulders were and I was absolutely amazed, not to say jealous. Why were *my* shoulders not as wide? But then I realised he was wearing my old motorcycle jacket and that that jacket had become too small for me which is why I had had to buy the new one that *I* was wearing. That meant my shoulders must be even *wider* than his! I had never seen myself from behind and so had never realised my own achievements before.

As I stood before my weight-training class I would always be the guy that wore a white ballgown for his twenty-first birthday party, but my pupils did not see me like that. They saw me as "Muscles" whose abdominal muscles were so strong that they would hurt their hand when I allowed them to punch me as hard as they could in the stomach without making me flinch.

It does not matter that both you and Mr Right may have once been the longed-for daughter. If you are now both able to express your anger sufficiently to delight (and even surprise) the other, the attraction of opposites will work its magic. You may both feel inside that you are longed-for daughters but, as no one can know what you are thinking unless you tell them, you will both judge each other by how you *appear* to each other, but now we are talking about behaviour, not merely physical appearance.

It does not matter that deep down inside you may actually be having difficulty in learning how to let so much anger out. As long as Mr Right does not find out that you are having difficulty in letting your anger out he will see only the anger that you *do* let out and that will delight him.

The mutual punching sessions that Andy and I engaged in have forged a powerful bond between us. Not only was each of us delighted by the show of anger that the other displayed (I love seeing the guy who is punching me distort his face with the effort – especially if the punch fails to hurt as it tells me I can beat him) but the final release of all the pent-up anger in ourselves gave us an inner peace for which we each depended on the other and for which we were grateful each to the other.

Deep down inside you may still feel like the longed-for daughter, but Mr Right will not be able to see that side of you unless you show it to him. If you are in your right mind you will show him only your ability to express your anger and not how much of a longed-for daughter you still feel inside.

In fact, we have seen that a relationship needs to be built on a common interest. Your common interest may well be pushing the anger boundaries away as you both learn to express more and more anger. More of that in the pages to come.

We have also seen that when I was wrestling twice a week my anger was sufficiently near the surface for me to be able to reach an orgasm without first fighting or wrestling in some way in order to provoke my anger. But, when I had to give up wrestling twice a week for health reasons, my anger soon became so buried once again that I was forced to box in order to bring my anger and my sexual feelings to the surface so that I could reach an orgasm.

You now no longer feel afraid of other men, or at least not as much as you used to. The fact that other (straight) men will still on average be 6.25 kg/13¾ lb heavier than you is still likely to leave you feeling inferior to them, as will the fact that they have many skills (standing up for themselves, playing body-contact sports) that you do not yet have.

You may like to put this book down for a few months at this point. You have come a long way since you started reading it and made many discoveries about yourself, and perhaps also about how you would like to become. I think you need to pause a while in order to perfect your self-assertion skills before continuing. The next stage is going to be building up your body so that you no longer feel inferior compared to other men on that score. You will find you need to be able to use your self-assertive skills when you go to a gym to train so you need to develop them enough to feel confident in using them to assert yourself. As soon as you feel you have achieved that then, by all means, pick up this book again and continue. (Of course, if you have already been training in a gym for some time, then read on!)

Spreading Your Wings and Flexing Your Muscles

Stage Three - BUILDING MUSCLE

WE discovered (page 60) that gay men are on average 6.25 kg/13¾ lb lighter than their straight counterpart of the same age and height. As gay men tend to play games less than their straight peers this is not surprising. A muscle has to grow bigger in order to become stronger so a lighter muscle is also a weaker muscle. Not only do you need to know the skills of asserting yourself but you need to present a body that shows people that you know how to handle yourself if push comes to shove.

I was in a gay disco one evening when a young lout kept crossing the dance floor pushing his way through by bumping into us who were dancing. After he had done it twice I was ready for him. The next time he barged into us I gave him a hefty push from behind that sent him flying across the floor nearly landing on his face. He turned round, furious, and swaggered back to deal with the person who had dared to push him so unceremoniously. When he reached me and saw that I was 5 ft 7 in and clearly weighed 79 kg/175 lb of muscle, he thought better of it, turned on his heel, and did not trouble us again.

On the other hand, if you look like a wimp, people will tend to treat you like a wimp.

Now that you are no longer frightened of other men it may, therefore, become of some concern to you that you have been deprived of developing your body as well as your straight counterparts have developed theirs. Cycling and running will develop your legs, swimming will develop your shoulders but the quickest way to develop your whole body is to train with weights.

Why should you develop your body? Well, a stronger body makes ordinary tasks seem easier. Physical pastimes such as dancing, mountain-climbing, cycling or aquaplaning become easier to do. You are able to play more games so you can enjoy yourself more and a muscular body is something to be proud of and will help to give you self-confidence (as the example in the disco above showed) that we have seen many gay men lack. A muscular body will add beauty to your face. A stronger, more muscular body will attract admirers. It will also attract Mr Right. That many gay men have already realised this, is borne out by the hordes of them that already work out with weights.

The first thing that may worry you is that a gym will be full of men like Arnold Schwarzenegger and you will feel too embarrassed to reveal your body there in training clothes.

I am a weight-training instructor and have worked in gyms either full- or part-time for nearly twenty years and I know that gyms are full of people who are thin or fat trying to normalise their bodies. In any one gym there are usually no more than one or two men with competition-level bodies, with the exception of those gyms that specialise in facilities for competition bodybuilders and there are only a few of those in the whole world and you would have to go to cities such as London, New York or Los Angeles to find them.

If you feel embarrassed about appearing in shorts in a gym then wear a tracksuit: a common sight in gyms especially during colder weather when it is necessary to ensure that you do not cool off between exercises.

Straight men have fathers who guide their sons in the things they want to do, but you are going to have to be your own father to help you take steps in the right direction. Phone up your local Gay Switchboard or gay phone helpline to find out where gay-friendly gyms in your city are located, or consult the Gay Guide pages in the local gay paper. Otherwise, consult the yellow pages of your phone book and then visit a few gyms so that you can see if you like the facilities available.

With most things you get what you pay for, and gyms are no exception. At the top end of the scale you will have all the latest electronic machines and chrome equipment with plenty of mirrors and carpeted floors. There will be an instructor on duty at all times for help and advice to guide you in planning a suitable exercise schedule and to ensure that you are performing the exercises correctly. There will be lockers in the changing area for each member, showers, television, a bar and wall-to-wall music. There may also be facilities for massage, a sauna and sun-beds. At the bottom end of the scale there may be only very basic barbells and dumb-bells, and primitive showers.

Go on a visit just to see what each one is like. Ask if there is an instructor who can provide a schedule of exercises for you and show you how to use the equipment. You also want to see what the other members are like to see if you think you will enjoy working out with them. A few muscular bodies around can be an encouragement to work harder, but members who hog machines or equipment can cause frustration and annoyance.

When I started using weights we used barbells (152 cm/5 ft or 183 cm/6 ft long) with loose weight discs that could be added to increase the poundage. There were also dumb-bells made up in a range of weights starting at 7 kg/15 lb. Nowadays these are called free weights and most gyms have machines for exercising each major muscle group.

They both have advantages and disadvantages. Free weights exercise only part of the muscle (owing to leverage and the pull of gravity) but you can perform a wider range of exercises with them to prevent staleness setting in and to develop certain parts of the muscles. Machines that have a cam or pulley at the fulcrum of the movement (such as Nautilus machines) exercise the whole muscle. They are safer to use as there is little risk of overbalancing and dropping weight discs on yourself or other members. The disadvantage is that as the machines are extremely expensive gyms often only have one machine for each major muscle group, resulting in queuing/standing in line to use the machines, especially at busy times, less variety and staleness setting in after eight weeks.

To engage in a programme of weight-training you need to ensure that you are in good health. If in doubt or if you are over the age of 40 consult your doctor first.

You should do an exercise for each major muscle group: the chest, the shoulders, the back, the arms (biceps), thighs, calves and abdominals. The triceps at the back of the upper arm are used in many exercises but one can also do an exercise for them individually.

At the first workout do 10 repetitions of each exercise with a weight that is light enough for you to be able to think about what you are doing rather than struggling to control a weight that is too heavy. Any number of repetitions performed without a break is called a "set". At the second workout you can change to doing 3 sets of 8 repetitions of each exercise (except the calves and abdominals) with a heavier weight to develop strength and muscle size, or 3 sets of 15 repetitions to give better definition. Calves and abdominals should always be at least 20 repetitions per set and you should do 3 sets of these too. The weight needs to be heavy enough so that you can only *just* complete the third set. The more repetitions one does in a set the lighter the weight has to be and the better quality muscle one builds as one burns off more fat. Increase the poundage

Spreading Your Wings and Flexing Your Muscles

when the exercise becomes easy to do.

If you are over the age of 40, do one set of 10 repetitions on each exercise at your first workout. Thereafter do 3 sets of 15 repetitions on all exercises except abdominals and calves which should be 20 repetitions. The reason for this is that, after the age of 40, the arteries tend to harden, and straining to press a heavy weight will increase your blood pressure; therefore avoid straining. This is not a problem when you are younger as the arteries are able to dilate to allow more blood through to cope with the extra effort. As you exercise count from 1 to 5 and perform 3 reps for each number for 15 repetitions. Do not increase the poundage more than once in three months as the arteries harden with age and it will take the body three months to normalise the blood pressure after you increase your workload. If you risk developing hypertension (high blood pressure) it would be useful for you to have your own sphygmomanometer (the instrument that doctors use to check blood pressure). You can buy this through your local chemist/pharmacy and use it in consultation with your doctor to ensure that your blood pressure normalises.

If you want to lose weight do a set of 10 repetitions on all exercises at your first workout and, thereafter, 3 sets of 20 repetitions increasing to 30 repetitions on all exercises. You will, in any case, be building muscle, but quality muscle, as you burn up the fat.

There comes a time for everyone who uses a gym when you find that someone else is using the machine or weight that you need. Should you do that exercise later instead? Definitely No. Never change the order of your exercises because an exercise you normally do first, when you are fresh, will be much more difficult with the same weight if you do it last when you are tired. Besides, the order will be planned by your instructor for reasons to do with starting and ending with a lighter exercise, the amount of blood in different parts of the body, and not using the same muscles (e.g., *triceps*) in consecutive exercises. It is common practice in gyms to share the equipment with another user. While you rest after a set, he does a set, by which time you should be ready to do your next set, and so on. Say to the person, "Do you mind if I do a set while you are resting?" The answer is usually "Yes, certainly" but if the person flounces off in a huff that is *his* problem. On the other hand if he become possessive of the equipment you will have to wait; but suggest to the gym owners that they purchase more equipment to avoid the problem. Everyone who pays their dues is just as entitled to use the equipment as anyone else. Add this to your Bill of Rights.

When one exercises a muscle, it tends to swell up as it becomes engorged with blood, popularly called "muscle pump" and this pleasing phenomenon becomes the pot of gold at the end of the rainbow for many bodybuilders who get bitten by the bug because the next day the muscle does not appear to be as big as it was during their workout the previous day.

After your workout you will be able to shower before putting your street clothes on again, therefore you need to take a towel, soap, shampoo and face-cloth with you besides the vest or T-shirt, shorts, gym shoes, gym socks and tracksuit you will need for your workout.

There are two golden rules which you should observe in the showers: keep your shower as short as possible and do not gaze at other men in the showers, *especially* not furtively. The exception is, of course, if someone speaks to you. The rules may be different in gay-orientated gyms but do not assume that the showers are for cruising. You may be peremptorily disillusioned, not to say called names.

If you strike up a friendship with a member in a straight gym do not assume that he fancies you unless you get incontrovertible proof such as noticing he has a gay periodical in his gym bag. You may only be engaging in male bonding which is an empathy that develops when men are sharing the same pastime and goals. Male bonding does not come with conjugal rights. Enjoy the friendship for what it is.

After attending the gym 2 or 3 times a week for a year you should achieve more than the small gain you are after if you are under forty. For the over-forties it may take a little longer, but it will be worth the effort. Then it is up to you to decide whether you want to be better than the average straight guy or not. Now that you find you can do it, why not? It may stand you in good stead later. Remember Mr Right?

TRUSTING YOUR FATHER

Now that you are entering the world where sports coaches and instructors reign there is another problem which might beset you.

Most gay men have had a jealous, competitive relationship with their fathers practically from day one because of the attention their mother lavished on them at the expense of their father. This leaves many of them feeling that they cannot trust their fathers.

How this affects them in later life is that they are unable to trust other men in a position of authority as their father was. They are frightened of flying because they cannot trust the pilot in whose hands they are putting their lives. They are frightened of riding pillion on a motorbike because they cannot trust the rider of the bike in whose hands they are putting their lives. And so on. This feeling of mistrust can spread to and include sports coaches and instructors in whose trust they are putting themselves. It is therefore important to lay this ghost as quickly as possible.

When I started out in training with weights in my early twenties I asked a fellow member of the gym I was attending how he had developed such big calves. He told me, but I simply did not believe him but, now that I am in my sixties, I am finally following the advice he gave me and my calves are responding as never before.

If you feel (even subconsciously) that you cannot trust your coach you will only make a half-hearted attempt at what he tells you to do. This may result in you failing at what you were attempting but, worse, you may even injure yourself as a consequence because you did not follow the coach's instructions correctly. (Not having your heart in it is one of the known and avoidable causes of sports injuries [which we will look at later in this chapter].)

The result of that is likely to reinforce your belief that other men are dangerous and not to be trusted and that your mother was right in keeping you away from them when you were a child (page 55).

Sports coaches or instructors may not give you enough attention because they are overworked, or because they imagine you are a lost cause, or because they are lazy, or because they are too tired (after the previous late night's capers) or because they are too busy sucking up to other students of theirs. They may give you wrong information because they are misguided or misinformed or because they do not know enough about human physiology, their sport or human psychology, or simply because, as coaches go, they are not very good at their job. Sports coaches and instructors are not perfect. They are human.

Given all of the above, I do not believe that the reason you cannot trust your father will apply to your coach or instructor. You did not have a jealous, competitive relationship with your sports coach over your mother when you were a child. You need to differentiate in your mind between them and your father. There is no way that your coach or instructor will be untrustworthy for the same reason that makes you feel you cannot trust your father. They are totally different from your father.

You need to regard them in that way. You need to judge the quality of their work by whether they are clever, good, efficient, knowledgeable, and expert at what they do. Some may be ignorant, misguided or misinformed. There are good coaches and there are bad coaches. That will determine how much trust you can put in them and the help they give you. Nothing else.

YOUR DATE WITH YOUR IDOL

Your body is a machine. You can neglect it as most gay men do so that it becomes so rusty it is hardly capable of doing anything or you can train it so that it becomes a high-powered engine like a Ferrari that can enable you to do things physically, jump higher, run faster, or push harder than you have ever done before. When it has been trained to be a high-powered engine you can then let out your anger and use your anger to make your engine run even faster, jump even higher, and push even harder and this is very exciting. It can be a tremendously exhilarating experience.

It is better than any theme-park ride because *you* are in charge. You *are* the ride. Your anger is your fuel. And this wonderful, powerful machine that is taking you on this hair-raising ride is you! It is your body! It is something you can be really proud of! The things it will enable you to achieve will be even more for you to enjoy and to be really proud of!

I have mentioned already that you need to become your own ideal father that you never had. Many (straight) sons have fathers who are handsome, have a muscular physique and are kind, helpful and encouraging to their sons. They want their sons to grow up into strong, brave men who can stand up for themselves and can enjoy the physical achievements that will help them to enjoy life and not spend it trapped in a straitjacket. Their fathers encourage their sons to build up their bodies and acquire the necessary skills.

We have already seen that it is necessary for you to build up your muscles to be level with your straight peers. I trust you are already advanced some way along that course.

It is also necessary for you to build up your stamina as, if you have never played games, you are probably sorely lacking in that department. By "stamina" we are talking about the ability of the heart to pump enough blood to the muscle to keep it working. This means increasing the through-put of your cardio-vascular system: the heart and blood vessels. You need stamina if you are going to be able to push yourself by using your anger that you want to express by doing all these exciting things that you have probably never done before.

Spreading Your Wings and Flexing Your Muscles

Suppose you had a father who looked like your idol, be he a film star, a sportsman or a physique champion, and he said to you, "Let's do a litttle jogging together. Do you want to come?" Would you go? I *bet* you would! You would be there like a shot just to be with your idol. For your imaginary father you need to choose an idol, someone that you will not want to disappoint by failing to turn up for your date to go jogging or training in the gym.

I have a friend Dave who, as a child, was very sickly. Consequently he was bullied at school. His father, as I have seen from family photos, was a very handsome man when he was young, and he said that he was not going to have a sickly child for a son. Against the doctor's orders he found a wrestling club that he took Dave to and both he and his son Dave joined in order to learn to wrestle. The stress of wrestling was just what his son needed in order to overcome his physical weakness and, spurred on by his father being at his side and constantly encouraging him, he became British freestyle-wrestling champion at middleweight and also at light heavyweight.

Dave and I became friends because he came to my gym to train and later invited me to his home to meet his wife and children. Dave always had his father as his best friend but today I have become his best friend. He does not wrestle any more and nor do I but we have our training that we both do and our interest in wrestling in common as the basis of our friendship. And, yes, now that his sons have reached maturity I am proud to have them as friends too.

Once you have trained your body and are strong enough and fit enough to do anything you like, you too will have something in common with any sportsman if you are attracted to particular sportsmen and so will have a basis for a friendship or a closer relationship if they happen to be gay too.

You need to imagine your idol as your father and that he is taking you on the training course I am prescribing and that he is encouraging you all along the way. Remember, if you disappoint him twice in a row he probably will not ask you again, so be sure to keep your training appointments with him.

To develop your general stamina I want you to go jogging once a week. Your idol is going to go with you so don't disappoint him! The first week you need to jog for ten seconds. Yes, that's right! Just ten seconds. As long as it takes you to count from twenty-one to thirty.

Don't fall victim to the veiled competitiveness that many gay men use. Don't try to, or think you need to, be better than everyone else right from the start. Training should mean doing only a small amount more than you have done before as the body takes time to adapt to the demands you will make of it. That is what training is. That is why you need to train. It does not mean having to do an enormous amount from the start.

If you try to do too much it will make you suffer so much that you will not want to train again. Whereas if it is a happy experience, one that you enjoy, you will want to do it for the rest of your life. That is why it is important for you to make that imaginary date with your idol every week!

The second week jog for ten seconds again. The third week I will allow you to make it fifteen seconds just so that you don't get too bored. The fourth week twenty seconds, fifth week thirty seconds, sixth week forty-five seconds and so on, increasing by 50% each week. Make a chart showing what you are doing on each date and paste it on the inside of the door of your wardrobe so that you can keep checking it, or write the details down in your diary. As your engine has been rusty for so long you want to ease it in gently so that it does not blow a gasket.

If possible jog on grass or sea sand. Do not jog on a hard surface such as a city street or pavement/sidewalk as these are too hard for your feet unless you make sure that you have running shoes that are properly designed (with a thick, compressible sole) for hard surfaces and these tend to be very expensive. Without the proper shoes jogging on hard surfaces can result in foot injuries.

It has been shown that to develop the strength of your heart you (together with your idol) need to keep your pulse rate over 120 beats per minute for at least five minutes. Therefore, I would recommend that once you have built up to jogging for ten minutes it would be more beneficial to increase the workload during the ten minutes than to increase any more the length of time you jog.

By this I mean you can sprint for a short distance and then return to jogging, or you should try jogging uphill as well as on the level. Either way limit the jogging to ten minutes.

My next book will be all about weight-training so keep an eye out for that. Watch the Power Books website!

It will take you a few months to settle down to your weight-training and jogging regime so this will be a good place to put this book down again. The next stage will deal with improving your rough-and-tumble skills as well as with how to avoid trouble, so you will need to have increased the strength of your muscles and your stamina before you can safely progress any further.

Stage Four - ROUGH-AND-TUMBLE

Most straight boys, as we have seen (page 55) engage in some rough-and-tumble as they grow up but most gay men, on the other hand, have been deprived of this by over-protective mothers and being kept from other boys who are seen as being too rough for them.

This is a pity for two reasons. The one is that if you have some wrestling skills you are less likely, should you be pushed over, to injure yourself when falling to the ground as you will have learned basic tumbling skills. Secondly, not being afraid of suddenly finding yourself in deep water will give you the confidence to handle a threatening situation calmly and authoritatively without inflaming it.

Without these skills you will remain frightened of other men, which will keep you in your straitjacket and keep you helpless, even though you may have learned how to assert yourself and may, by now, also have a muscular body. Remember, I had been wrestling unsuccessfully for some years before I learned how to let my anger out.

One of the essential techniques of fighting is feinting. If you want to catch your opponent's leg and simply dive down to catch his leg he will see you coming which will give him time to avoid your hand. This is known as "telegraphing" your moves. To succeed in catching his leg, for instance, you need to feint to his head, to pretend you are trying to catch him around the neck and, as he leans back to avoid your grasp, you dive down to his leg while he is still leaning back and off balance, to grasp his leg before he can recover his balance and dodge you. Gay men who have been taught (by their mothers) to be polite, honest and well-behaved will have a lot of difficulty, as I did, in readjusting to the real world of male competition where all is fair in love and war (and sports), as long as you *win*! It will seem very foreign and strange to you at first. This is what you need to learn, the better to understand other (straight) men and to be able to compete with them and (hopefully) beat them!

The card game of poker, for instance, is a game where you need to use bluff and deception to mislead your opponent into believing that you have a poor hand so that he increases his bet and ends up losing more money to you when you reveal you had four aces all the time! You will need to adjust your thinking to be able to beat other men at their own games. This is what you will learn from rough-and-tumble.

Again, I do not want you to become a black belt in judo. I only want you to follow a six-month course in freestyle wrestling, submission wrestling, judo or ju jitsu so that you will have some basic knowledge of rough-and-tumble that other (straight) boys have acquired as children.

It does not mean that you will become involved in a street fight on every street corner. It simply means that, if push comes to shove, you will not put your hand out to stop yourself landing heavily on the ground and end up by fracturing your wrist because you did that. You will learn the correct way to fall. With that knowledge you will be able to pick yourself up as though nothing had happened and talk an inflamed situation down.

Mothers who over-protect their sons or keep them away from their peers as children are sentencing their sons to a life in a straitjacket because they will never learn the skills to stand up to their peers and so will become frightened of other men for the rest of their lives. Men who are not in control of their lives are not seen as attractive when it comes to finding a mate and so their mothers have betrayed them on that score too.

It may seem to you unnecessary to venture out of your straitjacket as you have spent so much of your life safely there already but, believe you me, it will pay you handsome dividends if you *do* come out. If you go to a gay wrestling club you may well find Mr Right there also learning how to handle himself in rough-and-tumble.

I strongly believe that wrestling is the best sport possible for gay men for all kinds of reasons (some of which you can probably guess) but we have looked at the problem of gay men joining a straight wrestling club in their late twenties at a time when most straight men have wrestled for perhaps twenty years and are giving the sport up to get married (page 53). I therefore strongly recommend a gay-orientated wrestling club.

There are more and more gay wrestling clubs springing up, so contact Gay Switchboard, your local gay helpline, or look in the Gay Guide in your local gay paper. There is also a great deal of help in my book *Wrestling for Gay Guys*. Do not think that gay wrestling clubs will, however, understand all your problems and be sympathetic to your first-time nerves.

Gay wrestling clubs, in my experience, are run by wrestlers from the 10% of gay men who have had no hang-ups over playing body-contact sports. They are unlikely to have read this book or my previous one on wrestling for gay men. If they *have* read them they will believe that the problems I describe for gay men are a load of rubbish or "psychobabble" simply because they have not experienced them themselves. Not only will they not understand your problems, they will not want to be bothered by them. Their attitude is likely to be that, if you want to wrestle, why do you not just get on the mats and wrestle?

It seems to me that, regretfully, if you are from the 90% of gay men who have experienced pressure from your parents not to engage in body-contact sports, then you should seriously consider forming your own "gay-sensitive-sympathetic wrestling club" where you can give the members the special support they need with their psychological problems and hang-ups. There is a special chapter in my wrestling book on running and coaching your own gay wrestling club.

On the internet there are several directories of gay wrestlers where you might find individual wrestlers who are close to you. The problem here is that neither of you might have any experience nor the proper facilities like wrestling mats, so that it can be a case of the blind leading the blind and without the necessary equipment like guide dogs or white sticks.

Internet directories of wrestlers are located at

PB Directory of Wrestlers http://www.pb.clara.net/WresFGG/direct.htm
Gladiators' World Alliance http://www.vangar.com/gwa.htm
Choke's Takedown Wrestling Contacts   http://headrush.net/takedown
Wrestlemen Online Directory
                        http://members.aol.com/wrestlemen/directry.htm

Some guys on the internet directories have experience but if you are unable to link up with an experienced wrestler then there are some excellent books for beginners such as:

FORWARD ROLL: kneel on hands and knees. Place the back of your head on the mat then

Escape the Gay Straitjacket

Wrestling for Beginners by Tom Jarman & Reid Hanley
Wrestling Fundamentals and Techniques by Mark Mysnyk
Elementary and Junior High School Wrestling by Stephen L.
                     Hopke and Worden Kidder
Wrestling Teaching Guide by Richard C. Maertz
Wrestling Drill Book by Dennis A. Johnson

These should help you to learn basic techniques if you study them and practise the moves with a friend on a regular basis. Check the details in the Bibliography. To learn basic techniques you have to practise them over and over to master them. By regular I mean at least once a week and preferably twice a week to bring your anger to the surface as well as to master the moves so that they become automatic. It is no good reading the above books and thinking you now know what to do if you need to. That is not good enough. You need to have trained your body in executing these moves (this is called learning co-ordination) so that it will react automatically without your even having to think about. If you have not done this I can promise you that, when you need to use a technique, your mind will go blank and you will be useless. Remember, this is only for six months to get a grounding in rough-and-tumble.

Practice sessions should always begin with warm-up exercises and

push off by straightening your legs. Keep your back rounded so that you can roll.

Spreading Your Wings and Flexing Your Muscles

forward rolls which form the basis of correct landing technique. I cannot teach you a forward roll from this distance or coach you, but if you want to try it out for yourself, do it on a soft surface (not a household carpet) and round your back so that you roll. If you come down with a thump the first time you try it that means you did not round your back so that you could roll, you kept it flat. Think about that and then try it again. This first time you try the forward roll you may end up rather dizzy. As you practise it your body will adapt over time so that the dizziness disappears. Once you have mastered forward rolls reverse the movement to do a backward roll.

However, joining a club would be far preferable in order to learn basic techniques as you have the right equipment like wrestling mats, you might even have an experienced coach to teach you and you have a regular appointment and will not be stood up every other week by a training partner failing to turn up.

Besides wrestling, there are boxercise, non-contact karate, judo or ju-jitsu which are all suitable to help you to learn some basic rough-and-tumble skills.

Boxercise is circuit-training (see Glossary) based on boxing exercises and training. You will be able to practise punching on a punch-bag. There is no sparring or contests so you will be able to get very fit and learn boxing skills without having to enter into a fight and without having to spar with anyone. Many boxing clubs now offer boxercise as a separate training routine and so do many health clubs and weight-training gyms. Look in the yellow pages to help you find those that do.

Non-contact karate offers karate training which includes flexibility, strength, and both punching and kicking techniques. As the name implies, even where contests are arranged within normal training, students practise the striking moves without making contact with their opponents though, to be honest, there is a possibility that, if both contestants step forward and throw a punch at the same time contact will occur even though it is neither allowed nor intended. Look for non-contact karate clubs in the yellow pages of the phone directory.

Judo is a Japanese form of wrestling that includes choking, strangling and immobilisation techniques. A strong jacket is worn by which opponents can take hold of each other to execute throws. This is also an excellent way of learning rough-and-tumble techniques.

Ju-jitsu was originally invented as a system of self-defence but with the introduction of all-out fighting in competitions such as the Ultimate Fighting Championship held in the USA, ju-jitsu techniques are becoming incorporated into these fighting styles. Training in ju-jitsu involves strengthening and tumbling as well as the self-defence techniques. The moves are practised in simulated situations where they should be used but there are no contests. This is because ju-jitsu was invented, as I have said, as a method of self-defence rather than a fighting style. Also a good way of learning rough-and-tumble skills though with the emphasis on self-defence.

We will look at these sports again when I will describe them in more detail.

Would you go to learn any of these skills if your idol asked you to go with him? You bet you would! Make the appointment to go with him and do not let him down!

SAFETY FIRST

Participating in rough-and-tumble or in a sport can be fun, it can be exciting and give you a feeling of achievement that is very rewarding. It can make you feel better physically as well as psychologically, it can purge your anger, it can make you new friends that are valued and lasting, it could help you find Mr Right. But no one wants to be injured in pursuing these objectives.

According to the experts, 80% of sports injuries can be avoided: generally they occur

>through poor skills
>through tiredness causing poor co-ordination
>when your muscles and joints are stiff
>when you do not have your heart in it, or
>when you are using poor equipment.

No matter how slight your interest in a sport may be, you should take it extremely seriously: this will help to prevent you being injured. In tennis, for instance, the number of steps you have to take, the number of times you have to change direction suddenly, the number of times you swing your racket is the same during one game if you are Tim Henman or if you play only once a year.

The British School of Osteopathy recommends that you should get fit to play a sport and not play a sport to get fit. This is why **Stage Three** consisted of muscle-building and jogging.

Wrestling on domestic carpets causes terrible mat burns. If they are made of nylon the effect will be severe and almost immediate. For this reason you are advised NOT to wrestle on carpets.

If, for any reason, the skin is grazed it should be covered immediately with a self-adhesive bandage to avoid the risk of HIV infection. The bandage should be covered with an elastic bandage or clean old sock with the toe cut off to prevent the adhesive bandage underneath from rubbing loose. If you do not have these first-aid items, you should STOP wrestling immediately.

It is good practice, therefore, to carry basic items of first aid in your gym bag at all times. As with an umbrella, if you have it with you, you are more likely not to need it. It is always when you do not have it with you that you get caught out.

ACCIDENTAL KNOCKS

If you have never engaged in rough-and-tumble or have never taken part in other body-contact sports like football/soccer, rugby, hockey, boxing or wrestling, you have never subjected your body to the accidental knocks and bumps that are unavoidable in these types of games.

When you first get a knock or a bump it is really very painful, but the body then builds up special heavy tissue like armour-plating under the skin to protect the places where the bones are prominent, where taking knocks hurts the most, so that there will be less pain in the future.

Any man who has been involved in body-contact sports from early childhood will have taken all the painful knocks when he was a small child. His body will have had time to build up an excellent protective system under the skin around his body so that he will feel hardly any pain any more when he takes a knock or is involved in an accidental collision of bodies. This is why you can see rugby players on television involved in collisions with each other or throwing their bodies down on the ground to touch the ball to the ground beyond the opponent's scoring line, and then get up again as though nothing had happened to them.

Alas, you will still have to go through this phase. But the thing to remember when you get your first knocks is that the next time you get a knock on that part of your body it won't be as painful, and each time you get another knock there it will hurt less and less until you hardly feel anything at all. But it will take time for your body to build up its own armour-plating and, unfortunately, this will not happen until after you have taken a number of very painful knocks.

SOME BASIC PRINCIPLES

The techniques described here are commonly used in boxing and other martial arts. They should be learned under instruction from a qualified instructor. Neither the author nor the publisher can be held responsible for any injury caused by the correct or incorrect use of these techniques.

If you have seen a lot of cowboy films you may have the impression that you have to take every punch that anyone throws at you square on the chin. This may make cowboys look tough but in boxing the object is to get out of the way of any punch your opponent throws at you, if you can, so that he misses his target and you do not get hit or get hurt.

Only once in my life has anyone tried to punch me in the face in anger. Fortunately I dodged the punch so I came to no harm.

Only once in my life has anyone tried to head-butt me in anger. But I knew how to counter that so that my attacker got a sore head and I came off scot-free.

Only once in my life has anyone tried to knee me in the crutch in anger. Again I was able to counter it effectively so that he missed and I did not come to any harm.

I dread to think what the result would have been if I had not been able to dodge my attackers on all those occasions. Not only the pain but the psychological humiliation too. And if they had succeeded in hitting me they might not have stopped with one punch.

If someone is going to punch or knee you they usually pull their fist or knee back so that they can get more acceleration before striking you. This movement "telegraphs" their intention, giving you split-second time to get out of the way as the blow approaches you. If you stand still and let them hit you this will reinforce the fantasy that you used to have that men were dangerous whereas, if you read their body language, their "intention movements" correctly and take action to avoid getting hit you will feel superior to your aggressor and this will boost your self-esteem.

Only cowboys, masochists, 'pansies' and fools stand still when someone

Spreading Your Wings and Flexing Your Muscles

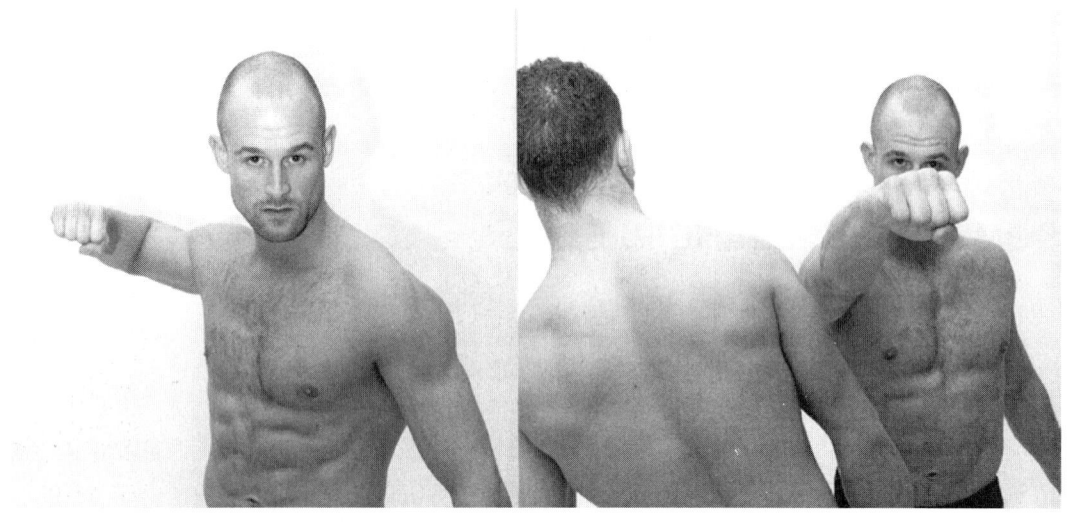

LOOK OUT! a jab is coming your way.   ACTION: step and lean to one side to avoid it.

tries to punch them so that they take the full effect of the punch. Let me tell you what you need to do to avoid being such an idiot as to stand still and get hit! If a car is coming towards you in the street you do not stand still and get hit, *do* you? The illustrations show you the "intention movement" that should be a warning and the action you need to take.

A jab is a punch that hits you in the front of your face: on the nose or in the eye. As the punch comes towards you, you need very quickly to lean sideways and take a step to the same side so that you do not fall over. The punch will then go hurtling past you and probably your attacker as well if he has thrown a lot of force or his own weight into it.

A hook is a punch that comes from the side and hits your cheek, dislodging your molar teeth, or hits the tip of your chin and knocks you out. As a hook comes towards you, you should sway backwards taking a step in the same direction so that you do not over-balance. By doing so the punch will fly past in front of you and you can get away from your attacker straight away.

An uppercut is a punch that comes from below and moves upward striking you under the chin. You will rarely see this used outside a boxing ring so you need not worry about how to avoid it It is only used in amateur boxing when an opponent is protecting the sides of his face from a hook.

If you watch amateur boxing matches on television you will see these manoeuvres demonstrated frequently. Notice I used the adjective "ama-

Escape the Gay Straitjacket

LOOK OUT! a hook is coming your way.   ACTION: take a step and lean backwards to avoid getting hit.

teur". Professional boxing is to a large degree entertainment.

Boxers often go into a clinch with their opponent by putting their arms around their opponent. It is difficult to hit someone when he is that close to you. That technique is all right in the ring, but in a street situation it is inadvisable to let your opponent grip you in this way as you may then have difficulty in escaping from him. If you do not want to get involved in a fight, run like hell. Having dodged a punch, it may be a good idea to run away and live to fight another day, as the saying goes. What is to be gained by getting involved?

You may wonder, as I did, how two people can bang their heads together and the one will get badly hurt and have a sore head for five minutes while the other will feel nothing. The trick to not getting hurt is to bounce your head Believe you me, it works!

The way to counter a head-butt goes like this. Your attacker plans to bounce his head on your head where you are standing (point A in the picture on the next page) so that he will not get hurt. As he comes forward you go forward and bounce your head on his, half-way to where he was standing (at point B in the picture). You bounce

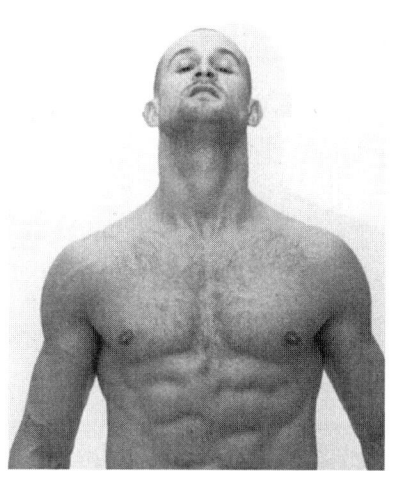

LOOK OUT! a head-butt is coming your way.

Spreading Your Wings and Flexing Your Muscles   **177**

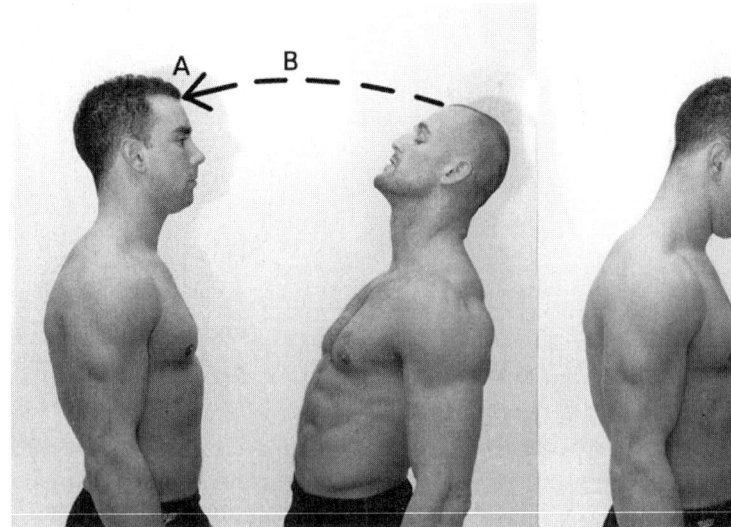

LOOK OUT! a head-butt is coming your way.    ACTION: meet him half-way and bounce your head at that point.

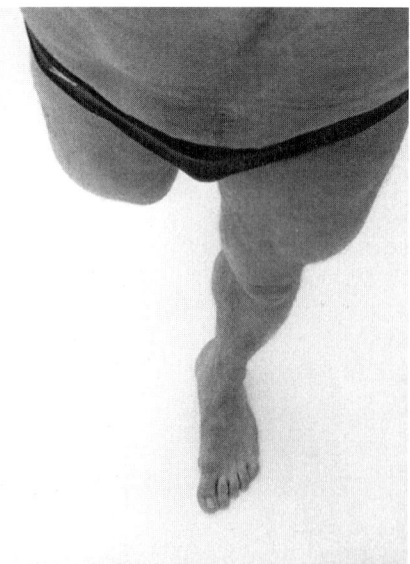

LOOK OUT! a knee in the crutch is coming your way.

your head at that point but he will not have been expecting to bounce his head so soon so he will come off with a sore head and you will not.

Simple when you know how! The guy who tried to nut me was left holding his head saying, "Don't hit me! Don't hit me!"

To knee you in the crutch your attacker's knee has to come up between your legs. It happens, but is not that easy to achieve. If you move one knee in front of the other he will not be able to do this as he will knee your leg instead. Or if you twist your hips clockwise or anticlockwise you will likewise prevent him getting his knee between your legs.

An easy way to deter someone and give yourself time to make an escape is punch him upwards with the butt of your open hand under his nose (see pages 180–181). The advantage of this is that he may not expect a punch to come from below and it does not telegraph your intention to strike him in the way that pulling your fist back before throwing a jab or a hook does. Of

Escape the Gay Straitjacket

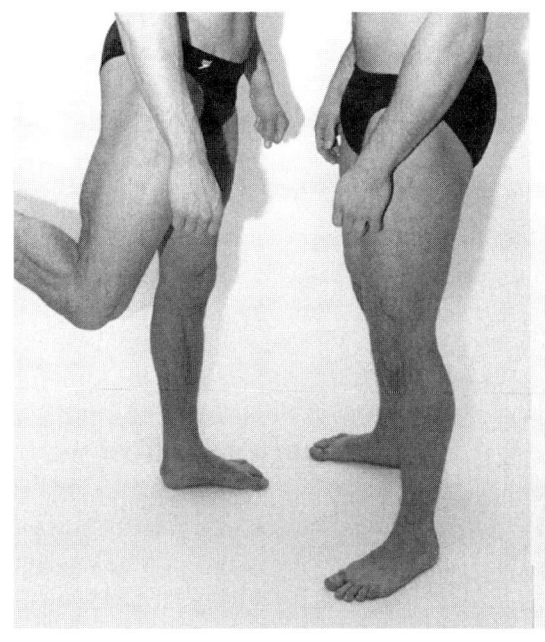

LOOK OUT! a knee in the crutch is coming your way.

ACTION: place one of your knees in front of the other to block your attacker's knee.

course, you should attempt to hit the ceiling with your hand in order to produce force at the point of impact. This will not knock him out. It will perhaps make him see stars for half a minute or so which should give you a head start in running away. Be warned: it will not work if you have not had frequent practice on a punch-bag beforehand so that you know how to punch. Be warned, also, that you need to consider the legal implications before you engage in this action.

BODY- BOXING

You will already have read, perhaps with some surprise and trepidation, how Andy and I punched each other and how Ken and I boxed.

We never used boxing gloves, and this is because we did not throw any punches aimed above the shoulders. The neck, face and head were out of

Spreading Your Wings and Flexing Your Muscles

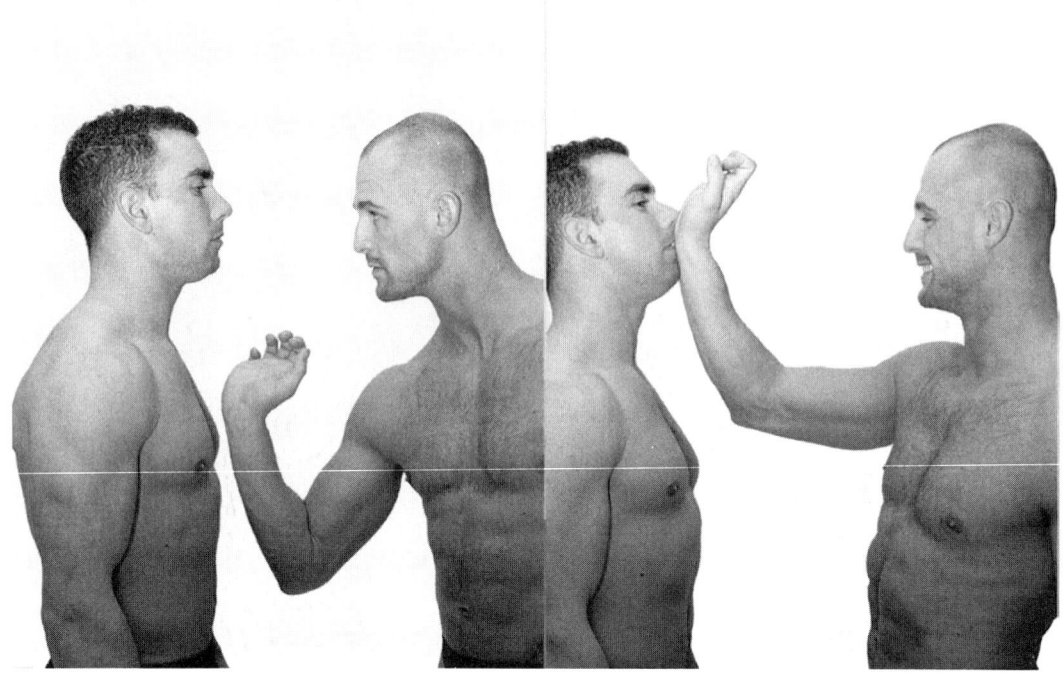

DETERRING AN ATTACKER: an uppercut to the nose delivered with the base of the hand.

bounds. You can call this body-boxing. You are not trying to incapacitate your opponent or knock him out. You are trying only to provoke him enough to rouse the anger that he has buried all his life and to allow each of you the opportunity to express the new-found anger by paying each other back.

When I had the one experience with Ken when I turned off – my mood changed from fight to flight – he insisted thereafter that we always start with body-boxing. I believe this was to pump enough adrenalin into our systems so that I would not turn off and it certainly seemed to work. I imagine he had learned this from his training in the paratroopers.

I have already mentioned (page 140) that some psychiatrists do not approve of people punching to express anger as, they believe, this only increases the anger people feel. This may well be bad for people who are expressing (too much) anger all the time, but your problem and mine, as you know, is that we are unable to express anger at all. Remember that when I was wrestling regularly I was able to enjoy sex without wrestling or boxing immediately beforehand because my anger and other emotions were near the surface but when, owing to high blood-pressure, I had to stop wrestling regularly, I found that my tender sexual feelings became buried again. With us the danger is that our anger will easily become buried again. One or two sessions a year over a period of, say, five years may be all that is needed for you to get in touch with your anger, but more frequent body-boxing sessions may put you more in touch with your anger.

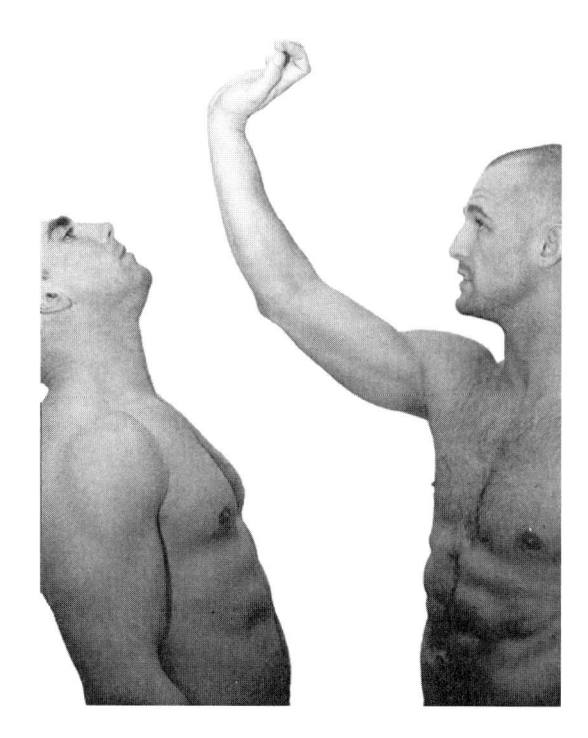

Why body-boxing is such good therapy for gay men who have buried all their anger in their unconscious minds all their lives is that perhaps the major problem for you is finding how to *feel* angry. If you have avoided feeling angry all your life by pushing anger out of your mind or by avoiding situations where you might feel angry, suddenly wanting to feel angry may present you with a real problem.

Being punched is extremely provoking. I do not pretend that you will enjoy it. It will make you feel angry that someone has the impudence to treat you that way and do that to you. But that is good. Because you are

Spreading Your Wings and Flexing Your Muscles

now allowed to retaliate and will feel able to pay him back and punch him back. And I am sure you will try to punch him back harder than he hit you and that will make you feel wonderful and very relieved. Relieved that you are able to express your anger and get rid of it!

Ken used to say to me, "I'm asking for it! Let me have it!" After years of bottling up my anger and feeling that I was doing something wrong when I wanted to wrestle, having someone actually *encourage* me to punch the other guy was, in itself, tremendously therapeutic. When you start body-boxing I would heartily recommend that you encourage each other in this way.

Do you remember how, when I arrived at Ken's house, he shut the front door behind me, made me put my bag down and then punched me three or four times to wind me up even before we took our clothes off?

Just as much as you will enjoy being encouraged to fight, so will the guy you are going to body-box with, so wind him up by punching him soon after you meet. When he is changing his clothes give him a push so that he falls over on to the floor then stand over him and say, "Come on, I'm asking for it!" After you have engaged in some punching he will soon get the idea and will welcome it from the second occasion you meet for body-boxing.

In case you are looking for other people wanting to body-box as anger therapy, Power Books has a directory on its website where you can look for sparring partners in your area. The address is:

http://www.pb.clara.net/ETGS/direct.htm.

If you feel butterflies in your stomach, that may be a new experience for you. This is not something to be frightened of. This shows your body is pumping adrenalin into your blood which will prepare you for competition: it will make your reactions quicker and increase your strength. As peculiar as it feels, you should welcome it as it will help you perform better. It is what makes little old ladies jump high fences to avoid a charging bull. When you participate in sport regularly you will not be aware of the adrenalin surge each time, as the body will learn to prepare itself gradually as the competition approaches.

When someone punches your torso, you should tense the muscles in the region to resist injury. If you take a breath and hold it while being punched your lungs act like a football and your ribs have tremendous ability to rebound. That is, as long as your back is not up against a wall or other hard object when you are punched: that is the classic way ribs are broken, being compressed between two immovable objects.

By the time you reach this point in the book you should have done some weight-training to build up your muscles as, in order to box, it is important that your abdominal muscles have been strengthened by exercising them with sit-ups and leg raises so that they will have the strength to resist punches to your *solar plexus*, the region just below the ribs.

It is an important precaution that BOTH of you should know how to revive someone who has been winded. This is a minor injury but, if it is not treated correctly or if it is not treated at all, it will develop into a major injury with serious consequences.

Being winded occurs when someone is hit unexpectedly in the region around the bottom of the ribs (the *solar plexus*) or when they have received a succession of punches to that area which has exhausted the muscles and left them too weak to protect it.

What happens is that the tendon of the diaphragm is stretched by the punch. That causes a reflex action which stops the muscle working and, as the diaphragm is one of the principal muscles (together with the intercostal muscles between the ribs and the abdominal muscles) used in breathing, breathing stops.

The method to revive the subject is mouth-to-mouth resuscitation (page 225). If the subject is revived within two minutes there will be no lasting effect as this is a minor injury. However, if the subject is given the wrong treatment or given no treatment, this minor injury will develop into a major injury. After three minutes permanent brain damage will occur, and after five minutes death will ensue. If you both know what to do should either of you be accidentally winded, disaster can easily be avoided and pleasure as well as progressive anger-expression therapy can continue.

I do not pretend that you will enjoy being

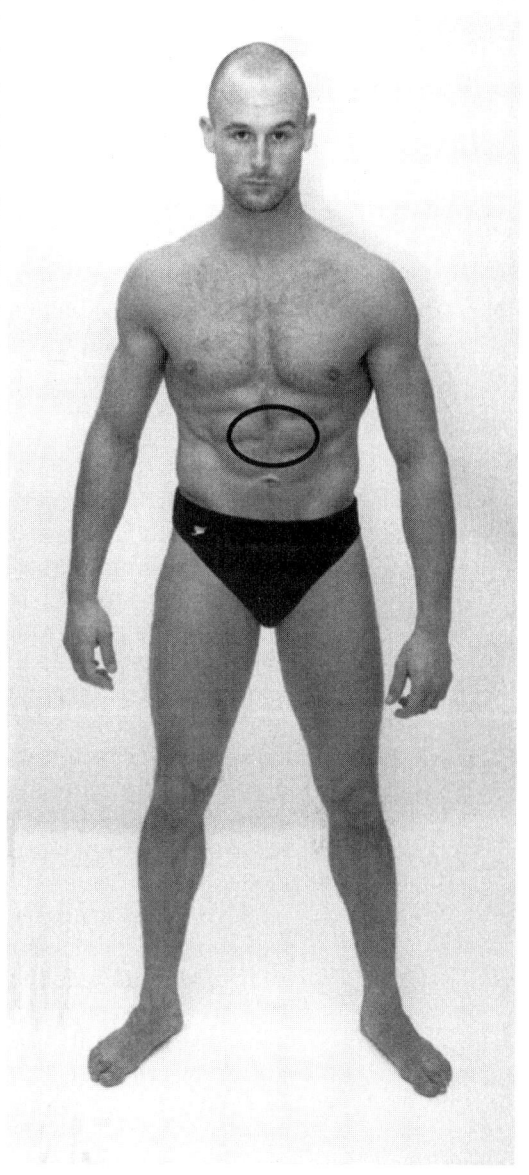

SOLAR PLEXUS: the sensitive area of the solar plexus (circled).

Spreading Your Wings and Flexing Your Muscles

punched by someone. Nobody does. It is being able to retaliate and hit back (that you have never been allowed or been able to do before) that is exhilarating, enormously satisfying and purging of all your pent-up anger. You will never know how wonderful the feeling is until you experience it for yourself.

There are, of course, other body-contact sports. Why not buy a plastic football/soccerball and spend an afternoon with a friend you like, kicking it back and forth to learn basic skills? The ball can be controlled with the feet, the knee, the chest and the head but not with the hands unless you are the goalkeeper.

I have a friend who is very effeminate and hates football but when we tried kicking a ball back and forth he displayed amazing natural skills in handling a football. If you choose the right friend you will enjoy being in his company whether you are walking through the woods, playing cards or kicking a football/soccerball about. Beware any friend who cannot control his need to express one-upmanship at your expense by giving you shots on purpose which are impossible for you to return. This will not give you the pleasure good fathers give their sons by spending whole afternoons giving them football practice to perfect their skills. It will only make you regret having asked him to play with you, and that is not what the exercise is about. Instead, that will reinforce your dislike of sport.

The next stage deals with becoming involved in body-contact sports. Before you started reading this book I am sure that, like me, you were not interested in getting involved in football/soccer, or rugby. We have gradually swept away your fears and helped you to grow stronger, more confident in yourself and more knowledgeable about how to handle yourself. You have gained some experience in wrestling and done some sparring with a friend, so body-contact sports are no longer as unapproachable as they once were.

Why bother to engage in them at all? For me the benefits have been in expressing my own anger sufficiently well in order to be able to reach an orgasm without wrestling first, and the same may apply for you too. You will know from reading chapter 1 what the consequences have been for you of repressing your anger. You will therefore now also know what the benefits for you will be.

I leave it up to you to decide whether you would like to put the book down for some time while you consolidate your present position and what you have managed to achieve so far, or whether you feel ready to plunge into body-contact sports and expressing anger freely in **Stage Five**.

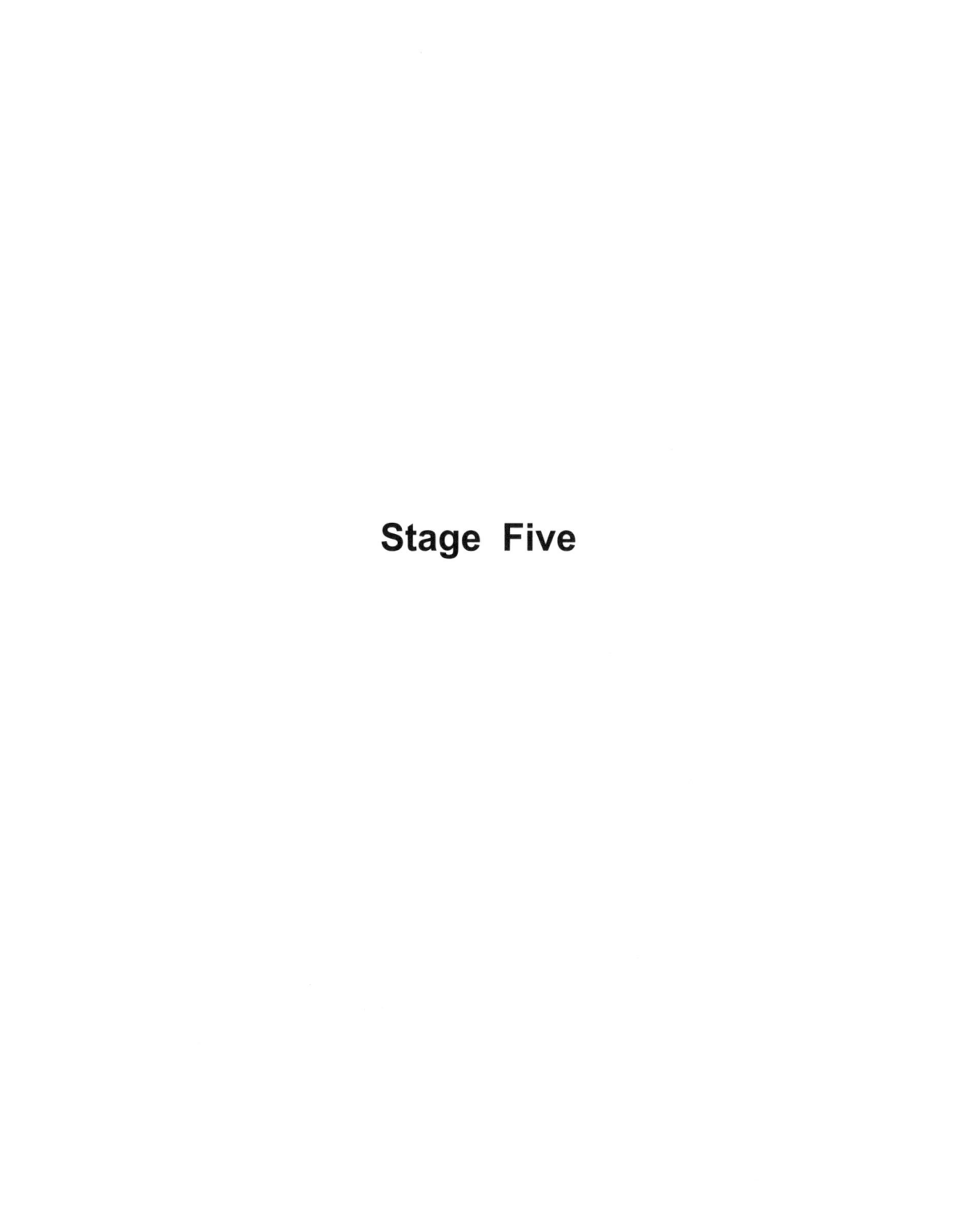

Stage Five

Stage Five - BODY-CONTACT SPORTS

If you read this book straight through because you are inquisitive to know what it has to say without leaving the long breaks recommended between some of the sections then you are going to say, "This is just a big trick to try to get me to play sports. I *hate* sports. I don't want to have anything to do with it, let alone take part in it."

You may well feel like that, as I used to, when you first pick this book up but after you have discovered the cause of your "fear of violence" neurosis, six months after you have learned how to assert yourself, have built your muscles up for six months, have done a little rough-and-tumble for six months I am sure that, like mine, your views will have changed.

I am not going to make any suggestions. Everybody is different. Look at the facts, that is, the evidence that has come to light through my own experiences that I have been describing throughout the book.

ACTION 1: I trained with weights (which is supposed to be a way of working off anger and aggression) three times a week. EFFECT: In order to reach an orgasm I needed to wrestle immediately beforehand.

ACTION 2: I had my "fear of violence" neurosis cured which helped me to wrestle more aggressively once a week. EFFECT: I still needed to wrestle immediately prior to reaching an orgasm.

ACTION 3: I began wrestling twice a week. EFFECT: I no longer needed to wrestle in order to reach an orgasm as I felt I had already wrestled enough during the week. The implication is that my anger was just under the surface and so were my tender sexual feelings, available when I wanted to express them.

ACTION 4: Owing to high blood pressure I had to stop wrestling regularly and training with weights. EFFECT: I then again needed to (wrestle or) box in order to reach an orgasm.

ACTION 5: I told Andy I was angry with him and he admitted he was angry with me. EFFECT: We were both able to reach an orgasm making love tenderly without any fighting to bring our emotions to the surface as our anger was no longer buried.

It is simply amazing how powerful a tool telling someone you are angry with them can be. You may like to remind yourself how I told Andy I was angry with him (page 21) and how Andy told me he was angry with me (page 22).

You may find that writing down the details of your anger in a journal or talking to a tape recorder may solve all your problems.

Many (straight) men find playing sports a wonderful way to let off steam. Are they wasting their time? Would it be easier and simpler for them to tell the people they are angry with that they are angry with them instead of having to stomp up and down a field for an hour and a half to let their anger out? Well, people are different.

Some people may never be able to admit to their boss or their wife/lover that they are angry with them. It is easier for them to go to the pub and cry into their beer or run up and down a field for an hour and a half letting their anger out by trying to do it faster than the opposing team. It will be difficult to know which category you would fall into until you try doing it.

Others, again, may find that running up and down a field does nothing for them even if they do it all day. What may work for them is having an opponent pick them up and fling them down on the mat. That may rouse all their ire and rage. "How *dare* he do that to me?" is what they may feel subconsciously though they could never say so. Others may need the opponent to punch them with a fist in order to bring their anger to the surface so that they can then express it by punching the opponent in retaliation.

There are more ways than one of skinning a cat. There are more ways than one of expressing anger. People are different.

What you need to do is to try them all to see which works best for you. And which you enjoy doing.

Perhaps it may be possible to forgo all these sports if you can simply go around saying to people, "I'm sorry to have to tell you this but I am angry with you." Would that work? I am sure it would if you were angry with them. It would be worth a try. It would be ironic if all our problems could actually be cured in such a simple, quick and efficacious way. That is what the evidence before us suggests, and what psychiatrists have been saying for years.

Did it work for Andy and me simply because, over the years, we had expressed so much anger with each other by punching each other that saying "I am angry with you" was all there was left to do to express the last of our anger with each other? I cannot say. I do not know. But it may well be the case.

If you say "I am angry with you" when you do not actually feel angry with the person for any reason at all, then it may have no effect. On the other hand, if you do feel angry with the person (given that as you have buried your anger all your life you may not be aware of your anger) then it would without doubt have an effect.

However, it is when you feel the anger that it becomes most difficult to put it into words. On the other hand, if you say that you are angry when you do not feel angry because your anger has been repressed, will that have the desired effect? I think it will. That is what psychotherapy is all about and how it works.

It may sound daft saying,"I'm pleased to meet you. I am sorry to have to say this but I am angry with you" but it could change your life with so little effort. Why not try it?

Of course, a statement like that is bound to elicit the response: "As we have never met before why should you be angry with me?" Then you will have to own up. "You are so handsome, so expensively dressed that you make me feel threatened, and that makes me angry with you."

The reply may not be so flattering because, for it to be effective, you would need to be honest.

"I overheard your loud conversation over there and you were so self-opinionated, bitchy and ill-informed that I am angry I have to put up with you."

The problem with 90% of gay men (as indeed it was with me) is that all their lives they have been burying their anger: the most difficult part of the problem is to bring the anger to the surface so that one can feel it, so that one can become aware of it.

Undoubtedly, this is what sports will do for you. I am not suggesting that you will enjoy boxing (even if it is only body-boxing). Getting hit is painful. If it is painful why do it? Because it brings your anger to the surface. You feel so angry that the other guy has had the effrontery to do that to you that you want to hit him back. And you *can* get a lot of pleasure from punching people you are angry with. Do not forget that or underestimate the pleasure that it will bring.

In rugby it is extremely annoying when you have run as fast as you could to have someone in the opposing team take the ball away from you. Your anger rises to the surface and you try to make yourself run even faster to catch up with him and to get your ball back. It may on the surface seem extremely childish, but it is an extremely powerful mechanism. Do not doubt that for a moment.

You may think it will be lovely to be able to wrestle with other guys and run your hands all over their beautiful muscles but when your opponent traps your legs and slams you down to the ground your anger rises up as you feel, "I'm not going to let him do this to me!" and you use your anger to struggle to reverse the situation you are in. If that is what it takes to feel your anger and to enable you to express it, believe you me it is going to be worth it!

Once you have had to run as fast as you can down a field to outrun your opponent you will learn to take long strides and, as a result, you will begin walking with long strides too instead of walking with short strides, commonly known as mincing, which is the hallmark of someone who has never played sports or learned to let his anger out. It tells everyone that this person is frightened of expressing his anger.

There is other body language that marks sportsmen. They learn to conserve their energy by not using it up in making useless movements, but making only strong, decisive movements which will have an effect. Once this lesson has been learned, it affects their behaviour off the sports field too.

All your life you have been prevented from expressing your anger. You have been prevented from expressing your aggression. You have been prevented from asserting yourself. You have been prevented from competing. You have been prevented from being a man and enjoying the things men do.

What has been the result? Are you one of the many gay men who are frightened of other (straight) men, limp, impotent, ineffective, sadistic, masochistic, and so on, and so on . . . ?

This is not love! This is not happiness! This is not life! This is being trapped in a straitjacket! Give yourself the power of your anger to empower you to a new, happier life!! If you need permission to be able to do this, I *give* you permission!

Let your anger out! Allow yourself to compete! Show people that you are not some wimp they can push around! Make a date with your idol and show everyone you are a force to be reckoned with!!!

Stage Six - EXPRESSING ANGER SAFELY

I have already described different ways of expressing anger safely, but for simplicity I have gathered them together here so that you can try each one for yourself and see whether it is comfortable for you for obtaining the right kind of release. This is the reason I will also cover sports I have already mentioned, but this time I will describe them in more detail.

It is difficult to suggest which is the most expedient for you because it depends on the person and how far your development has progressed. We are dealing with basically two extremes of people. There are those who smile a lot and have a "gay" façade and are probably totally unaware of having any anger inside them because they avoid anger-provoking situations as far as they can or push anger out of their minds (meaning repressing it) whenever they *are* provoked. Then there are those who are aware of having so much anger that they could never begin to let it out for fear of losing control completely and being very destructive in the process.

I will outline different ways of learning to express your anger so that you can try the ones that you feel may be most appropriate for you. At whichever point you feel safe to make a start you may feel, after letting some anger out, that you could also try another method which you would not have been able to do at first.

I think I have shown (page 21) that a simple statement to someone that you are angry with, can have the most surprising results by way of releasing other emotions such as tender sexual feelings that are repressed together with the anger.

However, if you feel you are seething with rage and might be frightened of losing control completely and being very destructive, then writing it down in a journal or letter to the person who made you angry may be the easiest solution to begin releasing anger, as long as you do not post the letter, but burn it. Making a drawing or painting may suit you if you are an artist. On the other hand, a workout on the punch-bag in the gym or someone's anger room may be beneficial because it would not really matter if you *did* lose control completely as there is not much damage you can do to a punch-bag apart from hitting it and it is made to be able to withstand punches from a man weighing up to 136 kg/300 lb or so.

Work down the list and if you feel it will be safe for you to do, then try it. Make your appointment with your idol to start tonight!

SAYING IT PRIVATELY

You need to make a list of all the people you are angry with. Then secrete yourself in your bedroom when others are out or turn the sound up on the television or hi-fi. Otherwise you need to go into a field or on to the beach where you are out of earshot.

Take the first person on your list. Imagine he/she is there and then say to the imaginary person all the things about which you are angry with them. You need to go on until you feel you have fully exhausted your anger with them. Then move on to the next person on your list and deal with them in the same way.

This is fine if you know that you are angry with someone and what it is you are angry with them about. The problem with most gay men is that, as they have been repressing their anger from day one, they face the world now with a "gay" façade and are completely unable to feel any anger at all. This was my situation. I knew I was angry because in the office at work I had an old-fashioned typewriter (in the 1960s) and I used to slam the carriage back with such violence that the typewriter used to slide off the desk. I felt rather guilty about taking it out on the typewriter, but whom was I angry with? Perhaps I felt oppressed by the world. As I was trapped in a straitjacket perhaps I was angry that I was so helpless.

SAYING IT PERSONALLY

I have already described (page 22) the most dramatic effect that telling someone to their face (or over the telephone as it occurred in this case) in a very quiet way that you are angry with them, can have. This is something you need continually to bear in mind and aim to copy in your own life. It needs some prior thought to discover why it is that you are angry with them.

If you realise that you must be repressing all your anger because you do not feel any anger, but you are displaying some of the symptoms of the gay straitjacket described in Chapter 1, I think you could make a habit of saying, "I'm sorry to tell you but I am angry with you." This would bring the reply, "What are you angry with me about?" To which you could reply, "When I find out I'll let you know." This may seem a very strange exchange but it is not as strange as it seems because of the way one's unconscious mind works. Some prior thought might bring reasons for your anger into your mind.

Of course, I am sure you will find that you are not really angry with everybody, but if you do not find you have any anger for a particular person no harm will have been done as the exchange sounds rather like a joke.

At worst, the only benefit will be that you will find you are not so trapped in a straitjacket any more, and that you are not so helpless. For example, if you told your lover that you were angry with him when you did not actually feel angry with him, the only benefit might be that you no longer need to use poppers when having sex with him if that had previously been the case. That would be an advantage worth having.

I would start saying it to your (gay) friends, then your family and then your workmates, and leave your boss till last by which time you will be better able to judge the effects the exercise may bring and also the supposed benefits.

Once you have practised asserting yourself and have developed, in particular, the technique of distancing yourself from your anger but being able to describe the way you feel as though you were a barrister representing yourself in a court case, you will find it easier to admit to people the way you really feel even when you feel angry. You can achieve this only when you are expressing your anger regularly so that you do not have a backlog that has mounted up over the years and is festering.

You may feel that someone is a conniving, low-down, cheating, selfish bully, but saying that is not going to help you or your cause. There are three things you need to say (and practise beforehand):

1. Sympathise with the person's point of view.
2. State how you feel.
3. Tell them what you would like them to do.

Examples of these might be:

> I can see you are having a lovely party. Your music has been keeping me awake since I went to bed two hours ago. I would like you to turn the sound down so that I can sleep. (Do NOT mention that you also think they are a bunch of layabouts if they do not have to work in the morning, drug addicts or inconsiderate delinquents.)

> I know the price of this suitcase was reduced when I bought it. I feel

very disappointed that the stitching has come apart and is not your usual high standard. I would like to have my money refunded. (Do NOT mention that you also think that the suitcase is cheap rubbish they imported from a third-world country and that they are behaving like sharks if they were trying to hoodwink you into giving them good money for it.)

I can see you are enjoying your game of football. You are kicking sand into our picnic sandwiches. Please move your game further down the beach away from us. (Do NOT mention that you also think they are a bunch of football hooligans or are inconsiderate louts.)

Do not allow yourself to be sidetracked. If the other person makes excuses or tries to pass the buck then repeat the statement, saying what you would like them to do over and over again, or repeat any of the other three statements you have prepared that you think are most appropriate over and over to them until you obtain satisfaction. Do NOT apologise as this will sabotage your case. It will show them that you mean business if you ignore anything else they say and repeat your demand for action .

CUSHION

You will need a large, well-padded cushion that you can punch, kick, throttle or do whatever you want to. You will need to go into your bedroom or somewhere else where you can be private. If necessary, turn up the sound of the television or hi-fi.
   You should imagine that the cushion is the person or persons that you are angry with. Place the cushion on your bed so that it has a soft support underneath. You should punch or do whatever you would like to do that person to the cushion until you feel completely exhausted.

PUNCH-BAG

When I started out training with weights in the 1950s and 1960s a punch-bag was a common sight in many weight-training gyms. Nowadays with the advent of machines for exercising they seem to have been eclipsed but they are a most valuable piece of equipment for "letting off steam" or expressing anger and will be used by many of the members if you can persuade the owner of your gym to acquire one.

Also suitable are torsos that can be used for wrestling practice. Although these are not cheap (GBP £200–300/USD $180–380), they are much better suited to being attacked and will prevent you from hurting your fist if there is something hard underneath the cushion. Check local martial arts and boxing shops and producers of wrestling mats and dummies. Consult the yellow pages or internet for suppliers.

Check the Power Books website for anger rooms in your vicinity that you can hire for a small charge:

> http://www.pb.clara.net/ETGS/angrooms.htm.

WRESTLING, JUDO OR JU-JITSU

Boxing is a perfect way of expressing anger, as you will find out when you throw a punch at a punch-bag. As a sport it appeals only to a certain type of person as you need to have so much anger in you that you do not mind getting hit in the face which can cause painful damage particularly to your nose and teeth.

Wrestling is a more suitable fighting sport for gay men. There are of course many different styles of wrestling and each has to be evaluated separately.

Professional wrestling, as seen on television, is all completely fake so not of any use at all in expressing anger though it may be an excellent way for spectators to enjoy anger vicariously.

Olympic freestyle/collegiate wrestling as practised in the Olympic Games is ideal for expressing anger as it is forbidden to use any holds or throws that endanger a wrestler's life or limb. You can be as aggressive as you like with minimum chance of getting hurt or hurting your opponent. All you have to do is to pin his shoulders to the ground for one second. Not as easy as you may think but plenty of opportunity to vent your anger through aggression.

Submission-style wrestling is gaining popularity and was what attracted me initially (once I had discovered professional wrestling was faked) since there was the sado-masochistic chance, I thought, of punishing your opponent and getting punished, too. In practice this is not what happens, as wrestlers tend to submit as soon as they have been trapped in a hold that is either painful or potentially harmful rather than writhe in pain in them for the opponent's especial delectation. My sadistic satisfaction was frustrated! The wrestling is merely a process of jockeying for a position where one can apply such a submission hold to gain victory.

Judo, sombo and ju-jitsu are styles of wrestling where a strong jacket is worn by which you can take hold of your opponent or which you can use to apply a hold, particularly strangle and choke holds, on him. These therefore have a special relevance in street situations. Judo and ju-jitsu were invented in Japan from indigenous wrestling styles, sombo was invented similarly in Russia. In judo, instructors have been known to use their students as dummies to perfect their own skills and this can contribute to injuries, particularly in practice sessions. Sombo is not as popular as judo and you may have trouble finding a club teaching it.

With any of these styles, whether you will be able to join a club locally to work off anger rather depends on where you live. That may be the chief reason why you choose one style over another but if you have a choice I would recommend Olympic freestyle wrestling first, then judo, sombo and lastly ju-jitsu. Consult the internet and yellow pages of your phone directory to find what clubs there are in your area. If you are really desperate you could try to form your own club. See my book *Wrestling for Gay Guys* for practical advice.

BODY-BOXING

Boxing is a painful and damaging sport that is not for the faint-hearted. But if you eliminate throwing punches to the neck, face and head you no longer need to use gloves and you can quite easily work off a lot of anger and aggression – as you will have seen with my exchanges with Andy and particularly with Ken (pages 95–99).

As the purpose of the sparring was to work off anger, it was agreed that we would not dodge or block punches, in true cowboy style. A word of warning first, however. It is essential that you have done some training to strengthen the abdominal muscles in order to protect your *solar plexus* (page 161) and also that BOTH participants know how to revive someone who has been winded (see Appendix A).

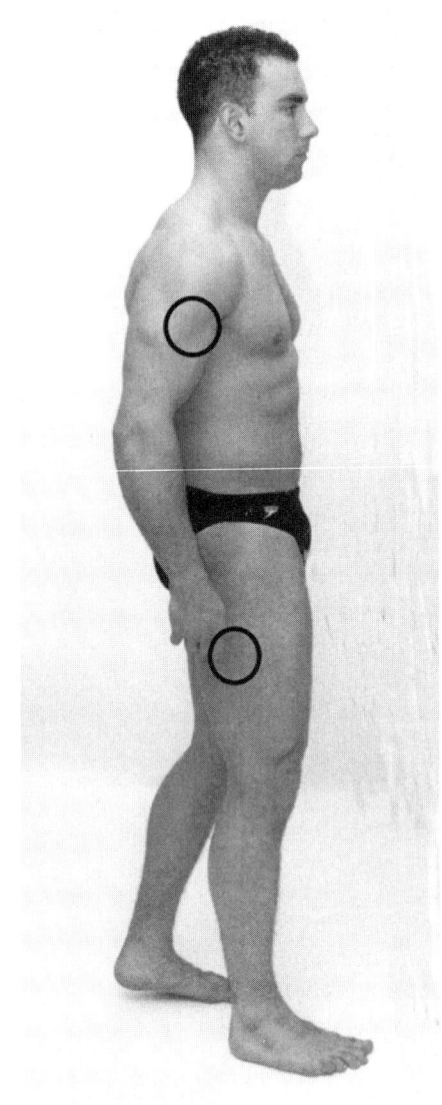

ARM-PUNCHING

Andy and I participated in punching each other on the side of the upper arm, and so did Ken and I. At the point where the deltoid (shoulder) muscle is inserted into the bone of the arm (see picture) punches are very painful and may appeal particularly to S & M devotees. Sometimes we simply took it in turns to throw a punch, on other occasions we agreed to have two punches each in turn.

Either way, the agreement was you had to take your turn within ten seconds, otherwise you lost your turn. After twenty seconds the fight could continue on the ground. Sometimes we called the end of a round by mutual agreement (with Ken) but with Andy it was often less formal and the ten-second and twenty-second counts did not always apply. Andy hit harder than anyone else his size that I have known. He was also a past-master at hitting you when you were not expecting it. Sometimes, though, to get him going I had to punch him twenty times before he would retaliate at all. His anger was terribly repressed.

Punches to the side of the thigh (see picture) on the lateral tendon are also extremely painful.

Arrange with your sparring partner what you would like to do. If you want to arm-punch, I would recommend doing a couple of rounds of body-boxing first to get your adrenalin flowing.

SENSITIVE POINTS: the side of the upper arm (circled) and the side of the thigh (circled).

MORE BODY-CONTACT SPORTS

I have emphasised that the only way you can get rid of

Escape the Gay Straitjacket

anger is to *express* it. It has also become apparent that, if you do not express your anger, you are piling up a lot of unnecessary problems and difficulties for yourself that will, at some time in the future, backfire on you or poison your whole life.

My own experience indicates that, in order to bring my anger to the surface sufficiently so that I could indulge in sex with someone else without first provoking my anger with boxing or wrestling, I needed to participate in body-contact sports, in wrestling in particular, at least twice a week regularly (once a week each in Olympic freestyle and submission style).

I have already mentioned the old adage: a healthy mind in a healthy body. What this signifies is that you need to participate regularly in sports in order to keep your mind healthy (by that I mean free from anger). This has always been denied you in the past by your "fear of violence" neurosis. Another adage which you could bear in mind is: Easy come – easy go: as a way of dealing with your anger. If something makes you angry, you need to let go of the anger just as easily and quickly.

You have also been too frightened to tell people that you were angry with them as that might have projected you into a conflict or made you appear to be a "bad" person.

I have shown (page 22) how expressing anger by telling someone quite quietly that you feel angry with them can at a stroke wipe away the problems caused by not expressing anger.

On the other hand, while this may be a route you can follow with friends and lovers, there may remain people like bosses whom you find it impossible to tell that you are angry with them. That residual anger, therefore needs to be channelled and expressed in a different direction.

To sum up the ways of dealing with your anger:

1 realising when you are angry – this may be your first great problem
2 writing down what made you angry, how it makes you feel and what you want to do about it
3 participating in a method of provoking your anger (e.g. body-boxing) so that you know when you are angry and are able to express the anger immediately by retaliating (easy come – easy go)
4 telling the person you are angry with that you are angry with them
5 expressing the anger, where you cannot tell the person (e.g. your boss), by channelling it into playing sport aggressively instead.

If you need to express anger through playing body-contact sports, there are a number you can choose from: basketball, boxing, five-a-side football/soccer, football/soccer, hockey, ice hockey, lacrosse, roller skating derby, rugby, volleyball, water polo and several different styles of wrestling. I will discuss them in order of suitability for gay men, starting with the most suitable.

If you have any doubts about whether you would like to try a particular sport go and watch a game and try to talk to someone who plays. Find out what they enjoy and what they do not like.

The following is a very rough guide to what each sport entails so that you could enjoy watching a game. It does not pretend to be a comprehensive set of rules.

Volleyball

For someone who has never participated in a team sport before, volleyball is a wonderful way to start. It is more of a body-contact sport than tennis or badminton, but not as rough as some of the others on this list as you are only bumping into members of your own team.

There are six players on each side of a high net. A large ball is thrown back and forth over the net until one side drop it. Then they lose a point – or actually, the opposing side gain a point. After a team serves the ball the members of that team rotate to the next position so that everyone gets a chance to serve.

However, what makes the game so easy for beginners and so much fun is that you do not have to put the ball over the net each time it is played (as in tennis). It can be played three times before it needs to go over the net, so if a player fumbles the ball, another player on the same side can play the ball, but a player may not play the ball twice in succession.

Beginners or players who are clumsy will not let their side down if they fumble the ball. This option can also be used to get the ball (when it does go over the net), into an area where the opposing team cannot play it because they do not have a player in that position.

The first team to gain 15 points wins. However, if the teams tie on 14 points one team needs to gain 2 points to win. As you are separated from the opposing team by a net there is not much aggression.

Volleyball is included in the Gay Games.

Five-a-Side Football
Correctly speaking this is "small-side football" as the rules allow for any number of players you like "up to seven" on each of two teams including the goalkeeper. The pitch is about one-third the size of the normal pitch and the game lasts for two equal periods of between four minutes and fifteen minutes. The goal at each end is 5 m/16 ft wide by 1.2 m/4 ft high.

There is no offside rule and the goalkeeper must return the ball to play by an underarm throw where there is a height restriction. Otherwise the game is the same as association football/soccer.

Football/Soccer
This is the most popular team game in the world – chiefly, I surmise, because so little special equipment is needed. Just a ball. And two goals.

The official name is Association Football and the term *soccer* comes from Assoc. which differentiates it from other styles of the game: e.g. A-merican football, Australian-rules football etc.

Each team has eleven players including a goalkeeper. The goal at each end of the field measures 2.4 m/8 ft high by 7.32 m/24 ft wide. The object is to put the ball in the opposing team's goal.

Matches last for two sessions of forty-five minutes each. Extra time can be allowed for stoppages due to injuries. Players can use a variety of kicking styles, heading the ball, or even using their thighs or chest to pass the ball or control it, but they may not use their arms or hands, except for the goalkeeper who is allowed to pick it up to throw it back to his team. Free kicks are awarded against teams for fouls.

A player is in an offside position if he is in the opponent's half of the field and nearer to the opponent's goal than both the ball and the second last opponent, but he will only be penalised if he is in active play while in this position.

Football/soccer is included in the Gay Games.

Basketball
There are five players in each team. Height is not a prerequisite but is a decided advantage.

At each end of the pitch is a horizontal hoop measuring 45 cm/18 in in

Spreading Your Wings and Flexing Your Muscles

diameter with open-ended netting into which the ball needs to be thrown to score a goal.

The (American) NBA play for four sessions of twelve minutes each. College games last for two sessions of twenty minutes each while high school games are for four sessions of eight minutes.

You are not allowed to run with the ball, which is why players bounce the ball continuously, called "dribbling". The team in possession of the ball have a very limited time to score otherwise the ball is given to the opposing team.

Although body contact is not permitted with the opposing team it occurs frequently in the region near the goal. One or two free throws can be given for a "personal foul".

Basketball is included in the Gay Games.

Olympic Freestyle Wrestling

The object is to force both your opponent's shoulders to the mat for one second to score a "pin" which ends the contest. No holds or throws are permitted that endanger life or limb. Strangleholds are therefore not permitted nor are kicking, punching, head-butting or taking hold of your opponent's leotard, the costume that is worn.

A match lasts for three periods of three minutes each. At the start of each period the wrestlers take hold of each other in a standing position, the "tie-up". One of the wrestlers may attempt to take his opponent down to the ground with a "takedown" or "throw" and then attempt to turn his opponent's back towards the mat, placing him in a "predicament" before trying to pin him.

Points are given to wrestlers who execute these moves or a "reversal" effectively so that, if there is no pin at the end of the allotted time, a winner can be declared on the basis of points.

If the bout reaches a stalemate situation, the referee can stop the wrestling and make the wrestlers start again on all fours on the mat in the "referee's position on the mat" with the wrestler who had an advantage when he stopped them in the top position. The same happens if the wrestlers move off the mat.

What is confusing to spectators (and even to wrestlers) is that tournaments are usually conducted, not by elimination ending in a bout to decide the champion, but on a league basis where all the wins and points are added up, to find a winner. Also included in the Gay Games.

Submission Wrestling

Submission wrestling is gaining in popularity. A contest lasts ten minutes if it is a qualifying bout or twenty minutes if it is the final. A bout ends if one of the wrestlers says he submits or taps his opponent or the mat three times, or if, in the referee's opinion, one of the wrestlers is in danger of having a bone broken or if his life is in danger – if, for instance, he is being choked or strangled. Punches, biting, eye-gouging, hair-pulling, finger or toe holds or touching the groin are not permitted.

Wrestlers try to win by putting their opponent in a strangle- or choke-hold, an arm-bar, arm-lever, shoulder lock or wrist-lock, a leg-lock or ankle-lock from which he is unable to escape and which will force him to submit to save his life or a bone being broken.

In the event that neither wrestler is forced to submit, points are awarded for certain moves so that the wrestler with the greatest number of points wins: 3 points for "passing the guard" and going behind the opponent; 4 points for taking an opponent down to the mat. For obtaining the "mounted position", that is, kneeling on all fours over an opponent lying on his chest on the mat 2 points; 3 points if the opponent is lying on his back in the mounted position; 2 points for placing a knee on the opponent's abdomen when he is lying on the mat on his back.

Body-boxing

There is no controlling body for this sport, but that does not stop you from arranging bouts or even tournaments amongst your friends.

Punches above the shoulders, that is, to the neck, head or face, are not permitted, nor are punches to the groin. No boxing-gloves are worn.

Bouts can be for a set number of timed rounds: e.g., five rounds of two minutes each, four rounds of three minutes each, or, less formally, by mutual agreement during the heat of battle. The winner is the competitor who makes his opponent say he has had enough.

Judo, Ju-jitsu, Sombo

Dr Jigorō Kanō (1860–1938) devised two modern forms of combat that he drew from different ancient Japanese (including Samurai) combat arts. He invented judo as a sport and for physical education, and he invented ju jitsu (or atemi-waza) as a form of self-defence.

JUDO Light cotton trousers and a loose jacket are worn with a belt. Men compete for five minutes. An *ippon* or full point wins the contest and can be gained by throwing an opponent cleanly on to his back, applying a stranglehold or immobilising an opponent pinned to the mat for thirty seconds. If these manoeuvres are executed imperfectly then a half-point or *waza-ari* is scored. Two *waza-ari* points equal an *ippon*.

Lesser points (*yuko* and *koka*) can be scored for other lesser manoeuvres or shorter periods of immobilising an opponent. Penalties are deducted for infringing the rules. If no *ippon* is scored to win the contest, a winner is declared on points.

JU-JITSU was invented as a form of self-defence but ju-jitsu techniques are being incorporated into submission wrestling and "ultimate fighting" contests (in the USA) which permit boxing and wrestling, Pankration (in Portugal and France), Vale Tudo (in Brazil) and Knockdown Sport Budo (in Britain).

SOMBO was invented in Russia from indigenous fighting skills. A loose jacket is worn which the opponent can take hold of. Contests last four, five or six minutes depending on the age and sex of the contestants. Putting an opponent flat on to his back from a standing position wins a bout if the attacker remains standing, called Total Victory. If a wrestler does not land flat on his back. the wrestling continues on the ground until one is forced to submit from a strangle- or choke-hold being applied on him or a lock that risks breaking a bone. Some submission holds are not permitted. Pinning an opponent chest-to-chest to the ground for ten seconds scores 2 points, and twenty seconds scores 4 points. A wrestler can signal defeat verbally or by tapping three times on the mat or anywhere on his opponent's body.

Water Polo

This game is played by two teams of seven men including a goalkeeper who must all be strong swimmers.

At each end of the pool is a netted goal 90 cm/3 ft high by 3 m/10 ft wide in which the ball must be placed to score. A game lasts for four sessions of five minutes each. Only the goalkeeper may hold, carry, catch or hit the ball with more than one hand. The ball must not be moved underwater at any time. Contact with another player is allowed only when he controls the ball. In spite of that I understand that a great deal of fouling is perpetrated under the water out of sight of the referee.

Water polo is included in the Gay Games.

Roller-skating Derby

This American sport faded out in the 1970s but has had a recent revival with television exposure under the name Rollerjam. Several cities have professional teams who draw their members from amateur talent.

There are two teams of five men and five women each with in-line skates (see Glossary). An oval cambered/banked track is used to enable the skaters to reach high speeds. The skaters wear protective pads and helmets. A match consists of four sessions of six minutes each of which the men compete in the second and fourth sessions.

Some of the skaters, called jammers, speed ahead to try to complete a lap so that they catch up with the other skaters. They score points by overtaking members of the opposing team, of which some of the members are blockers and try to prevent the jammers from overtaking them and scoring points.

The blockers use various physical contact tricks which are legal to waylay the jammers and the competition can become violent as tempers flare. An excellent way to express anger by aggression. Fighting, holding and tripping are actually fouls for which the penalty is sitting in the penalty box for a fixed period of time but worth it I would think and also satisfies the spectators.

Rugby

There are two forms of rugby: Rugby Union played by two teams of fifteen men and Rugby League played by two teams of thirteen men. The reason for this split is that Rugby Union used to be amateur whereas Rugby League has always been professional; however, in 1996 Rugby Union became professional as well. A game lasts for two sessions of forty minutes each.

There is a goal-line at each end of the field. The object is to put the oval-shaped ball on to the ground beyond the opponent's goal-line to score a "try". A try scores 4 points in Rugby Union or 3 points in Rugby League.

Extra points can be scored by "converting" a try by kicking the ball over the horizontal bar and between the vertical posts of the opponent's goal. Converting a try with a place-kick scores 3 points. A drop-kick over the horizontal bar and between the opponent's goal posts at any time during the game scores 3 points.

Players are allowed to run with the ball, to kick it or pass it backwards to another member of their team. A forward pass is illegal. They may also tackle an opponent who is carrying the ball. If the ball goes off the marked-out rectangle the point at which it went out is marked by a linesman with a flag and then the ball is returned to the players who stand in two parallel lines, a "line-out", to catch it.

When play is stopped owing to a minor infringement of the rules, the game re-starts with a scrum (short for scrummage) formed by eight players, called forwards, of each team, pushing against the opposing forwards. When the ball is thrown on to the ground between them they try to back-heel the ball to get it to the rest of their team.

There is lots of opportunity for expressing aggression by manhandling members of the opposing team. Much illegal mayhem is committed during the scrum out of sight of the referee.

Hockey, Ice Hockey, Lacrosse

FIELD HOCKEY is played by two teams of eleven players including a goalkeeper. For men, a game lasts for two periods of thirty-five minutes each. A goal cage is set at each end of the field. Wooden sticks with a curved end are used to hit a leather-covered ball into the opponent's goal.

ICE HOCKEY is played by two teams of six players including a goalkeeper. All the players wear protective padding. There is a goal cage 1.2 m/4 ft high by 1.8 m/6 ft wide at each end of the rink. The players use sticks with curved ends to sweep a hard rubber puck towards the goal. A game consists of three sessions of twenty minutes each.

As participating means lots of fast, continued skating, each team is backed up by two or three units of substitutes who are replaced as a team at frequent intervals.

LACROSSE is played by two teams of ten players including a goalkeeper. They use a stick of hickory at the end of which is a netted triangle which is used for catching, throwing or carrying the ball. The name of the game comes from the resemblance of the stick to a bishop's crosier or cross. A game lasts for four sessions of fifteen minutes each.

Boxing

Boxers need to undergo a medical examination and obtain a licence of fitness before being allowed to compete. Boxing-gloves, head-protectors and gum-shields must be worn by amateurs. A bout lasts for two or three rounds of two minutes each for novices or three rounds of three minutes each for experienced boxers. Professional bouts can be for ten, twelve or fifteen rounds of three minutes each.

The object is to score as many hits on the target area of your opponent as possible while defending yourself from the punches he throws at you. The target area is the front of the head and body down to the waist. A knock-out is declared if a boxer is knocked down with a punch and is unable to return to a standing position after ten seconds, and ends the fight. If a boxer collapses during a bout without being hit immediately beforehand this is termed a technical knock-out (TKO) and he is allowed ten seconds to return to a standing position or he loses the contest.

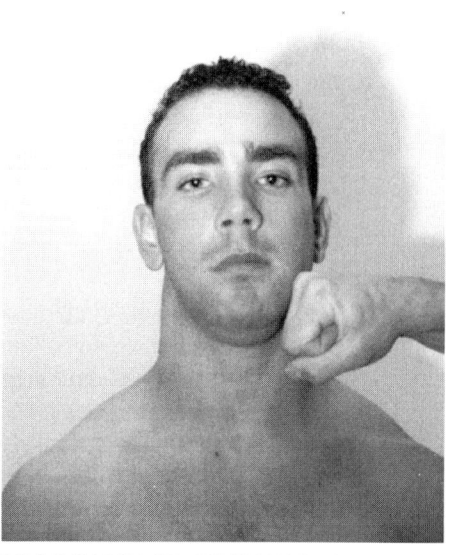

KNOCKOUT PUNCH: the classic knockout punch is a hook to the tip of the jaw.

Nowadays, on safety grounds, a referee can stop a fight if he believes that one boxer has taken too much punishment and give him a "standing count" of up to eight seconds before allowing the fight to resume. In the event that there is no knock-out, points are given for each punch that lands so that a winner can be declared on a points decision.

Karate

Karate is one of innumerable Eastern "martial arts" invented as methods of self-defence. In the West, participants felt they needed to prove its efficacy in a combat situation. Contests are held where the moves and coun-

Spreading Your Wings and Flexing Your Muscles

ter-moves are used without landing punches or kicks (non-contact karate) but are scored *as though* they had hit the opponent with full force. Some people believe the only way to test its efficacy is by using full force and so there are also full-contact karate tournaments for the hard-nuts.

The hands, elbows, knees and feet are used for punches and kicks to sensitive parts of the body (excluding the groin). Karate training can be divided into three main areas: free-standing exercises/calisthenics, *kumite* and *kata*. Free-standing exercises/calisthenics are to build strength and flexibility. *Kumite* consists of toughening the hands and feet and training them to deliver special punches, chops and kicks. *Kata* consists of acrobatic kicks and punches delivered with jumping or spinning movements.

My advice to you is to beware of any fighting method that does not also teach its students how to *avoid* the opponent's punches and kicks. Only film cowboys, masochists, gays and idiots stand still and allow themselves to be hit by an attacker without trying to avoid the blow.

WHAT NOW?

Whereas in the past you were frightened of participating in body-contact sports as you were unable to express aggression, the chances are you may now find that you need to participate in sports twice a week in order to keep your sex-life or the rest of your life simple and straightforward.

As you are no longer frightened of expressing your anger and are now even *allowed* to express your anger you may find, the more you are able to let your anger out, you actually get a buzz from seeing how much anger you can express, how aggressive you can be and how easy it is to use these to become better than your opponent and to beat him at his own game!

No more being pushed about! Wow!! Gay guys will be queuing/ lining up to get a date with you.

On the other hand, if you are able to tell people that you are angry with them then sports may be completely unnecessary for you. That depends on your being aware of when you are angry with people or taking my suggestion on board simply to tell everyone that you are angry with them – whether you are aware of feeling any anger with them or not – and waiting to see whether any anger surfaces later from your subconscious.

You may remember that adolescents need to be accepted by their peers (see page 92). Much of the inferiority and consequential low self-esteem that gay men experience stems from being rejected by their peers. The course in self-improvement in this book is aimed at redressing that inequality that began during your childhood. It needs to be said that the more equal with straight men you can make yourself, the less inferiority you will feel. You need to become equal with straight men in skills as well as in physique so that you can stand up to straight men and so that you can feel accepted (at last) by them as well as by your gay peers.

In Chapter 5 I mentioned that gay men who have had a jealous relationship with their fathers feel they cannot trust other men in authority such as gym instructors (page 163). You should be aware that, for the same reason, you may feel that I am not to be trusted and therefore you feel unable to believe what I have written in this book. If that is the case it will be very sad.

What now? The answer to that question rather depends on whether you read right through the book without pausing for the time periods that I suggested and without doing any of the things that I suggested, or whether you have done everything I suggested and are now playing body-contact sports or, at least, one body-contact sport.

If you did the former then you need to go back and re-read the book starting with Chapter 4 and putting all my advice into practice.

If you do not, you are only cheating yourself out of a happier life. You will find that, after ten or twenty years, when you learn how others have benefitted from my advice you will be wondering where this book is as you will feel you ought to re-read it and see if you, too, can benefit from it as others have done. Why lose those ten or twenty years of your life? The sooner you start changing your life the sooner you will be much happier, prouder of yourself, and more fulfilled as other people begin looking at you with pride and admiration, too.

If you have done the latter and followed my instructions, then my congratulations to you. It may not have been easy, but then things that are worth having often are not easy to acquire. As they say . . . join the club!

You can relate your experiences and development or problems you experienced on the Power Books website:

        http://www.pb.clara.net/ETGS/readers.htm

to inspire and encourage, and to help other gay or bisexual men to follow in your footsteps.

If you have particular problems you have been unable to solve that you need help with you can get help from the Problem Page on the Power Books website:

        http://www.pb.clara.net/ETGS/problems.htm.

I am sure your parents are very nice people as mine were (page 52). They know that they need to turn on the charm in order to be able to manipulate you. People who want to manipulate you always use all the charm they can muster. They know that that will make it more difficult for you to say "no" to them, but that is nevertheless what you have to do. There are three things you need to say to them (page 141) so turn on your own charm as you say "no" to them and use your anger to stand firm. That is what anger is for. I give you permission to be the person that you want to be. You do not have to be the person your parents hoped you would be. You are not obliged to turn their fantasy into reality. As you know, that is really impossible. As far down that road as you have already come there is always time to turn back and to take the right road to happiness.

Remember, too, there will be many new generations of gay and bisexual men following you who also need to learn to express their anger so pass on your knowledge to them and help them!

GLOSSARY

GLOSSARY

AUTOGENIC TRAINING

J.H. Schultz, a German neurologist, developed a system in 1970 to correct irregularities in the way internal organs worked and to provide physical and mental invigoration. This is achieved by breathing exercises and relaxing the muscles so that the person is able to relax, meditate and put himself into an almost hypnotic state.

AUTO-SUGGESTION

Also called self-hypnosis. The mind will carry out commands that you give it in much the same way as a computer will obey a command. Suppose you need to wake up at 6 a.m. to catch a plane. If you say to yourself very clearly the night before that you need to wake up at 6 a.m. your body clock situated in the hypothalamus will wake you at that hour.

It is, thus, very dangerous to say things such as, "I never remember people's names" as the mind is liable to interpret this as a command and ensure that you do not remember people's names even though it may make your life easier if you did remember people's names. A comment like that can, thus, become self-fulfilling.

Similarly, if a child breaks your best china ornament and you say to it, "You are a little devil!" the child's mind might well interpret that as a command to be a little devil and you should not be surprised, then, when the child turns into a delinquent.

In the 1960s I used auto-suggestion to put myself to sleep at night by imagining I was inhaling a sleep-inducing liquid gas from a glass cylinder.

As I inhaled, the level of the gas dropped in the cylinder. By the time I had inhaled two cylinders of the imaginary liquid-gas I would be asleep. By using the same technique I could put myself to sleep at any time or place during the day, and though I no longer have to use the auto-suggestion I usually fall asleep at night as soon as my head touches the pillow.

CIRCUIT-TRAINING

With weight-training each exercise is usually performed a number of times (repetitions) without stopping to form a "set" and then, after a rest, another set is performed totalling, for example, three sets of eight repetitions of each exercise or five sets of five repetitions. As the muscle needs time to recover before being used again, resting between sets can take up a lot of time, especially if people engage in conversation. The amount of rest required is perhaps two minutes, but this depends on one's general fitness.

Circuit training was therefore developed to allow the maximum amount of exercise to be performed in the shortest possible time. Instead of completing all the sets of each exercise before moving on to the next exercise, one set of each exercise is performed and then one moves on to the next exercise to do one set of that exercise, and so on. In order to do three sets of each exercise in this way, the whole course needs to be completed three times. This gives each muscle time to recover while other muscles are being exercised but the added advantage is that, because there are shorter rest periods between the sets, the pulse rate can be kept above 120 beats per minute and this benefits general (cardio-vascular) fitness too.

The disadvantage is that, owing to the short rests and the changes in blood flow to different parts of the body, the weights (resistance) needs to be lighter for each exercise than if the exercises were performed in the usual way.

DREAMS

The events of each day are stored in our short-term memory within the brain. Each night during sleep these memories are transferred to the long-term memory where each memory has a link to every associated memory. Thus the brain consists of millions of cells each with many links to other cells. Dreams are therefore probably the brain testing all the links it has set up.

For this reason, if during the day you have referred to your friend Charlie as a "randy old dog" you should not be surprised, then, if a dog called Charlie appears in your dream. It would clearly be referring to your friend.

As dreams have to do with the working of the innermost part of the brain, the unconscious, they form a way of finding out what is going on in the unconscious. Fears often present themselves in dreams. If you are frightened of losing control (of your anger) you might dream that you are walking down a street when, suddenly, the buildings all collapse around you. That is an illustration of your fear of the destructive power of your anger, should you lose control of it.

FANTASY

A fantasy is anything you imagine. Therefore fantasies can be good or bad.

A fantasy which is a goal to be striven for is a good fantasy. A bad fantasy is, for instance, when one imagines one knows what someone else is thinking. One can never know this unless they tell you and do not lie when they tell you. Consequently one's fantasy of what they are thinking may be incorrect.

Once one has a fantasy one often seeks evidence to prove that the fantasy is indeed true. One may *mistakenly* take something to be proof that one's fantasy is fact, and that will lead one to perceive the world incorrectly. Fantasies can be dangerous if people believe them to be true when, in fact, they are false.

FIGHT OR FLIGHT

When you are faced with a challenge or threatening situation the autonomic nervous system, comprising the sympathetic and parasympathetic nervous systems, in your body swings into action. Adrenalin (also known as epinephrine) and also some noradrenalin (also known as norepinephrine) are manufactured in the adrenal glands situated just above the kidneys, and are then secreted into the blood stream. These hormones stimulate other organs to act in different ways.

The sympathetic nervous system
- increases your mental alertness;
- increases the speed of chemical processes (your metabolism) in your skeletal muscle, heart muscle and nervous tissue;
- increases the breakdown of glycogen to glucose in the liver and releases fatty acids from fat cells (adipose tissue) and secretes them into the bloodstream to be used as energy;
- increases your breathing rate and dilates the respiratory passageways;
- increases the rate your heart beats at;
- increases the blood pressure; and
- activates the sweat glands to produce sweat.

At the same time the parasympathetic nervous system closes down your digestive system and stops producing urine.

The addition of adrenalin and noradrenalin to your blood stream produces the feeling known as "butterflies in the stomach". This puts your body on a "war footing" in the words of Walter B. Cannon (1871–1945), the American physiologist who discovered how the sympathetic nervous system worked to control the body's functions.

If the challenge or threat becomes too great, the body reverses these events by the parasympathetic nervous system reversing the changes made by the sympathetic nervous system and vice versa. You no longer feel able to deal with the challenge or threat and the feeling is to run away from it.

These reactions occur in animals as well as in humans and biologists call them the "fight or flight" mechanism.

GAY GAMES

In 1968, at the age of thirty, Dr Tom Waddell (1937–1987), an American, was a competitor in the decathlon event at the Olympic Games in Mexico City and placed sixth. Many people have to keep their sexual orientation secret in order to take part in their chosen sport in the Olympic Games owing to the homophobic attitudes of fellow sportsplayers. In 1980 he suggested the Gay Games which would be "conceived as a new idea in the meaning of sport based on inclusion rather than exclusion". Consequently, the San Francisco Arts and Athletics (SFAA) group was formed. They planned the first Gay Games to be held in 1982 in San Francisco as the Gay Olympic Games. However, the United States Olympic Committee (USOC) obtained a court injunction three weeks before the opening of the games forbidding the use of the word "Olympic" in the title although they had not objected to the Special Olympics, the Police Olympics, the Dog Olympics, the Nude Olympics and even the Rat Olympics. Such is the level of homophobia in most sports-organising bodies. The organising committee of the Gay Olympic Games was forced to delete every use of the word "Olympic" in all advertising, merchandise and printed material practically overnight, but the opening went ahead as scheduled. The name Gay Games was adopted instead: 1,300 male and female participants competed in sixteen sports.

Although it was never the intention that the Gay Games should always be held in San Francisco the second Gay Games took place there in 1986. With four years to prepare for the event a much more ambitious programme was arranged including a Procession of the Arts and a complementary series of concerts, plays, films, exhibitions, etc. as well. This time 3,482 athletes participated in seventeen sports.

The dispute with the USOC dragged on until 1987 to the Supreme Court where the original decision was upheld. The USOC then sued Tom Waddell for between USD $92,000 and $96,600 in legal fees although he was by this time dying of AIDS, but in 1993 they waived the costs against his estate.

In 1989 the SFAA was wound up and the Federation of Gay Games was established to take its place as the organisers of the Gay Games. The third Gay Games were held in Vancouver in 1990. They had grown, by that time, to a world-class event. Gay Games IV were held in New York in 1994, Gay Games V in Amsterdam in 1998 and Gay Games VI in Sydney in 2002. Gay Games VII will be held in 2006 in Montreal. The Gay Games are held every four years at a two years' distance from the Olympic Games.

The present form of the Games consists of a core of twenty-two sports. These are badminton, basketball, bowling (tenpin), cycling, diving, figure skating, football/soccer, golf, ice hockey, marathon, martial arts, physique, powerlifting, one of either racquetball or squash, softball, swimming, tennis, track and field, triathlon, volleyball, water polo, and wrestling (freestyle). To these the host city is allowed to add up to a further eight sports depending on the facilities that they have available up to a maximum total of thirty sports. On top of that they are able to stage "demonstration" sports which may have an indigenous quality. These are staged as exhibitions only and do not form part of the competitions.

No minimum level of ability is required in order to participate in any event: all are welcome. No one is excluded on account of sexual orientation, gender, race, religion, nationality, ethnic origin, political beliefs, athletic or artistic ability, physical challenge or HIV status. The website of the Federation of Gay Games is www.gaygames.org.

INLINE SKATES

Roller skates were invented in Belgium in the 1760s by Joseph Merlin and were first seen in Liège. They were later introduced into England and patented in 1819 in France. Improvements were made by James L. Plimpton of Medford, Mass. until they reached their present form in 1863, with four wheels of iron or wood arranged in a rectangle, the "quad". In about 1864 the mania for roller skating appeared in Austria, and by 1866 the roller-skating rink mania broke out in Australia and spread to England and the United States. Just before the end of the twentieth century plastic wheels of polyurethane were introduced which were lightweight and gave a much faster and smoother ride. In the mid-1980s the four wheels were placed in a straight line so that the skate resembled an ice-skate: the "in-line" skate was created.

MASOCHISM

Masochism is sexual pleasure obtained from pain or suffering inflicted on oneself by another person and even, sometimes, by oneself. The name comes from the writings of Leopold von Sacher-Masoch (1836–1895), an Austrian lawyer and writer, which often in his later stories described acts of sexual pleasure obtained from being whipped, choked or bitten, etc.

Masochism can also be applied to instances of suffering where sexual pleasure is not obvious such as martyrdom, humiliation, religious flagellation and asceticism. In psychiatry masochism is interpreted as aggression that is turned inward on the self when it is too frightening to express it.

MOODS

The conscious mind is unable to cope with every task at the same time, so it concentrates on the features of the task in hand, organising the physical execution of the task as well as recalling memories that will help to perform the task correctly while forgetting about everything else. These periods are called moods.

This is why you can put your car keys down and, five minutes later, when your mind is coping with other tasks and your mood has therefore changed, you are no longer able to recall where. The easiest way to remember is to try to return to the tasks that were in your mind at the time and therefore the mood your mind was in when you put the keys down.

While a fly is flying around looking for food, it will pay attention to evading you so that you will have difficulty in swatting it, but when it is copulating it cannot pay attention to attacks from enemies so it is quite easy to swat both.

This is also why when you are in a happy mood you are able to recall other happy times, but if you are depressed you are unable to remember the happy times; all you can remember are loads of other unhappy times.

NEUROSIS

A neurosis is a derangement in the mind that causes behaviour that seems to have no rational reason, but which the person is compulsively driven to perform.

For instance, if when you give Tom his dinner he smiles happily, sits down and starts to eat it, this is normal behaviour. If he scowls, sits down and pushes his dinner away, this is normal behaviour if he is not hungry.

If, however, he smiles happily but then smacks your arm very hard before sitting down to eat, this is neurotic behaviour or behaviour caused by a neurosis. There is no apparent reason why, when you give him something that he wants, he should have to hurt you. This is irrational.

However, if you are able to delve back into his childhood you may find that whenever he was given his food as a baby the family dog would pounce on it, hoping to have it for himself, frightening Tom who had to slap the dog to drive him off.

As an adult, Tom, having forgotten the reason for this behaviour, feels compelled to slap when he is given his food but, as the dog that caused the behaviour is no longer there to receive the blow, Tom delivers it instead to the only person who *is* there, the person who gives him the food. Neurotic behaviour is learned behaviour: only when the cause of the learned behaviour is forgotten is it called neurotic behaviour.

Ivan Petrovich Pavlov (1849–1936) was a Russian scientist who performed a now-famous experiment with dogs to prove that behaviour could be learned in this way. He rang a bell every time he fed his dogs and they salivated over the food. He discovered soon that if he rang the bell without giving the dogs their food, they would still salivate. In other words, the dogs had learned to salivate on hearing the bell, not only on seeing the food.

A person with such a neurosis often has a lot of anxiety too, perhaps because he does not understand why he acts compulsively in this way and becomes frightened of not being able to control his own behaviour and because of the social embarrassment it causes him.

PRECONSCIOUS

See Unconscious, Subconscious and Preconscious

RATIONALISATION

Hugo Münsterberg (1863–1916), one time Professor of Psychology at Harvard University, describes in his book *Psychology and Crime* an incident that occurred to him nearly a hundred years ago that is an excellent example of rationalisation. This incident was retold by W. M. S. and Claire Russell in their book *Human Behaviour*.

Professor Münsterberg was visiting a friend in a city that he had never been to before when the friend, a doctor, invited him to watch a hypnotic treatment that the doctor was to give to a wealthy lady of the town whom he was treating for a disorder.

The professor had never met the lady before and when she arrived he was introduced to her under a fictitious name. While the lady was in a hypnotised state the doctor gave her a post-hypnotic suggestion that she would return to his house during the afternoon and when the doctor took out his watch she was to say that she wanted to make her will and leave all her wealth to the professor. When she awoke from the hypnotic state she took no notice of the professor and took her leave.

During the afternoon she returned to the doctor's house where she found some other friends of the doctor's who had also come to watch the experiment. The lady was not quite sure of why she had come but said that she was passing and thought she would pop in so that the doctor could see how much better she felt. She also wanted to ask him if he thought she was well enough to go to the theatre. Professor Münsterberg chatted to her about opera and the theatre and she behaved quite normally.

When the doctor said he wanted to know how late it was and took out his watch the lady hesitated for a moment and then said, in a stammering voice, that she had not expected to find so many people there but then she continued normally that she wanted to make Prof. Münsterberg her heir and needed therefore to make her will.

The professor then said she must have made a mistake as she could not possibly have met him before. He said he lived in another city for which he invented a fictitious name. The lady replied that she had spent the last winter in that city and met him there in the street every day. She had decided right from the start to bequeath him her estate. The professor then protested that at least they had never spoken to each other before but the lady claimed they had met frequently at functions in the city.

The professor then said she should not leave all her wealth to a stranger and leave her children penniless. The lady claimed she had thought about it for years and considered that her children would be better off without the burden of her wealth whereas the professor would use the money in a philanthropic way. Some of the doctor's other visitors also protested in various ways but she had an answer for all of them.

Eventually, Münsterberg told her the truth – that during the hypnotic session she had had with the doctor that morning the doctor had made a post-hypnotic suggestion to her in his presence.

The lady smiled and replied that, yes, she knew all that but the doctor's suggestion actually coincided with the plans she had already made up in her mind a year previously. She said she had been on the point of writing to Münsterberg about it. To end matters, she insisted on being given a pen and paper and wrote a codicil to her will which the other people present had to witness, leaving her entire fortune to "the fictitious man from the fictitious town".

Once the professor had put the codicil in his pocket the lady seemed to forget about the whole incident and treated the professor like a stranger. After she left he, of course, burned the document in front of the doctor and his friends.

A rationalisation, therefore, is the false reason a person gives for an event that has occurred for which he or she is unable to give the real reason.

REPRESSION

Repression, in the psychoanalytical sense, is a way of protecting yourself by pushing painful feelings or unacceptable impulses out of your mind. You think you have got rid of them whereas, in fact, all you have done is to move them from your conscious mind into your unconscious mind where they remain to colour your personality and affect your behaviour in the future.

Anger that is shifted into the unconscious accumulates with all the previous angry feelings that have been treated in the same way until there is so much that they become uncontrollable and return to the conscious mind where they find uncontrolled expression in unexpected words or actions.

The only way to get rid of anger is to express it either in action or in words.

ROLLER SKATES

See Inline skates

SADISM

Sadism is sexual pleasure that is derived from inflicting pain, suffering or humiliation on another person. It can also mean cruelty in the general sense. It is named after the writings and personal behaviour of the Marquis de Sade, Donatien Alphonse François, Comte de Sade (1740–1814), French soldier, writer and rake.

SELF-HYPNOSIS

See Auto-suggestion

SKATES

See Inline skates

SUBCONSCIOUS

See Unconscious, Subconscious and Preconscious

UNCONSCIOUS, SUBCONSCIOUS, AND PRECONSCIOUS

Sigmund Freud theorised that the mind is divided up into parts: the conscious, and the subconscious which he further subdivided into preconscious and unconscious.

The *conscious* mind consists of the thoughts which are currently in our awareness. The *subconscious* contains memories and emotions which are not at present in our awareness. They can be subdivided into: *preconscious* (those memories and emotions which can easily be recalled into the conscious mind) and the *unconscious* (memories, emotions, wishes and hostility which are too painful to bring into the conscious mind).

What is going on in the unconscious can, however, be glimpsed from a person's dreams, slips of the tongue, fantasies, neurotic symptoms, as well as general demeanour and sudden uncontrollable bursts of anger, if there are any.

APPENDIX A

Mouth-to-mouth resuscitation

AN unexpected blow to the stomach, *solar plexus* or region around the bottom of the ribs (when the abdominal muscles are relaxed and unprepared) or a long succession of heavy punches to that area, tiring and weakening the muscles, can stretch the tendons of the diaphragm. This causes a reflex action which stops the diaphragm and the intercostal muscles between the ribs working, and breathing stops.

The victim drops to the floor, usually lying motionless on one side in a foetal position.

If the blow was sustained when the victim's back was up against a wall or against the floor there is a possibility of a broken rib as well, and mouth-to-mouth resuscitation should therefore be used for restoring normal breathing and preventing the broken rib penetrating a lung, the liver or spleen, causing major complications.

To resuscitate him, lie the victim on his back, clear the mouth of objects such as false teeth, and tilt the head backwards to clear the windpipe. To tilt the head backwards you may have to place a cushion under the shoulders.

Raise the person's chin with one hand (this prevents the tongue from blocking the windpipe) and with the other hand pinch his nostrils to prevent air escaping by that route; then take a deep breath and, making an airtight seal with your lips, blow into his mouth until his chest rises. Take your mouth away to allow the breath to escape from his mouth, and repeat every six seconds. Recovery is usually immediate.

This technique is not difficult but is potentially hazardous if not followed correctly. It should be learned by practising on a dummy during a first-aid course; *never* try it on a conscious person. It is recommended to have a cushion to hand before engaging in boxing.

WARNING: If the patient is left untreated and not resuscitated within three minutes permanent brain damage will result. After five minutes death will occur.

APPENDIX B

Body Opponent Bag

BOB manufacturer:

Century Incorporated,
1705 National Boulevard,
Midwest City, OK 73110
U.S.A.

www.centuryfitness.com

Phone: US and Canada 1-800-626-2787
       International   +1-405-732-2226
                       Central Standard Time

Fax: US and Canada 1-800-400-5485
     International   +1-405-732-3751

BOB (Body Opponent Bag) USD $299.99
                         plus shipping

British distributor:

Bytomic Distribution Ltd

Head office:
Unit 5a, Upper Barn Farm,
Bicester Road, Westcott,
Aylesbury.
HP18 0JX

Phone: 01296 658551
Fax: 01296 658553
E-mail: bytomic@aol.com

Retail price: GBP £299.00
              plus carriage

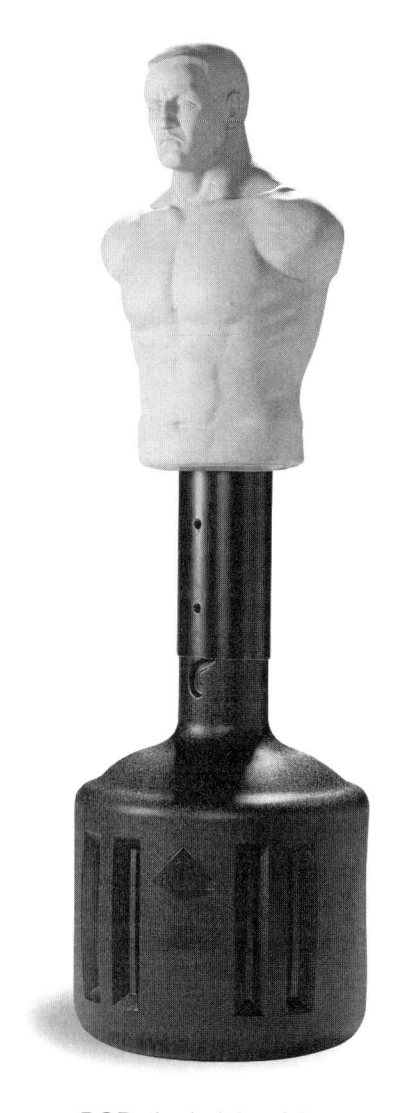

BOB: the height of the punch-bag is adjustable

Appendix B

BIBLIOGRAPHY

BIBLIOGRAPHY

ANGER

Anastasi, A., Cohen, N. and Spatz, D. "A Study of Fear and Anger in College Students Through the Controlled Diary Method", *Journal of Genetic Psychology* (1948) 73: 243–249

Averill, J.R. "Studies on Anger and Aggression: Implications for Theories of Emotion", *American Psychologist* (1983) 38: 1145–1160

Averill, J.R. "Anger" in *Nebraska Symposium on Motivation* (Vol. 26) (eds.) Howe, H. and Dienstbier, R., 1979 University of Nebraska Press, Lincoln, NE

Averill, J.R. *Anger and Aggression: an Essay on Emotion*, 1982. Springer-Verlag, New York

Gates, G.S. "An Observational Study of Anger", *Journal of Experimental Psychology* (1926) 9: 325–331

Kassinove, Howard (ed.) *Anger Disorders: Definition, Diagnosis and Treatment*, 1995. Taylor and Francis, Washington, DC

Luhn, Rebecca H., Ph.D. *Managing Anger*, 1992. Kogan Page Ltd, London

Meltzer, H. "Students' Adjustment in Anger", *Journal of Social Psychology* (1933) 4: 285–309

Richardson, F. *The Psychology and Pedagogy of Anger*, 1918. Warwick and York, Baltimore, MD

BISEXUALITY

Bem, Daryl. "Exotic Becomes Erotic: A Developmental Theory of Sexual Orientation" *Psychological Review* (1996) 103: 320–335

Blumstein, P.W. and Schwartz, P. "Bisexuality in Men" *Urban Life* (1976a) 5 (3): 339–358

Blumstein, P.W. and Schwartz, P. "Bisexuality in Women" *Archives of Sexual Behaviour* (1976b) 5 (2): 171–181

Coleman, Eli and Rosser, B.R. Simon "Gay and Bisexual Male Sexuality" in *Textbook of Homosexuality and Mental Health* (eds.) Cabaj, Robert P. and Stein, Terry S.), 1996. American Psychiatric Press, Washington DC

Fox, R.C. "Coming Out Bisexual: Identity, Behaviour and Sexual Orientation Self-Disclosure" (Doctoral Dissertation, California Institute of Integral Studies 1993) *Dissertation Abstracts International* (1995) 55 (12): 5565B

Golden, C. "Diversity and Variability in Women's Sexual Identities" in *Lesbian Psychologies Collective*, 1987 University of Illinois Press, Urbana, IL, pp. 18–34

Laumann, Edward O. *et al*. *The Social Organization of Sexuality: Sexual Practices in the United States*, 1994 University of Chicago Press, Chicago, IL

Matteson, D.R. "The Heterosexually Married Gay and Lesbian Parent" in *Gay and Lesbian Parents* (ed.) Bozett, F.W., 1987 Praeger, New York, pp. 138–161

Pillard, Richard and Weinrich, James. "Evidence of Familial Nature of Male Homosexuality" *Archives of General Psychiatry* (1986) 43: 808–812

Rust, P.C. "The Politics of Sexual Identity: Sexual Attraction and Behaviour Among Lesbian and Bisexual Women" *Social Problems* (1992) 39: 366–386

Rust, P.C. "Coming Out in the Age of Social Constructionism: Sexual Identity Formation Among Lesbian and Bisexual Women" *Gender and Society* (1993) 7 (1):50–77

Weinberg, Martin; Williams, Colin and Pryor, Douglas. *Dual Attraction: Understanding Biosexuality*, 1994 Oxford University Press, Oxford and New York

Weinrich, J.D. *Human reproductive strategy. I. Environmental predictability and reproductive strategy; effects of social class and race. II. Homosexuality and non-reproduction; some evolutionary models.* Unpublished doctoral dissertation, 1976. Harvard University.

Wellings, Kaye *et al*. *Sexual Behaviour in Britain (The National Survey of Sexual Attitudes and Lifestyles)*, 1994 Penguin Books, London

GENERAL

Bem, Daryl. "Exotic Becomes Erotic: A Developmental Theory of Sexual Orientation" *Psychological Review* (1996) 103: 320–335

Diamond, Milton. "Biological Aspects of Sexual Orientation and Identity" in *The Psycho-

logy of Sexual Orientation, Behaviour and Identity, 1995 (ed.) Diamant, Louis and McAnulty, Richard D. Greenwood Press, Westport, CT and London
Pronger, Brian. *The Arena of Masculinity*, 1990. Gay Men's Press, London
Wellings, Kaye, Field, Julia, Johnson, Anne M. and Wordsworth, Jane. *Sexual Behaviour in Britain: The National Survey of Sexual Attitudes and Lifestyles*, 1994. Penguin Books, London
Laumann, Edward O.; Gagnon, John H.; Michael, Robert T. and Michaels, Stuart. *The Social Organisation of Sexuality: Sexual Practices in the United States*, 1994. University of Chicago Press, Chicago, IL

HOMOSEXUALITY

Adkins-Regan, Elizabeth and Ascenzi, M. "Social and Sexual Behaviour of Male and Female Zebra Finches Treated With Oestradiol During the Nesting Period", *Animal Behaviour* (1987) 35: 1100–1112
Allen, David J. and Oleson, Terry. "Shame and Internalised Homophobia in Gay Men" *Journal of Homosexuality* (1999) 37 (3)
Bagemihl, Bruce. *Biological Exuberance: Animal Homosexuality and Natural Diversity*, 1999. Profile Books Ltd, London
Bailey, J. Michael and Pillard, Richard. "A Genetic Study of Male Sexual Orientation", *Archives of General Psychiatry* (1991) 48: 1089–1096
Bailey, J. Michael, Pillard, Richard and Agyei, Yvonne. "Heritable Factors Influence Sexual Orientation in Women", *Archives of General Psychiatry* (1993) 50: 217–223
Bailey, J. Michael *et al.* "A Family History of Male Sexual Orientation Using Three Independent Samples" *Journal of Personality and Social Psychology* (forthcoming)
Bahr, J.M. and Weeks, G.R. "Sexual Functioning in a Nonclinical Sample of Male Couples" *American Journal of Family Therapy* (1989) 17 (2), 110–127
Baum, M.J. *et al.* "Prenatal and Neonatal Testosterone Exposure Interact to Affect the Differentiation of Sexual Behaviour and Partner Preference in Female Ferrets", *Behavioural Neuroscience* (1990) 104: 183–198
Bawer, Bruce. *A Place at the Table: The Gay Individual in American Society*, 1993. Poseidon, New York
Beatty, R. "Alcoholism and Adult Gay Male Populations of Pennsylvania" Master's Thesis, 1983 Pennsylvania State University, University Park, PA
Behrendt, Andrew and George, Kenneth D. "Sex Therapy for Gay and Bisexual Men" in

The Psychology of Sexual Orientation, Behaviour and Identity, 1995 (ed.) Diamant, Louis and McAnulty, Richard D. Greenwood Press, Westport, CT and London

Bell, A.P. *et al*. *Sexual Preference: Its Development in Men and Women*, 1981 Indiana University Press, Bloomington, IN

Bell, A.P. and Weinberg, M.S. *Homosexualities: A Study of Diversity Among Men and Women*, 1978 Simon and Schuster, New York

Bieber, Irving *et al*. *Homosexuality: A Psychoanalytic Study*, 1962. Basic Books, New York

Bieber, Irving *et al*. *Male Homosexuality*, 1963. Basic Books, New York

Brown, Daniel G. "Homosexuality and Family Dynamics" *Bulletin, Meninger Clinic* 27 (1963): 227–32

Burr, Chandler. *A Separate Creation: The Search for the Biological Origins of Sexual Orientation*, 1996. Hyperion, New York

Buss, David. *The Evolution of Desire: Strategies of Mating*, 1994. Basic Books, New York

Cabaj, R.P. "Substance Abuse in Gay and Lesbian Community" in *Substance Abuse: A Comprehensive Textbook*, 1992 2nd Ed. (eds.) Lowenson, J.H., Ruiz, P. and Millman, R.B. Williams and Wilkins, Baltimore, MD

Cabaj, Robert P., and Stein, Terry S. (eds.) *Textbook of Homosexuality and Mental Health*, 1996. American Psychiatric Press, Washington, DC

Clinard, Marshall B. *Sociology of Deviant Behaviour*, 1974. Holt, Rinehart, London

Coates, S. and Zucker, K. "Gender Identity Disorder in Children" in *Clinical Assessment of Children: A Biopsychosocial Approach* (eds. J. Kestenbaum and D.T. Williams), 1988 New York University Press, New York

Coleman, Eli and Rosser, B.R. Simon "Gay and Bisexual Male Sexuality" in *Textbook of Homosexuality and Mental Health* (eds.) Cabaj, Robert P. and Stein, Terry S.), 1996. American Psychiatric Press, Washington DC

Corrigan, Carol. *In a Different Voice*, 1982 Harvard University Press, Cambridge, MA

Dardick, L. and Grady, D. "Openness Between Gay Persons and Health Professionals" *Annals of Internal Medicine* (1980) 93: 115–119

D'Augelli, A.R. and Hershberger, S.L. "Lesbian, Gay and Bisexual Youth in Community Settings: Personal Challenges and Mental Health Problems" *American Journal of Community Psychology* (1993) 21: 421–448

Deniston, K. (ed.) "Alcohol Awareness" in *Our Voice* Vol. 4: No. 1 March 1989, p.1

DeSlefano, G. "Gay Drug Abuse" *The Advocate*, 449, 24 June, 1986, pp. 42–47

Diamant, Louis, and McAnulty, Richard D. (eds.) *The Psychology of Sexual Orientation, Behaviour and Identity*, 1995. Greenwood Press, Westport, CT and London

Diamond D.L. and Wilsnack, S.C. "Alcohol Abuse Among Lesbians: A Descriptive Study" *Journal of Homosexuality* (1978) 4 (2): 123–142

Diamond, Milton see under "General"
Donnellan, Craig (ed.) *Homosexuality*, Vol. 23 issues 1998. Independence, Cambridge.
Dörner, Günter. *Hormones and Brain Differentiation*, 1976. Elsevier, Oxford
Dörner, G., Rohde, W., Stahl, F. *et al.* " Neuroendocrine Predisposition for Homosexuality in Men", *Archives of Sexual Behaviour*, 4(1) January 1975: 1–8.
Engel, George L. *Psychological Development in Health and Disease*, 1962 W.B. Saunders Company, Philadelphia
Evans, Ray B. "Childhood Parental Relationships of Homosexual Men", *Journal of Consulting and Clinical Psychology* 33 (1969): 129–35.
Ferveur, Jean-François *et al.* "Genetic Feminisation of Brain Structures and Changed Sexual Orientation in Male Drosophila", *Science* (1995) 267: 902–905
Fifield, L. *On My Way to Nowhere: Alienated, Isolated and Drunk*, 1975 Gay Community Services Center and Department of Health Sciences, Los Angeles, CA
Finnegan, D.G. and McNally, E.B. *Dual Identities: Counselling Chemically Dependant Gay Men and Lesbians*, 1987 Hazelden, Center City, MN
Flavin, D.K., Franklin, J.E., and Frances, R.J. "The Acquired Immune Deficiency Syndrome (AIDS) and Suicidal Behaviour in Alcohol-dependent Homosexual Men" *American Journal of Psychiatry* (1986) 143: 1440–1442
Friedman, Richard C. *Male Homosexuality: A Contemporary Psychoanalytic Perspective*, 1988 Yale University Press, New Haven, CT, and London
Gagnon, John H. and Simon, William (eds) *Sexual Deviance*, 1967. Harper & Row, New York
Gibson, P. "Gay Male and Lesbian Youth Suicide" in ADAMHA Report of the Secretary's Task Force on Youth Suicide, Vol. 3 (DHHS Publ. No. ADM-89-1623) 1989 US Government Printing Office, Washington, DC (pp. 110–142)
Green, Richard. *Sexual Identity Conflict in Children*, 1974. Basic Books, New York
Green, Richard. "One-hundred Ten Feminine and Masculine Boys: Behavioral Contrasts and Demographic Similarities", *Archives of Sexual Behavior* 5 (1976): 425–46
Green, Richard. "Childhood Cross-Gender Behavior and Subsequent Sexual Preference", *American Journal of Psychiatry* 136 (1979): 106–8
Green, Richard. The "Sissy Boy Syndrome" and the Development of Homosexuality, 1987. Yale University Press, New Haven
Green, Richard *et al*. "Specific cross-gender behaviors in boyhood and later homosexual orientation" *British Journal of Psychiatry* (1986)
Hamer, Dean H. and Copeland, Peter. *Living With Our Genes – Why They Matter More Than You Think*, 1998. Doubleday, New York
Hamer, Dean and Copeland, Peter. *The Science of Desire: The Search for the Gay Gene and the Biology of Behaviour*, 1994. Simon and Schuster, New York
Hamer, Dean *et al.* "A Linkage Between DNA Markers on the X-Chromosome and Male

Sexual Orientation", *Science* (1993) 261: 321–327

Harry, Joseph. *Gay Children Grown Up: Gender Culture and Gender Deviance*, 1982. Praeger, New York

Herdt, Gilbert and Boxer, Andrew. *Children of Horizons*, 1993 Beacon Press, Boston, MA

Hu, Stella *et al.* "Linkage Between Sexual Orientation and Chromosome Xq28 in Males But Not in Females", *Nature Genetics* (1995) 11: 248–256

Isay, R. *Being Homosexual: Gay Men and Their Development*, 1989 Avon Press, New York

Kallman, F.J. "Twin and Sibship Study of Overt Male Homosexuality" *American Journal of Human Genetics* (1952a) 4: 136–146

Kallman, F.J. "Comparative Twin Study on the Genetic Aspects of Male Homosexuality" *Journal of Nervous and Mental Disease* (1952b) 115: 283–298

Kallman, F.J. "Genetic Aspects of Sex Determination and Sexual Maturation Potentials in Man" in *Determinants of Human Sexual Behaviour* (pp. 5–18) (ed. G. Winokur), 1963 Charles C. Thomas, Springfield, IL

Kinsey, Alfred C., Pomeroy, Wardell B. and Martin, Clyde E. *Sexual Behavior in the Human Male*, 1948. W. B. Saunders Company, Philadelphia

Kleeman, James A. "The Establishment of Core Gender Identity in Normal Girls", *Archive of Sexual Behavior* 1 (1971): 103–29

Lebovitz, Phil S. "Feminine Behavior in Boys: Aspects of Its Outcome" *American Journal of Psychiatry* 128 (1972): 103–9

LeVay, Simon. "A Difference in Hypothalamic Structure Between Heterosexual and Homosexual Men", *Science* 253: 1034–1037

LeVay, Simon. *Queer Science: The Use and Abuse of Research into Homosexuality*, 1996. MIT Press, Cambridge, MA

LeVay, Simon and Hamer, Dean. "Evidence for a Biological Influence in Male Homosexuality" *Scientific American* (1994) 270 (May): 44–49

Lewis, C.E., Saghir, M.T. and Robins, E. "Drinking Patterns in Homosexual and Heterosexual Women" *Journal of Clinical Psychiatry* (1982) 43: 277–279

Lewis, C.W. et al "Drinking Patterns in Homosexual and Heterosexual Women" *Journal of Clinical Psychiatry* (1982) 43, 277–279

Lohrenz, L.J. *et al.* "Alcohol Problems in Several Midwestern Homosexual Communities" *Journal of Studies on Alcohol* (1978) 39 (11): 1959–1963

McDonald, Helen B. and Steinhorn, Audrey I. *Understanding Homosexuality*, 1993. Crossroad, New York

McKirman, D. and Peterson, P.L. "Alcohol and Drug Abuse Among Homosexual Men and Women: Epidemiology and Population Characteristics" *Addictive Behaviours* (1989) 14: 545–553

McKnight, Jim. *Straight Science: Homosexuality, Evolution and Adaptation*, 1997. Routledge, New York

Manners, Paul (producer). *Sex and the Single Gene?* (television) Human Biology and Health, 1997. British Broadcasting Corporation for the Open University

Martin, A.D. and Hetrick, E.S. "The Stigmatisation of the Gay and Lesbian Adolescent" *Journal of Homosexuality* (1988) 15: 163–184

Miller, Paul R. "The Effeminate Passive Obligatory Homosexual", *American Medical Association Archives of Neurological Psychiatry* 80 (1958) 612–18

Money, John and Russo, A. J. "Homosexual Outcome of Discordant Gender Identity/Role in Childhood: Longitudinal Follow-up", *Journal of Pediatric Psychology* 4 (1979) 29–41

Money, John and Tucker, Patricia. *Sexual Signatures,* 1975. Little, Brown, Boston

Mosbacher, D. "Lesbian Alcohol and Substance Abuse" *Psychiatric Annals* (1988) 18 (1): 47–50

Nadler, Ronald. "Homosexual Behaviour in Non-human Primates" in *Homosexuality/Heterosexuality: Concepts of Sexual Orientation*, 1990 (ed.) McWhirter D.P., Sanders, S.A. and Reinisch, J.M. Oxford University Press, New York

O'Connor, P. J. "Ætiological Factors in Homosexuality as seen in R.A.F. Psychiatric Practice", *British Journal of Psychiatry* 110 (1964): 381–91

Paluszny, Maria *et al.* "Gender Identity and Its Measurement in Children", *Comprehensive Psychiatry* 14 (1973): 281–90

Pattatucci, Angela and Hamer, Dean. "Development and Familiality of Sexual Orientation in Females", *Behaviour Genetics* (1995) 24: 407–420

Pauly, I.B. and Goldstein, S. "Physicians' Attitudes in Treating Homosexuals" *Medical Aspects of Human Sexuality* (1970) 4: 26–45

Pillard, R.C. "Sexual Orientation and Mental Disorder" *Psychiatric Annals* (1988) 18 (1): 52–56

Pillard, Richard and Weinrich, James. "Evidence of Familial Nature of Male Homosexuality" *Archives of General Psychiatry* (1986) 43: 808–812

Pillard, Richard. "The Kinsey Scale: Is It Familial?" in *Homoseuxality/Heterosexuality: Concepts of Sexual Orientation,* 1990 (eds.) McWhirter, D. P., Saunders, S. A., Reinisch, J.M. Oxford University Press, Oxford and New York

Pillard, Richard and Weinrich, James "Evidence of Familial Nature of Male Homosexuality" *Archives of General Psychiatry* (1986) 43: 808–812

Posner, Richard. *Sex and Reason,* 1992. Harvard University Press, Cambridge, MA

Remafedi, G. "Adolescent Homosexuality: Psychosocial and Medical Implications" *Pediatrics* (1987a) 79: 331–337

Remafedi, G. "Male Homosexuls: The Adolescent's Perspective" *Pediatrics* (1987b) 326–330

Remafedi, G., Garrow, J.A. and Deisher, R.W. "Risk Factors for Attempted Suicide in Gay and Bisexual Youth" *Pediatrics* (1991) 87: 869–875

Rice, George *et al.* "Male Homosexuality: Absence of Linkage to Microsatellite Markers at xq28" *Science* (1999) 5: 631–660

Roesler, T. and Deisher, R. "Youthful Male Homosexuality" *Journal of the American Medical Association* (1972) 219: 1018–1023

Ross, M.W. "A Taxonomy of Global Behaviour" in *Bisexuality and HIV/AIDS: A Global Perspective*, 1991 (ed.) Tielman, R.A.P., Carballo, M., Hendriks, A.C. Prometheus Books, Buffalo, NY

Rosser, B.R.S. "Male Homosexuality in Minnesota: A Psychosexual Study of Safer Sexual Behaviour, Affect and Cognitions of Man-to-Man" Report to the Minnesota Department of Health, 1994

Ruse, Michael. *Homosexuality: A Philosophical Enquiry*, 1988. Blackwell, New York

Stein, Edward. *The Mismeasure of Desire*, 1999. Oxford University Press, Oxford.

Saghir, Marcel T. and Robins, Eli. *Male and Female Homosexuality*, 1973. Williams and Wilkins, Baltimore, MD

Saghir, M.T. *et al*. "Homosexuality: IV Psychiatric Disorders and Disability in the Male Homosexual" *Journal of Psychiatry* (1970) 126, 1079–1086

Schneider, S.G., Farberow, N.L. and Kruks, G.N. "Suicidal Behaviour in Adolescent and Young Adult Gay Men" *Suicide Life-threatening Behaviour* (1989) 19: 381–394

Skinner, William F. and Otis, Melanie D. "Drug and Alcohol Use Among Lesbian and Gay People in a Southern United States Sample: Epidemiological, Comparative and Methodological Findings from the Trilogy Project" *Journal of Homosexuality* (1996) 30 (3)

Socarides, Charles W. *Homosexuality*, 1978 Jason Aronson, New York

Stall, R. and Wiley, J. "A Comparison of Alcohol and Drug Use Patterns of Homosexual and Hetersexual Men: the San Francisco Men's Health Study *Drug and Alcohol Dependence* (1988) 22: 63–73

Stephan, Walter G. "Parental Relationships and Early Social Experiences of Activist Male Homosexuals and Male Heterosexuals" *Journal of Abnormal Psychology* 82 (1973) 506–13

Stoller, Robert. *Sex and Gender*, 1968. J. Aronson, New York

Stonewall. *Public Opinion on Homosexuality*, 2001. Stonewall Lobby Group, London

Sullivan, Andrew. *Virtually Normal: An Argument About Homosexuality*, 1995. Knopf, New York

Thio, Alex. *Deviant Behaviour*, 1978. Houghton Mifflin, Boston

Thompson, Norman L. *et al*. "Parent-child Relationships and Sexual Identity in Male and Female Homosexuals and Heterosexuals", *Journal of Consulting and Clinical Psychology* 41 (1973): 12–27

Thompson, Spencer K. *et al*. "Gender Labels and Early Sex Role Development" *Child Development* 46 (1975): 339–47

Tripp, C. A. *The Homosexual Matrix*, 1987. Meridian, New York

Vasey, Paul. "Homosexual Behaviour in Primates: A Review of Evidence and Theory", *International Journal of Primatology* (1995) 16: 173–204

Weinberg, M. and Williams, C. *Male Homosexuals: Their Problems and Adaptations*, 1974 Oxford University Press, Oxford and New York

West, D. J. "Parental Relationship in Male Homosexuality", *International Journal of Social Psychiatry* 5 (1959): 85–97

Whitam, Frederick L. "Childhood Indicators of Male Homosexuality", *Sexual Behavior* 6 (1977): 89–96

Whitam, Frederick L. "Childhood Predictors of Adult Homosexuality", *Journal of Sex Education and Therapy* 6 (1980) 11–16

Whitam, Frederick L. and Mathy, Robin M. R. *Male Homosexuality in Four Societies*, 1986. Praeger Publishers, New York

Zuger, Bernard. "Effeminate Behavior Present in Boys From Early Childhood: I The Clinical Syndrome and Follow-up Studies" *Journal of Pediatrics* 69 (1966): 1098–107

Zuger, Bernard. "The Role of Familial Factors in Persistant Effeminate Behavior in Boys", *American Journal of Psychiatry* 126 (1970): 1167–70

Zuger, Bernard. "Effeminate Behavior Present in Boys from Childhood: Ten Additional Years of Follow-up" *Comprehensive Psychiatry* 19 (1978): 363–69

PSYCHOLOGY

Berne, Eric, M.D. *Games People Play*, 1968. Penguin Books, London

Berne, Eric, M.D. *What Do You Say After You Say Hello?*, 1981. Corgi Books, London

Birch, Cathy. *Asserting Your Self*, 1999. How To Books, Oxford

Bradshaw, John. *Healing the Shame That Binds You*, 1988. Health Communications Inc., Deerfield Beach, FL

Brearley, Gill and Birchley, Peter. *Introducing Counselling Skills and Techniques*, 1986. Faber & Faber, London

Fensterheim, Herbert, and Baer, Jean *Don't Say "Yes" When You Want to Say "No"*, 1984. Futura Publications, London

Foulkes, S. H. and Anthony, E. J. *Group Psychotherapy: The Psychoanalytic Approach*, 1965. Pelican, Harmondsworth, Middx.

Freud, Sigmund. *The Psychopathology of Everyday Life*, 1980. Pelican Books, Harmondsworth, Middx.

Freud, Sigmund. *Jokes and their Relation to the Unconscious*, 1978. Pelican Books, Harmondsworth, Middx.

Kermani, Kai S. *Autogenic Training: The Effective Way to Conquer Stress*, 1992. Thorsons, London
Malan, David H. *Individual Psychotherapy and the Science of Psychodynamics*, 1979. Butterworth-Heinemann Ltd, Oxford
Malan, David. *Anorexia, Murder and Suicide*, 1997. Butterworth-Heinemann Ltd, Oxford
Münsterberg, Hugo. *Psychology and Crime*, 1909. T.F. Unwin, London
Rushforth, Winifred. *Something Is Happening*, 1983. Gateway Books, London
Russell, W. M. S. and Russell, Claire. *Human Behaviour*, 1961. André Deutsch, London

SPORTS

Black, Donald. *Wrestling for Gay Guys*, 1995. Power Books, London
de Vries, Herbert. *Physiology of Exercise*, 1966. W.C. Brown Co., Dubuque, IO
English Basket Ball Association *Basketball* (Know the Game), 1994 A. & C. Black, London
English Hockey Association *Hockey* (Know the Game), 1998 A. & C. Black, London
English Olympic Wrestling Association *Wrestling* (Know the Game), 1979 EP Publishing Ltd, East Ardsley, Yorks.
English Volleyball Association *Volleyball* (Know the Game), 2000 A & C Black, London
Football Association *Soccer* (Know the Game), 2000 A. & C. Black, London
Gleeson, Geof *Judo* (Know the Game), 1995 A. & C. Black
Hopke, Stephen L. and Kidder, Worden. *Elementary and Junior High School Wrestling*, 1977. A. S. Barnes & Co. Inc., New York/Thomas Yoseloff Ltd, London
Jarman, Tom and Hanley, Reid. *Wrestling for Beginners*, 1983. Contemporary Books, Chicago, IL
Johnson, Dennis A. *Wrestling Drill Book*, 1991. Leisure Press, Champaign, IL
Maertz, Richard C. *Wrestling Teaching Guide*, 1973. A. S. Barnes & Co., New York /Thomas Yoseloff Ltd, London
Mitchell, David *Karate* (Know the Game), 1994 A. & C. Black, London
Muckle, David S. *Sports Injuries: a practical manual for trainers, coaches, players and schools*, 1971. Oriel Press, Newcastle-upon-Tyne
Murray, Alistair. *Modern Weight Training*, 1981. Kaye & Ward, London/A. S. Barnes & Co., New York
Mysnyk, Mark. *Wrestling Fundamentals and Techniques*, 1982. Human Kinetics Publishers, West Point, NY
Read, Dr Malcolm with Wade, Paul. *Sports Injuries: A Unique Guide to Self-diagnosis and*

Rehabilitation, 1984. Breslich & Foss, London
Rugby Football League *Rugby League* (Know the Game), 1994 A. & C. Black, London
Rugby Football Union *Rugby Union* (Know the Game), 2001 A. & C. Black, London
World Jiu Jitsu Federation *Jiu Jitsu* (Know the Game), 1995 A. & C. Black, London

INDEX

INDEX

Bold entries indicate headings in the text.
Underlined numbers indicate illustrations.

10% of gay men 5, 11, 39, 47, 52, 53, 54, 65, 66, 67, 169
10% of gay men: definition 47
10% of gay men not displayed feminine need 46, 47
10% of gay men expressing anger 11
21st birthday drag party 50, 155
80% became homosexual 46, 48
90% of gay men 4, 5, 11, 37, 38, 47, 48, 51, 52, 53, 54, 65, 66, 67, 75, 78, 79, 116, 169–170, 188
90% of gay men: definition 46–47
90% of gay men unable to express anger 11
90% of gay men displayed feminine need 46, 47
abandoned, feeling 32
accepted by all peers, need to be 133
accepted by peers, need to be 92, 129
accepted, feeling 207
accepted, need to be 24, 25
accident, no such thing as 104
accident-prone 13, 136
Accidental Knocks 174–175
acting career 58
Acting Out 32–34
acting out 33, 73, 93
actions and effects 186
Adkins-Regan, Elizabeth 81
Admiral Duncan, The 24
adolescence 23, 24, 26, 91, 92
adolescents 133
adolescents need to be accepted by peers 206
adrenalin 112, 144, 180, 182, 196, 214
ads for younger, more handsome men 113
Advocate, The 16
aggression xiii, 8, 54, 129, 138
aggression and destructive behaviour 129
aggression ended, lack of 123
aggression, lack of 61, 122
aggression, not able to be expressed 29
aggression, repressing 108
aggression, working off 186, 195
aggressive, becoming 67
aggressive, being 5
aggressive, not 11
aggressive, not wanting to be 11
aggressive, prevented from being 102, 189
aggressive, unable to be 8, 30, 146, 206
aggressiveness, developing 114
aggressiveness, testing 147
Agyei, Yvonne 80
AIDS 74, 80, 82
AIDS and Ken 105
AIDS TV campaign 28
alcohol 13, 16, 17, 26, 27, 31
Alcohol Abuse 26–29
alcohol abuse 36
alcohol and drugs, trying to avoid 28
alcohol: heavy drinkers 28
alcohol, needing 79
alcoholic 37
alcoholic drinks 28
Alcoholics Anonymous 37
alcoholism, crisis stage, 27
alcoholism: high risk 27
All or Nothing 14–15
all-or-nothing law 21
Alternate Explanations 63
Alternative Explanations 67–69
ambulance 6, 119
amphetamines 17
Amsterdam xv, 88, 215
amyl nitrite 15, 22
Anastasi, A. 5
androgens, levels of 68
Andy 18–22
Andy 18–22, 32, 35, 98, 114, 155, 179, 186, 187, 195, 196
Andy admits anger on phone 22, 191
Andy: admitted not cramp 20
Andy: arthritis 21
Andy: bisexual 20
Andy: expressing anger 35
Andy's fear of rejection 115
Andy: going to Rio 21, 22
Andy has child 115
Andy in prison 19
Andy, jealous of 19
Andy: laughing reflex 20
Andy: never showed pain 18, 114
Andy: opposites attract 18
Andy: punching upper arm 20
Andy, reasons I was jealous of 21
Andy repressing anger 19
Andy's repression 115
Andy's self-confidence 114
Andy: unexpected hard-on 20

Index **247**

Andy: what he is really like 22
anger xiii, 44, 67
anger, able to express 11, 36, 74, 125, 155, 156
anger a good emotion 9, 116
Anger and Self-assertiveness 123
Anger and Self-assertiveness 138
anger as aggression, expressing 123
anger bad for you, repressed 136
anger became buried 156
anger bottled up 35, 93, 107, 136
anger, bottling up 11, 106, 105, 138, 143
anger boundaries 156
anger, buried 9, 181, 188
anger, channelling 29, 197
anger coming out of ears 18, 28, 32
anger, curing repressed 53
anger, destructive power of 8, 35, 213
anger, difficult to express xi, 187–188
anger, effects of 12–13
anger, encouraged to express 100
anger entwined with sexual feelings 15, 18
anger evaporated 21
anger exploding 79, 107, 116
anger, expressing xiii, 8, 14, 20, 22, 51, 69, 100, 103, 106, 138, 141, 143, 144, 146, 152, 184, 187, 194
anger, expressing new-found 180
anger. expressing too much 140, 180
anger expression, enabling 188
anger-expression therapy 183
anger, express your 145
anger, feeling 187–188
anger, finding 116
anger for effect 10
anger, getting rid of 10, 196–197, 220
anger, greater the restraint, greater the 23
anger, happy not expressing 10
anger, hidden 44
anger in subconscious mind 11, 44
anger into sports, channelling 12
anger is for, what 208
anger is your fuel 165

anger just under surface 186
anger, learned to express 168
anger, learning to express 136, 154, 156
anger, level of 9–11, 12, 35, 138
anger, losing control of 9, 35
anger mounts up 10, 11
anger, need to express 11, 73
anger, not able to be expressed 29
anger not entwined with sexual feelings 22
anger, only way to get rid of 14
anger out, letting 93
anger out of mind, pushing 181, 190
anger out of proportion 32, 33
anger, pent-up 73, 184
anger, perpetual 32, 33, 79
anger, prevented expressing 38, 102, 136, 189
anger, provoking 180
anger, release of pent-up 155
anger, repressing 10, 11, 12, 13, 14, 18, 19, 21, 22, 23, 25, 28, 31, 39, 44, 54, 69, 75, 80, 83, 92, 108, 111, 119, 125, 140, 154, 184, 188, 190, 191
anger rising to surface 188
anger-rooms 140, 190, 194
anger, rousing 187
anger safely, expressing 67
anger safely, venting 140
anger, safety valve for 12
anger, saving oneself from another's 145
anger, scale of 9, 11
anger, small amount of 143
anger, steps of 9
anger, symptoms of repressed 38
anger terribly repressed 196
anger to surface, bringing 187, 188
anger, unable to express 8, 30, 52, 79, 92, 93, 100
anger, unable to feel 116, 187, 190, 191
anger uncontrollable 79
anger, uncontrollable bursts of 222
anger uncontrolled 138
anger, unexpressed 32
anger used constructively 69
anger, using 10, 136, 147, 149, 188

anger: using in a controlled way 35
anger, voicing 139
anger, ways of dealing with 197
anger, ways of expressing 190
anger, working off 186, 195
angry, aggressive, encouraged to be 100
angry and loving same person 43, 44
angry, being 150
angry, how to feel 181
angry, not feeling 188
angry, makes me 188
angry, not feeling 44
angry?, safer not to be 8
angry with parents 38, 43, 52
angry with you, I'm sorry I'm 187–188, 191
animal pack, position in 147
anxiety 13, 16, 17, 88, 90
anxiety caused by guilt 74
apathy 16, 17
Arena of Masculinity, The 36
Arm-punching 196
armour-plating 174, 175
Arousing Anger 102–103
arts and crafts, African 77
Ascenzi, M. 81
ashamed, feeling 61, 71, 92
assert themselves, able to 76
asserting yourself 138, 141, 156
asserting yourself, prevented from 189
Asserting Yourself 140–143
Asserting Your Self 141
Asserting Yourself 149
assertiveness 129
Athens 94
attacker, deterring 178–179, 180–181
attraction to professional wrestlers 109
attraction to construction workers 109
attraction to Hell's Angels 109
attraction to sportsmen etc. 109
attraction to footballers 109
attraction to labourers 109
attraction of opposites 154, 155
Attraction of Opposites 109–110
Australia 216
Auto-suggestion 211–212

248   *Escape the Gay Straitjacket*

Autogenic Training 211
Autogenic Training 139
Averill, J.R. 5
avoiding provoking situations 11, 190
baby xv, 11, 59, 68, 122, 136
baby and father 120–121, 123, 124, 127, 133
baby feels guilty 127
baby helpless 120
baby's fantasy 120–121
baby with ringlets 50, 65, 80
back pain 12
badminton 215
bad person 197
Baer, Jean 151
Bagemihl, Bruce 81
Bahr, J.M. 15
Bailey, J. Michael 62, 63, 68, 80, 81
ball commandeered by sister 128
ball-throwing skills, lacking 128
Banks, John xvi
baptism of fire 45, 106
Barcelona 29
Barometer of Bisexuality, A 82–83
Barrett, Elizabeth 32
barrister 141, 192
bar in Soho 95, 102, 106
bars 26, 28, 37, 76, 103, 152, 187
basketball 198, 215
Basketball 199–200
Baum, M.J. 81
Bawer, Bruce 81
BBC radio programme 130–132
Beatty, R. 28
behaviour, discouraging 52
Behrendt, Andrew 15
Being Bullied 7–8
Bell, Alan P. 25, 48, 127
Bellville 125
belt fight with Ken 96, 101
Bem, Daryl 82, 109
Berne, Eric xv, 67–68, 93, 94, 104, 140
Beyer, Alex xv
biceps 154–155
Bieber, Irving 46, 48, 49
Bill of Rights 149, 162
biologists 45. 62, 81, 102
Birch, Cathy xv, 141–143, 149
birth, difficult 56
bisexual youth 26

bisexuality xiii
bisexuality, hypothesis of 110
bisexuality, types of 82
Bisexuality and HIV/AIDS 82
Bisexuality Revisited 110
bisexuals 39, 82, 83, 110, 208
bitchiness 14
Bitching 29
bitching 79, 113, 136
blood glucose rises 12
blood pressure increases 13
blood pressure, normalising 162
Blumstein, P.W. 82
BOB 139, 229
bodies, developing 114
body language 189
body is a machine 165
Body Opponent Bag 139, 229
body-boxing 102, 136, 181, 188, 196
Body-boxing 179–184, 195–196, 201
body-contact sports xii, xiii, xiv, 25, 53, 54, 56, 169, 170, 174, 184, 197–198
Body-contact Sports 186–189
body-contact sports, avoiding 5, 108
body-contact sports, kept from 52
body-contact sports, now playing 207
body-contact sports valued by role model 129
body-punching, with Andy 19, 20
bodybuilding 71, 135, 156, 159,162
bombing of gay pub/bar 24
bondage fetish 14
bondage 17, 23, 70, 74, 108, 111
Bondage Fetish 22–23
boredom, apathy 16, 17
boss 187, 192, 197
bowling (tenpin) 215
Boxer, Andrew 25
boxercise 172
boxing 12, 52, 62, 66, 67, 95–106, 119, 156, 174, 175, 181, 186, 194, 195, 197, 198
Boxing 205
boxing-gloves 2, 8, 94, 96, 195, 201
boxing on TV 176
boxing, professional 177

boxing skills 172
boxing, will not enjoy 188
boxing with schoolmate 8
boy, polite, honest, well-behaved 168
boy with ringlets 50, 65, 80
boys too rough, other 136
Brandhorst, Hennie xv
Brazil 46
Brighton 95
British School of Osteopathy 173
British Social Attitudes xii
Brixton 30
Brown, Daniel G. 49
Browning, Robert 32
Bryant, Anita 62
Building Muscle 159–163
bullied, being 8, 79
bullied by schoolmates 7, 166
bullies 123
burning candles 18, 74
Burr, Chandler 63
Buss, David 81
butterflies in stomach 112, 144, 182, 214
Butterworth-Heinemann xv, 44
butyl nitrite 15
Cabaj, Robert 28, 31, 37
California 68
campaign of hate and persecution
Can You Express Your Anger? 100
Cannon, Walter B. 214
Cape Town station 125–126
Cape Town 33, 91, 125, 132, 148
cardio-vascular system 165
cat, ways of skinning a 187
cathartic stimulus 103
cats 32
Central YMCA 61
Century Incorporated xv
change in British law xii, 27, 29–30
charm, turn on 208
chemically dependent 27
Chicago 56
child xv, 124, 128
child and father 128
child kept from peers 127
childhood 92, 174
children 23, 26, 43, 48, 68, 133
children in cellar 9, 13, 32
Children of Horizons 25

Index **249**

children, troublesome 9, 13
children will do anything to be loved
    43, 75, 108
children's emotions 31
Chips 91–92
Christ 30
Christian religion 24
chromosome 63
church-going diminished 24
Cinderella 93
circuit-training 172
Circuit-training 212
Classic Guilt Complex, The 53
Classic Guilt Complex, The 88–90
clean, purged etc., feeling 106, 136
clinch 177
club, forming a 195
clumsy and maladroit 128
co-operative network 147
co-ordination 171
coach, not trusting 164
Coates, S. 129
cocaine 16, 17, 105
coercion 81
cold soup 140
Coleman, Eli 15
come out, cannot 27
come out, not allowed to 28
coming out xv, 24, 25, 74, 82
coming out to straight sportsmen 67
common interest 152, 156, 166
communication between both parties 144
companion, life 75
companion, sexually-fulfilling 76
compete, being allowed to 113
compete, need to 113
compete, unable to 30, 79, 108, 112, 113, 130
competing, prevented from 70, 189
competitive games 147
competitive pyramid 147
competitive relationship 164
compulsive 13
compulsive mistakes on piano 59, 70, 73, 134
Conclusion 37–39
confidence 168
conflict with other men 11, 120, 124, 138
confrontation with workmate 6, 119
congenital heart defects 56

conscious mind 90, 127, 217, 220
conserving energy 189
contract killer 95
control, losing 190, 213
control of lives, not in 169
control of rage, losing 140
control people, able to 76
controlling anger 138
conversation, starting a 151, 152
Copeland, Peter 81
Copeland, David 24
court case 6, 119, 192
cowboys 175, 195
cross-dressed by parents 50
cross-dressed, wrestling friend 65–66
Cross-dressing 46–47
cross-dressing 47, 48, 65
cross-dressing as children 47–48, 50
cross-dressing, persistent 46, 48
cross-gender behaviour 47, 48, 65
cross-gender behaviour, no 65, 66, 67
Crushing Your Father 57–58
Crushing Your Mother 58–59
crutch 132
cushion 139
Cushion 193
cycling 159, 215
D'Augelli, A.R. 26
Dalai Lama 148
dancing, ballroom/old-time 149
Dardick, L. 15
daughter, desire for 75
daughter, longed-for 51, 52, 54, 57, 65, 67, 78, 88, 122, 154, 155, 156
daughter, not longed-for 66
daughter: passive-aggressive behaviour 34
daughter, playing role of 76
daughters 66
daughters wanted by parents 49, 51–52
Dave 166
dead, wish and someone drops 126
Deisher, T. 25
denial xiv
Denmark 27
Dentemaro, Christine 13, 17, 34
Depression 31–32

depression, not 71
depression: bereavement 31
depression 13, 17, 31, 33, 70, 79, 134, 145
derogatory remarks 29
DeSlefano, G. 16
despised, feeling 111
destructive, being 190
Destructive Power of Anger, The 35
detached retina 96
detachment, feelings of 17
deterring attacker 178–179, 180–181
Diamant, Louis 38
Diamond, Milton 81
Diamond, D.L. 28
Digging Deeper 79
directories of gay wrestlers 170
directory of body-boxers 182
discipline standards 81
Discoveries Through Wrestling 51–53
discrimination against homosexuals xii
dishes, plate broken, doing 128
diving 215
DNA 51, 63
Does He Take Sugar? 130–131
dog 32, 213
dogs put down 91
Dominant Mothers 135–136
domination 92
Don't Say "Yes" When You Want to Say "No" 151
Dörner, Günter 51, 64, 65, 66, 67, 69, 80, 81
Dörner's work discounted 65
drawing 138, 190
Dreams 212–213
dreams 222
drug abuse 13, 14, 15, 28, 79
drug-dealer 95
drugs 16, 18, 27, 133
drugs and Ken 105
Drury Lane 57
easy come, easy go 197
Ecstasy 17
Eddy, Mary Baker 7
effeminate adult men 47
effeminate homosexuals 82
electricity switched off 32

250 *Escape the Gay Straitjacket*

emerging research programme 81
emotions, releasing 190
emotions, repressing 14, 109
emptiness, inner 17
Ending Your Fear of Violence 119–121
Engel, George 74, 124–125
engine, body an 165, 167
England, return to 91
England 132, 216
equal rights 23
erection in swimming trunks 2
Escaping Low Self-esteem 133–135
Escaping the Gay Straitjacket 79
Evans, Ray B. 48, 49
evolutionary model 81
ex-convicts 93, 95, 106
exercise equipment, sharing 162
exercises 161
exercises, warm-up 171–172
exercises, schedule of 161–162
exotic becomes erotic 109
explode, liable to 107
exploited etc., being 9, 30, 79
exploited etc., not being 36, 76
exploited, preventing being 116
Expressing and Repressing Anger 143–145
Expressing Anger Safely 190–206
expressing how you feel 144
fag 23, 146
failures, personal 134
fairy story, favourite 93–94
fall, learning to 169
family 27, 68, 192
fancy dress, wearing 36, 154
fantasy 52, 108, 122, 135, 175, 208, 222
Fantasy 213
fantasy exacerbated 129
fantasy of child 127
fantasy of violence 124
fantasy, reinforcing 164
fart 146
father 43, 57, 91, 132, 166
father, absent or distant 62
father a giant 120
father and sister playing ball 128
father, becoming your own 133
father catatonic 58
father, crushed 58

father, crushing my 91, 134
father feeling unwanted 135
father feels ignored 124
father feels neglected 124, 125
father figure 19
father had died 72
father jealous and angry 124–125
father, jealous conflict with 122
father, jealous relationship with 207
father loses interest 49, 124
fathers 46, 49, 50, 108, 160
fathers, absent 49, 50, 90, 108, 124
fathers, bad relationships with 50
father's brain haemorrhage 126
father's disappointment 122
father's friend taken my place 71
father's friend trapped me 4, 71, 72
fathers, good 184
fathers, good relationships with 49
fathers, hostile 49
fathers, jealous, competitive 163
fathers not sporting 57
father's retaliation 120
fathers showed loss of interest 49
Fear of Rejection 115–116
Fear of Violence 61
fear of violence xi, 7, 38, 61, 120, 121, 122, 124, 128, 129, 135, 136, 186, 197
fear of violence description 6–7
fear of violence ended 123–124
Feeling Angry 116
Feeling Oppressed 29–31
Feeling Purged 106
Feeling Threatened 111–112
feinting 168
feminine attributes 147
Fensterheim, Herbert 151
Ferveur, Jean-François 81
field hockey 204
Fifield, L. 27, 28
fight, avoiding getting into a 129
fight!, I'll give you a 95
fight or flight 180
Fight or Flight 101–102, 213–214
fighting 95–106, 156
fights, needle 102
figure skating 215
Finding Mr Right 154–156
Finnegan, D.G. 28
fist, making a 139–140 <u>139</u>
Five-a-side Football 199

flagellation 17, 70, 111
Flavin, D.K. 74
flood-gates opened 35, 138, 143
foetus 64, 65, 68
football 7, 10, 12, 52, 66, 67, 182, 215
football/soccer 92, 147, 174
Football/Soccer 199
football at school 5
football club 55
Football Fan, The 55
football fan 152
football fisticuffs 12
football, five-a-side 198
football, peers playing 87
football, prevented from playing 56
football/soccer skills, learning 184
force to be reckoned with 189
forgetful 136
forgetting appointments/dates 13
forward roll <u>170–171</u>, 172
Fox, R.C. 82
fractured skull 6, 119
France 216
Frances, R.J. 74
Franklin, J.E. 74
freestyle wrestling 168–169
Freestyle Wrestling 200
Freud, Sigmund 20, 44, 124, 221
Friedman, Richard C. 23, 24, 26, 38, 74, 127, 129
friend invited to theatre 78
friend needing sex often 111
friend, pressuring 78
friend sickly as child 166
friend who cut face with razor blade 90
friend who sold me his motorbike 153
friend with gonorrhoea 74
friend wrestling champion 166
friends 192, 197
frightened 106
frightened of aggression 8
frightened by anger 31
frightened of body-contact sports 38, 206
frightened of confrontation 8
frightened of expressing anger 33, 35, 120, 189
frightened of expressing anger, not 206

Index **251**

frightened of other men, no longer 159
frightened of riding motorbike 164
frightened of straight men 189
frustration, feeling of 14
Fuller Mental Health Centre 62
Further Research 79–81
fuss, don't want to make a 140–141
Games People Play xv, 68
Gates, G.S. 5
Gay Adolescence 23–26
gay disco 159
gay façade 14, 190, 191
Gay Games 198, 199, 200, 203
Gay Games 214–216
Gay Games website 216
Gay Games, woman wrestler 88
Gay Gene, The 51
Gay Gene, The 62–63
gay gene 51, 63, 69, 80
Gay Liberation xii
Gay Men and Straight Men 59–60
gay men and straight men 59, 60, 63, 80
gay men avoid sports 54
gay men clumsy and maladroit 128
gay men not aggressive 5
gay men playing sports xiii, 12
gay men unable to reach orgasm 16
gay men's brains not correctly wired 128
gay movement 30
Gay Politics Rears Its Head 61–62
Gay Pride xiii, 79
gay rights 62, 69, 81
gay scene 26, 29, 36, 71, 72, 73, 108, 133, 145
gay scene abhorred 130
gay teachers 62
gay theorem xii
Gay Times 24
gay wrestlers 54
gay wrestling club 51, 170
Gay Wrestling Clubs 54
Gay Wrestling Group 49, 51, 54, 61, 89, 106, 150
gay youth study 26
gay-bashing 24
General Social Survey xii
genetic factor 68

genetic linkage 81
George, Kenneth 15
get where the action is 55, 152
getting back 33
getting hit painful 188
getting phone number and address 145
getting pleasure from punching 188
getting punished more 102
Getting Rid of Anger 11–14
Gibson, P. 25
Gilligan, Carol 147
girls, taken to play with 129
glass-eye 95
God xii
Golden, C. 82
Goldstein, S. 15
golf 215
gonorrhoea 28, 74
good about yourself, feeling 146
Grady, D. 15
Graham 131–132
Grapevine, The 56
Green, Richard xv, 48, 49, 50, 51, 55, 57, 59, 63, 65
Griffith, Bobbie 25
Griffith, Mary 25
ground needs to be prepared xiv
Guatemala 46
guilt 13, 17, 44, 74, 91, 93, 99, 101, 104, 111, 119, 122, 123, 126, 134, 139
guilt complex 88–90
guilty, feeling 74, 104, 111, 122, 127, 135
gym 111, 119, 139, 154, 156, 160, 162, 172, 190, 194
gym, gay men going to xiii, 36
gym, jealous boyfriend in 92–93
gym machines 161
gym, training in 166
gym visit 160–161
gym-master at school 56, 128
Hamer, Dean 62, 63, 67, 80, 81
hand-butt to nose 178–179, 180–181
handcuffs 18
handling a threatening situation 168
Harry, Joseph 48
Harvard University 218
head-butt 175, 177–178, 177–178
headaches 12

healthy mind in healthy body 12, 197
heart and blood vessels 165
heart disease 13, 136
heart strength, developing 167
helpless 72, 79, 106, 113, 141, 168
helpless, feeling 111
helplessness 7, 17, 71
helplessness, feeling of 14
helplessness, less 74
Henman, Tim 173
Herdt, Gilbert 25
heroin 16
Herschberger, S.L. 26
heterosexual couples 18
heterosexual, expected to be 23
heterosexual dancing 149
heterosexual, pretending to be 23
heterosexual relationship 109
heterosexual sexual climax 92
heterosexuality 82
heterosexuals 109
Hetrick, E.S. 25
hidden gay population 28
high blood pressure 71, 95, 162, 181, 186
HIV 28, 82, 174
hockey 174, 198
Hockey, Ice Hockey, Lacrosse 204–205
holding back 6, 61
Homdok-LAA xv
homophobia 24, 25, 27
homophobia, negative 24
homophobic physicians 15
homophobic families 36
homophobic society 74
homophobic doctors 15
Homosexuality 111
homosexuality abhorrent 23–24, 26
homosexuality acceptable xii, 24
homosexuality, cure for 74–75
homosexuality in animals 81
homosexuality runs in families 67, 80
homosexuality wrong xii, 24
homosexuals, mentally-ill 46
hook 176, 177, 178
hormones, imbalance of 65, 66, 80, 81
hospital 119
hospitalised in early life 55

Hove 21
How To Books 142
How to Say "No" 148–150
Hu, Stella 81
Human Behaviour 219
Human Rights Campaign 63
humiliated, feeling 57, 71, 111, 146–147
humiliated, stop being 73
humiliation 7, 17, 24, 61, 70, 72, 73, 74, 75, 92, 93, 105, 108, 111, 175
humiliation mentioned, times 134
humiliation, public 25
humiliation, punished for 75
humiliation vanishes 73, 74
humour, basis of 20
hurt, feeling 69, 146
hustler 16
hypothalamus 64, 66, 67, 109, 110
hypothalamus masculinised 68
hypothalamuses, comparison of 80
hypothesis 110
I Love Andy, Andy Loves Me 114–115
ice hockey 198, 204, 215
idol, your 166, 173, 189, 190
If People Knew What I Am Really Like 90
if people knew what I am really like 108, 116, 127, 133, 135
illness in early life 55, 124, 127
I'm asking for it! 102, 182
imbalance due to illness 81
immune system, suppressing 15
impostor 154
impotence 14, 15, 16, 22, 136
Impotence and Drug Abuse 15–18
In a Different Voice 147
inadequate, feeling 24, 92, 111
Indian Deathlock 19, 21
Individual Psychotherapy and the Science of Psychodnamics xv, 44
ineffective 79
inferior, feeling 9, 25, 30, 70, 73, 113, 114, 124, 133, 156
inferior no longer, feeling 135
inferiority due to rejection by peers 206–207
inferiority, less 73
inhibitions, lowering 28

injuring self intentionally by accident 89
Inline Skates 216
instructor 92, 162, 163, 164, 175, 207
intention movements 175, 176
internet 170
interpretation, psychological xiv
invitation to dinner 148
Iron City Wrestling Club 56
irrational behaviour xiv
Isay, R. 127
isolation, feelings of 17
Italy 32
jab 176, <u>176</u>, 178
Jack and the Beanstalk 93–94
Japan 195
jaw, might break 119
Jealous Fathers 124–126
jealousy 16, 17
Jenkins, Tony xv–xvi
jogging 166–167, 173
jokes, basis of 20
ju-jitsu 169, 172–173, 195, 202
Judaism 24
judo 12, 52, 67, 169, 172, 195, 202
Judo, Ju-jitsu, Sombo 201–202
jump higher etc 10, 165
Just Good Friends 35–36
just good friends 109, 154
Kadish, Joyce 58
Kallman, Franz 80
Kano, Jigoro 202
Karate 205–206
karate, non-contact 172
Karr, Alphonse xii
Kassinove, Howard 140
Ken 95–96
Ken 93, 95–106, 113, 133, 136, 153, 179, 180, 182, 195, 196
Ken and Donald: punishment 96
Ken, body-boxing with 102
Ken, boxing with 95–106
Ken, cocaine and 105
Ken cuddling me 105
Ken, Donald punishing 106
Ken draws out anger, aggression 106
Ken, fighting with 95–106
Ken, macho combat with 100–101, 136

Ken not turning up 102–103
Ken punching me at front door 103
Ken, stood up by 102–103
Ken tattooed 96
Ken's father 104
Ken's father: bicycle chain 101, 104
Ken's Guilt 103–105
Ken's guilt 133
Ken's suicide 105
Ken's wife's hint 103
kept from other boys 55, 70, 87, 124, 129, 136, 164, 168, 169
Kerkuon 94
Kermani, Kai 139
key stimuli 67
kicking sand in sandwiches 10, 193
killing father and dog 134
Kingsley, Charles 94
Kinsey scale described 64, 65
Kinsey, Alfred C. 25, 64
Kinsey scale 82, 110
Kleeman, James A. 48
knee in crutch 175, 178, <u>178–179</u>
knife fights, Ken's 103–104, 133
knocked out, fear of being 99
knockout punch <u>205</u>
knowing someone else's mind 107
Krantz, Rachel 13, 17, 34
Kuils River 5, 33, 125, 132, 148
lacrosse 198, 204–205
last trains missed 125
late for appointments/dates 13, 136, 144
laughter reflex 20
Laumann, Edward O. xii, 83
Lavrikovs, Juris xv
Learning the Hard Way 97–100
Lebovitz, Phil S. 48
let him be a boy! 56, 114
Let me have it! 102, 182
letter 190
letting off steam 187, 194
LeVay, Simon 80, 81
Levels of Anger 9–11
Lewis, C.W. 27, 28
licence to rude, not 144
Liège 216
life companion 75
like-minded people 26
little boys taught 135, 147
Locked in the Closet 36–37

Index **253**

locked in closet 79
Lohrenz, L.J. 27, 28
London 21, 56, 57, 58, 61, 71, 95, 119, 150, 160
loneliness 17
longing 17
lordosis 65
Los Angeles 27, 48, 160
loud music 140, 192
lout crossing dance floor 159
love 70, 71, 111
love and hate 44
Love and Hate 105
Love, Attraction and Rejection 108
love gives power to reject 115
love/hate tattoos 18
love, not 189
love that dare not speak its name 26
loved by parents, need to be 133
loved, need to be 108
lover 31, 187, 192, 197
lover, losing 108
loving and angry with same person 43, 44
Loving Yourself 70–72
Low Self-esteem 92–93
low self-esteem 7, 14, 27, 31, 71, 79, 99, 101, 104, 111, 114, 123, 126, 130, 133, 134, 150
low self-esteem due to rejection by peers 206–207
low self-esteem, eliminating 124
LSD 17
Luhn, Rebecca 12, 14, 17
machine, body a 165, 167
Macho Combat 100–101
macho combat 96, 100–101, 102, 104, 136
Making a Start 138–140
making a tape recording 138
Making Anger Evaporate 21–22
making babies 25, 133
Making Conversation 150–152
making new friends 151
making silly mistakes 13
Malan, David xv, 31, 44, 71, 72
Male Animal Pack, The 69–70
Male Animal-pack Psychology 147

male bonding 155–156, 163
Male Homosexuality in Four Societies 46, 49
Male Homosexuality: a Psychoanalytic Perspective 37–38, 74, 129
male pack, gays in 147
male prostitute 16
man-at-work sign 132
Managing Anger 12
manic depression 71, 132, 134
manipulated behind back, being 56
manipulated etc , being 9, 30, 51, 52, 78, 79, 208
manipulated etc., not being 36, 76
manipulated, preventing being 10, 116
manipulation, allowing 108
manipulation by mother 78, 145
manipulation by parents 50, 75
\manipulation, resisting 148–149
manipulation, sensitive to 145
manipulative, being 149
manipulative women 150
Manners, Paul 63
marathon 215
marihuana 16
martial arts 215
Martin, A.D. 25
Martin, Clyde E. 64
masculine attributes 147
Masoch, Leopold von 216
masochism 17, 70, 71, 72, 73, 75, 108, 111, 133, 175, 189
Masochism 216–217
masochism engineered 74
masochism, unconscious 74
masochistic, realised I was 8
masochists than sadists, more 74
master-and-slave relationship 92, 108
masturbation 16, 111
mat burns 53
mate for life 75
mates, good 76
mates, not good 76
Mathy, Robin 46, 47, 49, 65, 67
Matteson, D.R. 82
McAnulty, Richard 38
McDonald, Helen B. 25, 26, 28
McKirman, D. 28
McKnight, Jim 81

McNally, E.B. 28
MDA 17
meeting through contact ads 145
Meltzer, H. 5
men biological enemies 108, 112, 130
men not to be trusted 163–164
men repress, what straight 109
men, sexually-attractive 35–36
men who are in control 76
Mentzer, Mike 112
Merlin, Joseph 216
Mescaline 17
Methadone and Ken 105
midwest, American 27
migraine 13
militant gay men xi, 15, 30, 45, 46, 62
Miller, Paul R. 49
mincing 189
mind in balance xv
Miracle Merchant, The 57
Mismeasure of Desire, The 63, 81
Missing the Boat 53–54
model theatres 57, 125
Montreal 215
Mony, John 48
Moods 217
moods, different 127
Mopping Up 136
Morales, E.S. 28
More Body-contact Sports 196–206
More Discoveries Through Wrestling 106–107
more handsome, younger etc. 112
Mosbacher, D. 28
mother 43, 57, 58, 91, 120, 140, 148, 149, 168
mother Christian Scientist 7
mother cooking Sunday lunch 32, 33
mother, crushing my 91
mother disapproved of wrestling 53
mother, dominating 62
mother ignoring husband 135
mother invalid 78
mother lavished attention 163
mother: passive-aggressive behaviour 34
mother playing piano 58
mother shatters knee 132

mother was right 164
motherfucker 146
mothers 46
mother's boy 35
mothers, close-binding-intimate 46, 62
mother's fault 126, 135–136
mothers, gays manipulated by 150
mothers, over-protective 49, 127, 168, 169
mothers spend time with baby 124, 126
mothers' fear of male aggression 129
motorbike 19, 71, 77, 95, 103, 106
mouth-to-mouth resuscitation 183, 195–196, 225
movement, useless 189
movements, decisive 189
movements, useless, ineffective 124
Mr Right 36, 76, 154–156, 160, 163, 169, 173
Mr Right, finding 36, 151
Mrs Malmesbury 148–149
mummification 17, 23, 79
Munro, H.H. 57
Münsterberg, Hugo 218–220
murder 72
Murder, Anorexia and Suicide 71
muscle, building 162, 186
muscle is weaker, lighter 159
muscle pump 162–163
muscle, smaller is weaker 60
muscle-building 173, 183
Muscles 8, 155
muscles, building my 111
muscles, developing 159
muscles, guy with biggest 154
muscular body 154, 160, 168
Mykonos 29
Nadler, Ronald 81
name-calling 23
narcotics 16
National Household Survey on Drug Abuse 15, 27
National Cancer Institute 62
National Health Service 16
Nature of Homosexuality, The 79, 82
Nature of Love, The 111
nature's way of protecting us 9, 116

Need for Love 75–76
need to be valued by parents 129
need to be your own father 160, 165
need to love yourself 70
need to speak for yourself 132
negative homophobia 27
negative Oedipus Complex 125
Netherlands 27
neurosis xi, xiv, 38, 69, 82, 122, 186, 197
Neurosis 217–218
neurotic symptoms 222
New York 16, 160, 215
nice guy 108
nice, polite ineffectual boy 52
nice people do not express anger 31
nice people, parents 52, 132, 208
no cure for sick man who believes he is well 14
"no", difficult to say 208
nonsense, absolute xiv
nonsense, utter xiv
O'Connor, P.J. 49
Oedipus Complex 124
Oedipus freaked out 43, 116
Olympic Games 215
Olympic symbol 154
open-heart surgery 56
opposites attract: heterosexual couples 18
oppressed by society, feeling 13, 30, 78, 79, 85, 141, 191
Orange Free State 58
Orange Juice Queen 62
ostracised 24, 92
Other Boys Are Too Rough for My Little Johnny, The 55–56
Other Boys Are Too Rough For My Little Johnny Revisited, The 127–133
Otis, Melanie 15, 16, 27
Ottawa 152
Our Voice 27
over-protected 56
pain of conflict 44
Painful Truth, The 122
painting 138, 190
Palacios, Luis 16
Paluszny, Maria 48
pansy 23, 52, 146, 175

Paratroop Regiment 95, 104
Parental Disapproval 87–88
parents 28, 31, 37, 38, 43, 44–45, 49, 57, 62, 66, 67, 68, 69, 75, 67, 87, 89, 116, 170, 208
Parents and Homosexuality 48–51
parents, colluding with 52, 76
parents, daughter wanted by 49, 51–52
parents important to you 76
parents nice people 52, 132, 208
parents not told about wrestling 51, 52, 88
parents, repressive 60
parents: repressive attitudes 52
parents, role of 44
parents, tacit manipulation by 87
parties, not good at 150
party in drag 50, 155
party 150
passive-aggressive behaviour 10
Passive-aggressive Behaviour 34
passive, compliant attitude 125
pathology 65, 67, 81
Pattatucci, Angela 81
Pauly, I.B. 15
Pavlov, Petrovich 218
penis erect 2
Periphetes 94
permission, give 189, 208
Perpetual Anger 32
Perpetual Anger 33
pet or daughter 133
Peter Pan's mother 130
Peter and Paul, blaming 13
Peterson, P.L. 28
Philippines 46
physical development 124
physique 215
piano, not able to play 72
picnicking on beach 71
pictures of fighting, etc. 16
Pillard, Richard 28, 62, 68, 80, 81
Pittsburgh 56
Plimpton, James L. 216
poisoning your life 197
poker 168
politeness, excessive 106–107
political goals 81
polls xii

Index **255**

polycarbonate vinyl 23
Pomeroy, Wardell B. 64
poof 146
poofter 23
poppers 13, 14, 15, 16, 17, 18, 23, 192
Posner, Richard 81
power 70
Power Books website 54, 140, 167, 182, 194, 207
powerlifting 215
President of the United States 148
Presley, Elvis 111
pressured, feeling 150
prevented from being a man 189
pride, feeling 116
pride in themselves 73
Pride Institute of Minneapolis 27
prior engagement 149
problem page 54, 207
problems and hang-ups 52, 53, 54, 169
problems for gays taking up sports 60
problems, constellation of 17
problems with sexual climax 14, 15
Procrustes 94
prone to accidents 74
prone to bad relationships 13
prone to changing jobs 13
prone to injury 74
prone to surgery 74
Pronger, Brian 36
proof fantasy is true 89, 120, 128, 129, 213
protecting body 182
proud of yourself, becoming 72
proud of yourself, feeling 135
Pryor, Douglas 82
psychiatrist xi, xiv, 17, 24, 52, 58, 59, 61, 68, 70, 71, 92, 108, 109, 111, 119, 120, 124, 127, 128, 129, 132, 140, 187
psychiatrists xv, 33, 38, 46, 62, 72
psychiatrist's interpretation 120
psychiatrists' waiting rooms 93
psychiatrists when patients laugh 20
psychiatry in infancy 17
psychological baggage 68
psychological inheritance 63, 80

psychological interpretation xv
Psychological Development in Health and Disease 74, 124
psychologist xi
psychologists 33, 45, 62, 104
psychology 38
Psychology and Crime 218
Psychology of Sexual Orientation 38
psychology, people who abhor 120
psychology, people who discredit 122
psychotherapist 16, 17, 180
psychotherapy xi, 21, 73, 134, 188
psychotherapy course xiv
psychotherapy group 120–121
psychotherapy, group xiv, 58, 59, 108, 119–120
psychotherapy: more an art xiii
pub/bar in Soho 18, 95, 102, 106
puberty 23, 27, 48, 49, 59
pubs/bars 26, 28, 37, 76, 103, 152, 187
pulse rate rises 13
punch 176, 179
punch back 182
punch-bag 139, 140, 172, 179
Punch-bag 193–194
punch-bag, workout on 190
punch-up on sports field 12
punches, succession of 183
punches to thigh 196
punching 8, 175
punching Andy 155
punching me any time 19, 20
punching opponent 187
punching upper arm 97, 99, 100–101, 196
punished, being 89
punished, deserved to be 7, 8, 73
punished, need to get 98–99, 101
punishment 70, 75, 93, 104
punishment, self-induced 89
push harder etc. 10, 165
pushed around, etc., being 9, 30, 79
pushed around etc., not 36
pushed around, preventing being 116
pushed to limits 100
put upon, etc., being 9, 79

put upon etc., not being 36, 76
put upon, preventing being 10, 116
put-downs 69–70, 146, 147
Put-downs 145–147
put-downs, repeating 147
Quaaludes 16
Queen of England 148
queer-bashing 23
quick fix, sexual 76, 109
racquetball 215
rage 16, 17
Rationalisation 218–220
re-heat soup 143
Red Riding Hood 93
rehearsal for play 148
rejection 27
rejection by peers 92
rejection, sensitive to 108, 122
relationship, self-destructing 10
relationships, bad 14, 136
relationships, poisoning 33, 34, 79
Remafedi, G. 26
reminded of bad aspects of oneself 144–145, 146
renter 16
Reply to My Critics, A 69
repress one, repress all 14, 21, 83, 114
repressing gay side 83
repression 110
Repression 220
research in southern-state cities 15
restraints 18
retaliation 12, 187
Revealing Yourself in a Handshake 152–153
revenge 10, 70, 73, 92, 99, 103
Rice, George 63
Richardson, E. 5
RNA synthesis 63
Robins, Eli 28, 48, 49
Roesler, T. 25
role models 129, 134
role models, lacking 135
roller skates 216
roller-skating derby 198
Roller-skating Derby 203
Roman toga 30
Ross, M.W. 82
Rosser, Simon 15
rough-and-tumble 56, 60, 92, 128, 129, 136, 169, 171, 173,

256   *Escape the Gay Straitjacket*

174, 186
Rough-and-tumble 168–173
rough-and-tumble, child frightened of 128
rough-and-tumble, learning from 168
rough-and-tumble skills 167, 172, 173
rough-and-tumble valued by role models 129
rough-house forbidden 56
rubbish xiv
rugby 7, 12, 52, 66, 67, 70, 174, 184, 188, 198
Rugby 203–204
rugby at school, playing 5–6, 87
rugby fisticuffs 12
rugby news met with silence 6, 87
rugby players 174
run faster etc. 10, 165, 187, 188
running 159
Ruse, Michael 81
Rushforth, Winifred 9 , 10, 11, 12, 13, 32
Russell, Claire 67, 219
Russell, W.M.S. 67, 219
Russia 195
Russian roulette 74
Russo, A.J. 48
Rust, P.C. 82
S & M devotees 196
S & M sub-culture 72, 73, 74, 92, 133
Sade, Marquis de 221
sadism 17, 70, 71, 72, 73, 75, 108, 111, 133, 189
Sadism 221
Sadism and Masochism 72–75
sadists 35
sado-masochism 70, 102, 134, 195
Safety First 173–174
Saghir, Marcel T. 27, 28, 48, 49
Saki 57
sample bill of rights 141, <u>142</u>
San Francisco 56, 215
San Francisco Examiner 25
SAS 95
Saying It Personally 191–193
Saying it Privately 191
scapegoated 24, 92
scar tissue 75
Schneider, S.C. 26

school, first day at 5, 87
schoolmate, demi-god 8
schoolmates wrestling on beach 102
Schultz, J.H. 211
Schwartz, P. 82
script 68, 93, 140–141, 150
sculpting 138
scum 146
Scyron 94
seedlings xiv
self-confidence 56, 160
self-confidence draining away 71, 72
self-confidence, lacking 71
self-defence 173, 180–181, 195, 202
self-esteem 129
self-esteem, drop in 9
self-esteem, improving your 135
self-esteem mentioned, times low 134
self-hatred 7–8, 24, 92, 111
self-hatred, less 73
self-hypnosis 211–212
self-loathing 27,71, 72, 73, 79, 111, 133, 134
self-loathing increases 75
self-punishment 17, 70, 71, 73, 74, 133
self-punishment, need for 92
self-worth, feeling 133
sensitive points of body <u>196</u>
Separate Creation, A 63
serves you right! 53
sex, opportunistic 74
sex, safe 28
sex, unsafe, unprotected 28
sexual aid 16, 17
sexual desires 81
sexual climax without hesitation 22
sexual attraction fades 36
sexual climax 15, 23, 92
sexual crutch 17
sexual dysfunction 15
sexual enabler 16
sexual feelings 156
sexual feelings coming to surface 20
sexual feelings repressed 18
sexual fulfilment 31
sexual orgasm 20, 70, 184, 99,

111, 186
sexual orgasm, difficulty in reaching 17
sexual orgasm impossible 21, 111
sexual orgasm impossible with gay friends 16
sexual orgasms, multiple 18
sexual satisfaction 18
sexual orgasm, unable to reach 79
sexual orgasm, reaching 156
Sexual Behaviour in the Human Male 64
sexually attractive 36
sexually attractive, not 35
sexually fulfilling 76
Shakespeare 150
shame 16, 17
shot of masculinity 111
should not have to tell them 10
shoulders wider from behind 155
sidestepping your rage 141
silhouettes of sexual attraction 64, 67, 109, 110
sissy 23, 48
Sissy Boy Syndrome and the Development of Homosexuality, The xv, 49
sister 32
Skinner, William 15, 16, 27
slamming door 10
slamming down phone 10
slamming typewriter carriage 191
Sleeping Beauty 93
sleeplessness 13
small talk 150
small-time villain 95
smile, sardonic 144
Smuts, Bill 57
Socarides, Charles 111
soccer 7, 10, 12, 198, 215
soccer fisticuffs 12
Soccer 199
social goals 81
sociologists 45, 46, 61–62
softball 215
Soho 95, 102, 106
solar plexus 97–98, 183, <u>183</u>, 195
sombo 195, 202
Some Basic Principles 175–179
someone they love, used to love, etc. 33, 44
someone who is a failure 130

Index **257**

Something is Happening 9
something one should not do 31, 52, 53, 55, 60, 66, 80
sons nice, gentle and good 129
South London Gay Community Centre 30
South Africa, 3, 58, 77
southern metropolitan areas 27
speaking in low voice 151
sphygmonanometer 162
spine, congenital curved 56
spiral, downward 75
spiral slows down, downward 73
spiral, upward 73, 135
spontaneity, lacking 110
sport teaches you, what 130
sports coaches 163
sports field, fisticuffs on 12
sports, fouling in 12
sports injuries 164
sports injuries, causes 128, 173
sports injuries, fewest 89
sports, playing 114
sports, withdrawal from competitive 8
sports-master at school 5, 56
sportsmen 10, 12, 124, 154, 166, 189
squash 215
Squirrel Club, The 57
Stage Five 184
Stage Five 186–189
Stage Four 168–184
Stage One 119–136
Stage Six 190–206
Stage Three 159–167
Stage Three 173
Stage Two 136
Stage Two 138–156
stamina 165, 166, 167
stand up for oneself, unable to 25, 30, 76, 78, 79, 146
standing up for oneself 8, 37, 52, 89, 116, 120, 129, 133, 134, 136, 147, 153, 156, 165, 169
standing up to straight men 207
Stein, Edward 63, 81
Stein, Terry 37
Steinhorn, Audrey 25, 26, 28
Stephan, Walter G. 49
Stevenson, John xvi

stimulants 17
stitches in Ken's hand 103–104
stitching on suitcase 192–193
Stoller, Robert 48
stomach aches, ulcers 13, 136
Stonewall xii, 27
Stonewall Action Lobby xii, xv
Story of Theseus, The 93–95
straight men, equal with 207
straight men using poppers 16
straight boys 38, 43, 128, 129, 134–135, 168, 169
straight men 5, 7, 9, 11, 12, 16, 30, 49, 52, 53, 69, 72, 111, 114, 121, 125, 133–134, 135, 146, 147, 153, 156, 159, 160, 165, 168, 169, 187, 189
straight men and gay fashions 13
straight men free to express anger 16
straight men: alcohol 28
straight, passing for 83
straight sports clubs 60
Straight Talk About Anger, A 13, 34
straight wrestlers 53, 54
straight wrestling club 53, 106
street situations 195
sub-text 88
subconscious engineers punishment 89
subconscious mind 9, 10, 11, 14, 20, 25, 90, 93, 102, 104, 121, 124, 127, 164, 187, 221
submission wrestling 168–169, 194–195, 197
Submission Wrestling 201
submissive, repressed men 35
subservience 111
suicidal, feeling 44, 59
suicide 25, 26, 38, 44, 45, 62, 105, 133
suicide attempt 25, 26
suicide when mothers die 130
sulking, 10
Sullivan, Andrew 81
superior 73, 113
superior, feeling 73, 175
superior, feeling others 114
superior position 29
surrogate husband 132

swimmers 152
swimming 159, 215
swimming club 152
swimming pool 71, 72
switched off 102
Sydney 215
symptoms will vanish 136
syphilis 28
Table Mountain 132
talking about ourselves enjoyable 151
Tamboerskloof 132
tape-recording 186
taunts 123, 127, 146
Tavistock Clinic xi, xiv, xv, 59, 61, 119, 123
telegraphing intention 175, 178
Telscombe Cliffs 95
Temple, Shirley 65
tender feelings of love 18, 71, 111
tender love impossible 75
tender sexual feelings 22–23, 114, 186, 190
tennis 51, 52, 215–216
testosterone 64
Textbook of Homosexuality and Mental Health 28, 37
that is the way it is 38
Theatre Royal 57
Theseus 93–94
thigh, punching point <u>196</u>
Thompson, Spencer K. 48
Thompson, Norman L. 49
threatened, feeling 72, 108, 112, 114, 188
Three Groups of Homosexuals 47–48
three things you should say 141, 149, 192, 208
Tooting Lido 71
tough guy 105
Tourist Guide, The 77–78
towel fight 101
trapped in legs, 4, 71, 72
track and field 216
Transactional Analysis xv, 68
treated badly by fathers 93, 107
triathlon 216
trick to make me play sports 186
triple shock 108
triumph, feeling 146–147
Trout, Hank xv, 56, 114

Escape the Gay Straitjacket

trust men in authority, cannot 163, 207
Trusting Your Father 163–165
Tucker, Patricia 48
turd 146
turned off 180
twins studies 62, 68, 80
Two Sets of Feelings 127
Two Sides of a Coin 112–113
UCLA 48
Ultimate Fighting Championship 172
unconscious mind 74, 79, 181, 213, 220
Unconscious, Subconscious and Preconscious 221–222
Understanding Homosexuality 25
university lectures 125
unlovable 70, 72, 90, 108, 123, 127, 135
upper arm, punching point 196
uppercut 176
uppercut to nose 178–179, 180–181
Upward Spiral Begins, An 122–124
USA. xii, 27, 46, 62, 63, 172, 216
Valium 16
Value of Anger 9
Vancouver 215
Vasey, Paul 81
Veiled Competitiveness 29
veiled competitiveness 79, 166
vermin 7
Viagra 16
victimisation 27
volcano, sitting on a 113, 138, 140
volleyball 198, 216
Volleyball 198
Waddell, Tom 214
Wages of Repressed Anger, The 79
walking away from situations 11
wanker 146
washing-up, plate broken 128
water polo 198, 216
Water Polo 202–203
water sports 111
web of connectedness 147
web-sites 54, 140, 167, 170, 182, 194, 207, 216
week later xiv

Weeks, G.R. 15
weight difference 59, 60, 153, 159
weight-training instructor 160
weight-training xiii, 135, 183, 186
Weinberg, Martin 27, 28, 82
Weinberg, A.S. 25
Weinrich, James 80
Weinrich, J.D. 60, 153
Wellings, Kaye 83
West, E.J. 49
West End 95
What is a Gay Straitjacket? 4–7
What Now? 206–208
what the world is like 129
where did we go wrong? 66
whipping 74
Whitam, Frederick 46 , 47, 48, 49, 65, 67
Williams, Colin 82
Williams, C. 27, 28
Wilsnack, S.C. 28
wimp 105, 153, 159, 189
winded, being 97, 183, 195–196, 225
Winding Me Up 102
Windy City Wrestling Club 56
women repress, what straight 109–110
workmate taunting you 123
workmate who sent me up 6, 119
workmates 192
wrestle, learning to 53, 54, 60, 88
wrestle, needing to 17, 186
wrestle, wanting to 108
wrestler friend dissuaded by mother 87–88
wrestler with muscular thighs 61
wrestler with video camera 61
wrestlerball 100
wrestlers 152
wrestlers, running hands over 188
wrestling 12, 30, 52, 53, 60, 66, 70, 71, 72, 77, 93, 111, 156, 166, 172, 174, 180, 181, 184, 194, 195, 197, 198
wrestling a provoking sport 107
wrestling and guilt 88–90
wrestling books 171
wrestling champion 166
wrestling club 53, 152, 166
wrestling club, gay-sensitive-sympathetic 170

Wrestling for Gay Guys 45–46, 50, 54, 66, 95, 169, 195
wrestling, freestyle 168, 194, 197, 216
wrestling good for gay guys 107
wrestling ideal for gay men 67
wrestling inappropriate 52
wrestling, interested in 66, 94
Wrestling, Judo or Ju-jitsu 194–195
wrestling on carpets 174
wrestling oppressed gay men 30
wrestling practice torsos 194
wrestling, professional 194
wrestling skills 119, 168
wrestling, stopped 95
wrestling: straight wrestling club 169
wrestling takedown 6, 119
wrestling teaches you, what 130
wrestling techniques, basic 172
wrestling, telling parents about 88
wrestling, turned on by 6
wrestling unsuccessfully 168
wrestling, watching 55
wrestling with Andy 19
wrestling with Ken 95, 103
wrestling without problems 67
wrestling without psychological problems 80
writing 186, 190
writing a letter, etc. 138
wrong hormones 51, 80
Wrong Hormones in the Womb 51
Wrong Hormones in the Womb 63–67
x-chromosome inheritance 63
X-linked transmission 63
Xq28 63
young man in wheelchair at hotel 131–132
Younger, More Handsome, More Muscular 113–114
Your Date With Your Idol 165–167
Zucker, K. 129
Zuger, Bernard 48

Index

NOTES

Finished reading Stage One on

Finished reading Stage Two on

Finished reading Stage Three on

Finished reading Stage Four on

Finished reading Stage Five on

Finished reading Stage Six on

(continued from back cover)

. . . unable to assert themselves, needing to use poppers and other drugs, bondage or sado-masochism to achieve sexual satisfaction. Being unable to do what they see straight men doing leaves them with low self-esteem, even self-hatred, depression, stifled personalities behind a "gay" façade, resorting to "bitching" or other behaviour that results in bad relationships.

Why am I trapped by this single cause for all these problems? you may ask. Why does it affect most gay men? How can I solve all these problems, find Mr Right and become happy?

Donald Black is a gay man who has discovered how to escape from this crippling fear of "violence". He will answer all your questions and offers to guide you through the explanation, release, development and fulfilment that you have been deprived of up to now to make you a more effective, more fulfilled, prouder, and happier gay or bisexual man.

By the same author:

WRESTLING FOR GAY GUYS

GYM AND HEALTH CLUB GUIDE